MW00324788

The Metaphysics of German Idealism

Martin Heidegger

The Metaphysics of German Idealism

A New Interpretation of Schelling's *Philosophical Investigations into the Essence of Human Freedom and the Matters Connected Therewith* (1809)

Translated by Ian Alexander Moore and Rodrigo Therezo

polity

First published in German as GA vol. 49, *Die Metaphysik des deutschen Idealismus. Zur erneuten Auslegung von Schelling*: Philosophische Untersuchungen über das Wesen der menschlichen Freiheit und die damit zusammenhängenden Gegenstände *(1809)* © Vittorio Klostermann GmbH, Frankfurt am Main, 1991. 2nd, revised edition 2006.

This English translation © Polity Press, 2021

Polity Press
65 Bridge Street
Cambridge CB2 1UR, UK

Polity Press
101 Station Landing
Suite 300
Medford, MA 02155, USA

All rights reserved. Except for the quotation of short passages for the purpose of criticism and review, no part of this publication may be reproduced, stored in a retrieval system or transmitted, in any form or by any means, electronic, mechanical, photocopying, recording or otherwise, without the prior permission of the publisher.

ISBN-13: 978-1-5095-4010-5

A catalogue record for this book is available from the British Library.

Library of Congress Cataloging-in-Publication Data
Names: Heidegger, Martin, 1889–1976, author. | Moore, Ian Alexander,
   translator. | Therezo, Rodrigo, translator. | Heidegger, Martin,
   1889–1976. Metaphysik des deutschen Idealismus.
Title: The metaphysics of German idealism : a new interpretation of
   Schelling's Philosophical investigations into the essence of human
   freedom and the matters connected therewith (1809) / Martin Heidegger ;
   translated by Ian Alexander Moore and Rodrigo Therezo.
Other titles: Metaphysik des deutschen Idealismus. English
Description: Cambridge ; Medford : Polity Press, [2021] | Includes
   bibliographical references. | Summary: "A major work by one of the most
   influential philosophers of the 20th century, published here in English
   for the first time" – Provided by publisher.
Identifiers: LCCN 2020057294 (print) | LCCN 2020057295 (ebook) | ISBN
   9781509540105 (hardback) | ISBN 9781509540129 (epub)
Subjects: LCSH: Schelling, Friedrich Wilhelm Joseph von, 1775–1854. |
   Schelling, Friedrich Wilhelm Joseph von, 1775–1854. Philosophische
   Untersuchungen über das Wesen der menschlichen Freiheit. | Idealism,
   German.
Classification: LCC B2898 .H4513 2021 (print) | LCC B2898 (ebook) | DDC
   193–dc23
LC record available at https://lccn.loc.gov/2020057294
LC ebook record available at https://lccn.loc.gov/2020057295

Typeset in 10.5 on 12 pt Times New Roman by
Servis Filmsetting Ltd, Stockport, Cheshire
Printed and bound in the UK by CPI Group (UK) Ltd, Croydon

The publisher has used its best endeavors to ensure that the URLs for external websites referred to in this book are correct and active at the time of going to press. However, the publisher has no responsibility for the websites and can make no guarantee that a site will remain live or that the content is or will remain appropriate.

Every effort has been made to trace all copyright holders, but if any have been overlooked the publisher will be pleased to include any necessary credits in any subsequent reprint or edition.

For further information on Polity, visit our website: politybooks.com

Contents

RECAPITULATIONS AND COURSE OF THE INTERPRETATION

APPENDIX

GLOSSARIES

Translators' Introduction

The decision to translate Heidegger into English is in many respects a difficult one. Not simply because Heidegger's thought remains irreducibly tied to language and to a certain artisanal craft of writing – a *"Hand-werk der Schrift,"* as he calls it in "The Letter on 'Humanism'"[1] – but also because English, to all appearances, at least, was not a language Heidegger particularly esteemed. This *would* be philosophically irrelevant were it not for the utmost significance Heidegger himself ascribes to "the essential danger" that the "English-American" language poses, a threat to nothing less than the "shrine" of being in which "the essence of the human is held in store."[2] It is difficult to overlook, then, a certain irony at the heart of any English translation of Heidegger, particularly of a Heidegger text, such as *The Metaphysics of German Idealism*, dating back to the early 1940s, when Heidegger's most explicit condemnation of English takes place. Would it not be an ontological disaster to translate the thinker of this ontological disaster precisely into the language in which this disaster is supposed to unfold?

Yet we maintain that such an undertaking is nevertheless in keeping with *another* Heidegger, more open to a non-Greek other and capable of writing – in 1946 – that "in the most diverse ways, being speaks everywhere and always, through *all* language," even, dare we say, the English language?[3]

---

[1] Martin Heidegger, "Brief über den 'Humanismus,'" in *Wegmarken*, Gesamtausgabe vol. 9, ed. Friedrich-Wilhelm von Herrmann (Frankfurt am Main: Vittorio Klostermann, 1976), p. 344.

[2] Heidegger, *Hölderlins Hymne "Der Ister,"* Gesamtausgabe vol. 53, ed. Walter Biemel (Frankfurt am Main: Vittorio Klostermann, 1984), pp. 80–81.

[3] Heidegger, "Der Spruch des Anaximander," in *Holzwege*, Gesamtausgabe

Translated here in its entirety for the first time is volume forty-nine of Heidegger's *Gesamtausgabe* or "Collected Works," a volume comprised of a lecture course delivered at the University of Freiburg in the first trimester of 1941 and of material for a seminar held there in the summer semester of that year. Previously, excerpts from this volume, occasionally revised, had appeared in the appendix to Heidegger's first lecture course on Schelling from 1936, whose 1971 publication (English 1985) was overseen by Heidegger himself.[4] As indicated by the title of the present volume, here Heidegger again takes up Schelling's 1809 treatise on freedom, which, he argues, marks the peak of German Idealism. Only, this time, Heidegger more explicitly distinguishes his own thought from that of his German predecessor, whose work he situates within the continuum of Western metaphysics. Along the way, taking up Schelling's important distinction between ground and existence, Heidegger provides an extensive history of the concepts of existence and ground, with detailed discussions of Jaspers, Kierkegaard, Hegel, and his own opus magnum *Being and Time* – including its unpublished third division.

The style of the present volume is uneven. Some of the material appears as fully worked-out prose. Other portions resemble notes. We have endeavored to remain faithful to the character of the text, at the expense of occasional inelegance or grammatical incompleteness.

The reader can consult the glossaries to see how we have typically rendered Heidegger's terminology, but there are four sets of terms which we believe it will prove helpful to discuss in advance.

1. We have rendered the noun *das Sein* as "being" and the nominalized present participle *das Seiende* as "beings," "the being," or "that which is." When it is unclear in the English which is meant, as in the phrases "the being {*Sein*} that human Dasein itself is" and "the proper being {*Seiende*} in itself," we have, as here, inserted the German. Heidegger's use of the archaic German spelling *Seyn* has been translated by the obsolete English *beyng*. Since, in Schelling's time, *Seyn*, with a "y," was standard, we have used "being" when translating authors from that period, although here too we have included the German. The abstract *Seiendheit* appears as "beingness." Although, in Schelling's later philosophy, which Heidegger occasionally references, Schelling does not

---

vol. 5, ed. Friedrich-Wilhelm von Herrmann (Frankfurt am Main: Vittorio Klostermann, 1977), p. 338 (emphasis added).

[4] Martin Heidegger, *Schellings Abhandlung über das Wesen der menschlichen Freiheit (1809)*, ed. Hildegard Feick (Tübingen: Max Niemeyer, 1971) / *Schelling's Treatise on the Essence of Human Freedom*, trans. Joan Stambaugh (Athens: Ohio University Press, 1985).

use *Sein* and *Seiendes* in the same way Heidegger does, we thought it important to maintain terminological consistency. In cases where confusion might result, we have interpolated the German.

2. Heidegger uses numerous words for existence and for the human being in particular. In order to keep them apart, we have, with two exceptions, consistently rendered *Existenz* as "existence," *Ex-sistenz* as "ex-sistence," *existenzial* as "existential," *existenziell* as "existentiell," *Mensch* as "human," and *Menschsein* as "the being of the human," "human being" (no article), or, in one instance, "being-human." (In two cases, in which we include the German, it seemed more appropriate to translate *das Existenzielle* in Schelling as "the existential.") Unless indicated by a German interpolation, we have, as in point 1, left *Dasein* and *Da-sein* in the original. In § 11, θ, Heidegger claims this term is "*untranslatable*," although he does provide – translating from within German, as it were – an explanation as to how one should understand it, which we reproduce here:

> The word "*Da*" {there, here}, the "*Da*," means precisely this clearing for *Sein* {being}. The essence of Da-sein is *to be* this "*Da*." The human takes this on, namely, to be the *Da*, insofar as he exists {. . .}. What is meant is not "*Da*sein" in the sense of the presence of a thing or of the human that is here and there and "*da*"; rather, what is being thought is "Da-*sein*," that the clearing for being in general essences and is (p. 47).

3. The verb *essences* translates the rare verb *wesen*, which, in its noun form, *Wesen*, means "essence." Although *Wesen* can refer to *a* being, as in the term *Lebewesen*, "creature" or "living being," we have either translated it as "essence" or, when not, supplied the German, since this is a crucial term for both Heidegger and Schelling. Heidegger occasionally accentuates the verbal character of the word with the noun *Wesung*, which we have translated by "essencing." "Presencing" and "to presence" translate *Anwesung* and *anwesen*.

4. Heidegger exploits the etymology of numerous words built on the root verb *stellen*, "to place." *Darstellen* appears as "presenting" or, when hyphenated, as "presenting forth"; *Vorstellen* appears as "representing" or, when hyphenated, as "re-presenting," although one should bear in mind that it also has the literal spatial sense of "placing before"; *Herstellen* appears as "producing"; and *Zustellen* as "delivering."

Since Heidegger uses both parentheses and square brackets, we have placed all of our notes and interpolations in curly brackets. We have also included, in the margins, the pagination of the original

German.[5] For foreign phrases that cannot readily be found in a lexicon, we have provided common translations in footnotes. For individual Greek and Latin words, we have supplied, at the end of the volume, a lexicon with typical translations. Readers consulting the lexicon should bear in mind that it is intended as a resource for beginning to work through Heidegger's own use and interpretation of these words, not as a replacement or definitive rendering.

Following Anglophone conventions, we have italicized foreign words and phrases. When Heidegger himself emphasizes them, or when the words are already emphasized in material he is quoting, we have added underlining. In his citations of Leibniz, several words are written *gesperrt*, spaced out for emphasis. We have retained this spacing in order to distinguish it from other types of emphasis. Words appearing in Greek script have been transliterated.

We would like to thank Katie Chenoweth, Tobias Keiling, Richard Polt, Philipp Schwab, Tim Steinebach, and two anonymous reviewers for their helpful comments on the translation.

Ian Alexander Moore
Rodrigo Therezo

---

[5] Martin Heidegger, *Die Metaphysik des deutschen Idealismus. Zur erneuten Auslegung von Schelling: Philosophische Untersuchungen über das Wesen der menschlichen Freiheit und die damit zusammenhängenden Gegenstände (1809)*, Gesamtausgabe vol. 49, ed. Günter Seubold, 2nd edn. (Frankfurt am Main: Vittorio Klostermann, 2006).

Introduction:
The Necessity of a
Historical Thinking

§ 1 Schelling's Treatise as the Peak of the Metaphysics of German Idealism

According to the announcement,[1] we will deal with *the Metaphysics of German Idealism* here. We shall attempt to do so by way of an interpretation of Schelling's "Freedom Treatise." We have thus singled out an isolated writing of *one* single thinker from this epoch. This procedure is in order if we generally limit ourselves to learning about only this text of this thinker, thereby becoming familiar with a limited sphere of the thinking of German Idealism. Yet this procedure becomes questionable as soon as there lurks in the background the claim to think through, by way of such a path, "*the* metaphysics of German Idealism *as such.*" This claim will guide us nevertheless.

But then the intended one-sided approach requires a particular justification. How else should this be accomplished than by a knowledge of what is thought in this isolated treatise by Schelling? In this, we already presuppose that this isolated treatise reaches the peak of the metaphysics of German Idealism. However, the earliest we can discern this is at the end of a completed interpretation, or perhaps even only after a *manifold* interpretation.

When is it the case that this apparently isolated and arbitrary path is justified and even necessary?

1. If Schelling's treatise is the *peak* of the metaphysics of German Idealism.

2. If all the essential determinations of this metaphysics are borne out in this treatise.

---

[1] {TN: i.e., the advertisement about the lecture course made available to students.}

2   3. If, *at all*, the essential core of all Western metaphysics is able to be exposed in complete determinacy on the basis of this treatise.

The procedure therefore remains violent, at least at the beginning. Put more precisely: the procedure always appears violent to the commonplace opinion that only the frequently mentioned "historiographic completeness" provides the guarantee for the knowledge of history. But *perhaps* this opinion is *only* an opinion, an assumption that is ungrounded, or poorly grounded, or even altogether ungroundable in terms of the essence of history. Perhaps that is so. In order to raise this conjecture to the level of certainty and, in this way, to justify our undertaking, we would admittedly have to engage in a consideration whose extensive scope and difficulty hardly take a back seat to an interpretation of the selected treatise. For it would have to be shown that, and in what way, the historicality of the history of thinking is unique, that this history can, to be sure, look like historiographic reflection, but in truth has, rather, an essence of its own and also does not coincide with what one in this field otherwise tends to oppose to historiographic presentation, namely, "systematic" reflection.

These brief indications already make clear that, at the beginning, our undertaking remains surrounded by a tangle of different sorts of misgivings and all too easily misleads one to untangle and iron them all out prior to the proper work, thereby deferring, however, the proper work of interpretation time and again. In order to avoid this danger, there is evidently only one good way out, namely, to begin blindly with the elucidation of Schelling's treatise and to trust that some benefit will come of it.

3   ## § 2 Historical Thinking, Historiographic Explanation,
                         Systematic Reflection

This seemingly "natural" carefreeness would certainly be allowed to guide us if it were *only* a matter of drawing out what Schelling meant. To be sure, the correct rendering of his thought already requires enough of our ability to think. And yet – thinking it once again does not already guarantee that we *ourselves* would presently also be those who think, in the sense of those whom we call thinkers. But we are not willing to renounce this. Why not? Out of some stubbornness and will to thought? That would be too little, essentially too little, to let us persevere with thought.

But from where else can a necessity come to us? If we could reckon this necessity up for ourselves of our own accord, as it were, it would, then, not be a necessity that compelled us. Are there, then, mysterious experiences in play, which destine us to persevere with thought and to awaken a thinking which questions? This can suffice least of all in the realm of thought; here, cold audacity alone has the word. But this, too, is again only an assertion, which, moreover, takes it to be already decided that we are actually placed into a necessity to think. We appear thus again, only in another direction, to rush ahead endlessly on the path of misgivings. And is it not by now already clear that misgivings {*Bedenken*} most of all hinder us from thinking {*Denken*}?

Then, *as a point of fact*, everything hinges precisely on "making" a beginning in thought without having any misgivings. But should we then still engage with "the historiographic" at all? If not, where should we begin? How insignificant the aforementioned misgivings – regarding the restriction to a particular text of a single thinker – now seem in relation to the objection that, in reflecting on the metaphysics of German Idealism, we are already running after something past and "orienting" ourselves "historiographically." This sort of orientation contains, after all, the admission that philosophy would only be the historiographical making-present of its past, which it admittedly must be when it no longer finds "a measure or rule" in itself. Schelling expressed himself clearly enough on this matter in the final paragraph of his Freedom Treatise (415):[2]

> If the dialectical principle, that is, the understanding which is differentiating but thereby organically ordering and shaping things in conjunction with the archetype by which it steers itself, is withdrawn from philosophy so that philosophy no longer has in itself either measure or rule, then nothing else is left to philosophy but to seek to orient itself historiographically and to take the *tradition* as its source and plumb line [. . .]. Then it is time, as one intended to ground our poetry through acquaintance with the literature of all nations, to seek for philosophy a historical norm and foundation as well.

But Schelling turns against this time and says:

> The time of merely historiographical faith is past, if the possibility of immediate cognition is given. We have an older revelation than any written one – nature. (Ibid.)

---

[2] {TN: For bibliographic information, see § 3 and the relevant note in that section, below.}

Yet does this hold straight away for our time as well? Or is this time – our time – a different one? Which law, then, requires that thinking conform to its time? Or is thinking untimely, and indeed always and necessarily so? But how could this be the case, if the untimely were but the inversion of the timely – a still fiercer dependence on "time" { *"Zeit"*}? In accordance with what should "an age" { *"Zeitalter"*} be determined in order for it to be definitive for a thinking? But how, if essential thinking first decides an age in what is most proper to it, and does so without this age having or being able to have a public consciousness of its own historical essence? But then this decisive thinking must in turn be so originary that it cannot lose itself to a past epoch, so as to reckon up from this epoch
5   what is necessary for the present, making what is necessary conform with the present. That reckoning up is the essence of "historicism"; and this making-conform is the essence of "currentism" { *"Aktualismus"*}. Both belong together. They are the sometimes overt, sometimes covert enemies of decisive thinking (see § 5).

   If, however, as our undertaking suggests, we do *not* abandon the historical reflection on the metaphysics of German Idealism – but perhaps first introduce it, in fact, and thereby nevertheless act only from the *one* necessity {*Notwendigkeit*} to think in the sense of essential thinking – then that is a sign that our necessities are different, different because the need {*Not*} has become a different one. Or is it perhaps even the *same* need, not the need of an age, not the need of a century, but the need of two millennia, the need arising from the fact that, ever since then, thinking has been "metaphysics"? Perhaps this need has meanwhile become more pressing, which does not preclude that it has become even less visible. Indeed, our thinking, when it attempts to reflect on German Idealism historically, is not a historiographic orientation; but neither is it "immediate cognition" in the manner of the metaphysics of German Idealism. The thinking that has become necessary is a *historical* thinking. An actual attempt should clarify what this means.

   We will therefore now leave all misgivings about our undertaking to the side; we will, however, attend to how they resolve and sort themselves out in due course. For a long time to come, we will perhaps not be able to distinguish historiographic explanation from historical thinking. Yet this we shall keep in mind, namely, that the historical thinking attempted here can be subsumed neither under philosophical-historiographic explanation nor under "systematic" reflection, nor under a mixture of both. It suffices if we glean from what has been said, even if only in broad strokes, the manner in which we do not arbitrarily and blindly take up Schelling's treatise so as to publicize it for erudite ends.

Several tools of the trade are necessary for the work of interpreta-   6
tion. But all this remains obtuse if we do not question and think from
out of what presses and determines us, no matter how confused all
this may be, and how beset it may be with habits of thought that have
converged from often unknown sources and impetuses.

§ 3 Elucidations of the Title of the Treatise

Schelling's treatise bears the title: "Philosophical Investigations into the
Essence of Human Freedom and the Matters Connected Therewith."
It appeared in the year 1809 as the final part of a collection of investigations that Schelling had already published earlier and that were
selected from the totality of his existing publications in order to serve
as an introduction to the "Freedom Treatise."

Cite the four preceding parts (do not at first go into the "works" and
biography):

I.   Of the I as Principle of Philosophy, or, On the Unconditional in
      Human Knowledge (1795)
II.   Philosophical Letters on Dogmatism and Criticism (1795)
III. Treatises on the Elucidation of the Idealism of the Doctrine of
      Science (1796–1797)
IV.   On the Relation of the Fine Arts to Nature: An Academic Speech
      (1807)

The text of the Freedom Treatise will be cited according to volume
and page numbers of the edition of Schelling's *Sämtliche Werke*, 1856–
1861, fourteen volumes.[3] The Freedom Treatise can be found in volume
VII, pp. 336–416. These page numbers are printed on the inner margin   7
of the edition of the *Philosophische Bibliothek*.[4]

The title of the treatise: *philosophical* investigations: "*philosophical*"? – *zētēsis*; "*freedom*": arbitrary topic? freedom of the will? Kant;

---

[3] *Friedrich Wilhelm Joseph von Schellings sämmtliche Werke*, ed. Karl Friedrich
August Schelling (Stuttgart and Augsburg: J. G. Cotta, 1856–1861).

[4] F. W. J. Schelling, *Das Wesen der menschlichen Freiheit. (Philosophische
Untersuchungen über das Wesen der menschlichen Freiheit und die damit zusammenhängenden Gegenstände, 1809*), newly edited with an introduction, index of
names, and index of subjects by Christian Herrmann (Philosophische Bibliothek,
vol. 197) (Leipzig: Felix Meiner, 1925). {TN: Translations of Schelling's treatise
come, with occasional modifications, from Jeff Love and Johannes Schmidt's rendering in F. W. J. Schelling, *Philosophical Investigations into the Essence of Human
Freedom* (Albany: SUNY Press, 2006). This edition also includes the pagination of
Sämtliche Werke.}

"*human*": essence of the human; "*essence*": inner possibility (formal concept) and *ground of actuality (centrum)*,[5] the absolute; "*and {. . .} therewith*": with the "essence" (that is, with the absolute); "*connected*": nexus – *sustasis – system*; "*matters*" {*Gegenstände*}: (formally) what *stands* {steht} 'there' in such a *standing-together (system)*; "*the*": not a few – arbitrary ones, but, rather, eminent ones.

Depending on how human freedom in its essence belongs to this nexus or even determines it, the treatise on human freedom either is an isolated and separate reflection or comprises the "innermost center-point of philosophy . . ." (Preface 1809, p. VIII).

The treatise goes into the center of the system as the "*system of freedom.*"

In his Berlin lectures on the history of philosophy, Hegel also dealt with Schelling's philosophy – he calls it "the latest interesting, true shape of philosophy." He assesses the Freedom Treatise in particular as follows:

> Schelling published a separate treatise on freedom that is of a pro-found, speculative character, but it stands apart and for itself; in philosophy, nothing that stands apart can be developed.[6]

8   To what extent Hegel's assessment is mistaken, to what extent it hits the mark, this can be gleaned already from the precise elucidation of the title. What stands "apart and for itself" here in this treatise is the *center* of the system, that is, it does *not* stand *apart*. Quite the contrary, what stands apart in this system is not carried out, above all not in the manner that Hegel demands and has himself actualized. The question must remain open as to what extent Hegel's demand conforms with and does justice to Schelling's system.

§ 4 The Organization of the Treatise

As typeset, the treatise is, to be sure, organized into segments and para-graphs. At important places we also find remarks on the present state

---

[5] {TN: Heidegger writes both *Centrum* (without italics) and *Zentrum*. We distin-guish them in the translation by italicizing the former. *Mitte* appears as 'center.'}

[6] G. W. F. Hegel, *Vorlesungen über die Geschichte der Philosophie*, 3 vols. (Stuttgart 1928), p. 682 [XV, 682], *Sämtliche Werke*, ed. Hermann Glockner, vol. 19. [In what follows, all Hegel citations and references are based on this edition.]

of the investigation; but an explicit table of contents and organization are lacking. We should not let this belie its rigorous internal structure.

We shall begin by providing here the missing table of contents; it can serve as a guide to a first understanding.

Introduction *(336–357)*

On the Question of System in General and the Question of the "System of Freedom" in Particular by Way of the Clarification of the Concept of "Pantheism"

Primary Investigation *(middle of 357 – beginning of 415)*

I.   The Inner Possibility of Evil (middle of 357 – beginning of 373)
II.   The General Actuality of Evil as Possibility for Particular Evil (373 – beginning of 382)
III. The Process of Particularization of Actual Evil (382–389)
IV. The Shape of Evil Appearing in the Human (end of 389 – middle of 394)
V.   The Justification of God's Divinity in View of Evil (394–399)
VI. Evil within the Whole of the System (399 – beginning of 406)   9
VII. The Highest Unity of Beings as a Whole and Human Freedom (406 – beginning of 415)

Concluding Remark *(415/416)*

On the Only True System

From the basic contents of the primary investigation and its trajectory, it becomes clear that the Freedom Treatise is a treatise on "*evil.*" Thus, "human freedom" and "evil" must be essentially connected; and this connection must essentially determine how beings stand together as a whole – the system.

§ 5 Brief Excursus on a Further Misgiving (the Historiographic – the Current – That Which Has Been)

In reflecting on what is treated in the Freedom Treatise, we find our way into essential relations to that which "is"; or, better put, we experience that and how we "are" in such relations. We experience and consider that which "is." Fine; but what merits the distinctive designation: it "is"? What is called "being"?

This chair over there – "is." Is that which "*is*," in the manner of the chair? With this, do we have a yardstick for measuring what "is"? All sorts of things "are" in such a way; whence the measure of being? Is there a measure here at all? The relation to that which "is," and even the essential relations: difficult to experience. Wherein lies the ground of the "difficulty"? (the abandonment of beings by being – the forgetting of being by the human)

So, not only, nor first of all, to learn about something or other; not some sort of "instruction" about learned matters. But surely still less a snatching at what is "practically" useful and "germane to life."

If, however, a reflection on essential relations in which "we" stand – we, here and now – why then a treatise from a bygone age?

10   *Historicism!* The making-present of the past – and explaining on the basis of what lies further back in the past {*Vor-vergangenen*}; flight into a holding onto the past; *counting on ways out of the present*; "restoration" – "eschatology"; (the essence of historicism is not mere "relativizing");

Or, alternatively,

Currentism – as its flipside; *to settle the past on the basis of its value for the present*, and the "future" as the extended "present" (its plans); – "untimeliness" as the fiercest dependence on time; constantly staring at it. Even the relation to the "future" changes nothing if the latter is but the forward extension of the present – indeed of a present in its congealment. (See, for example, Pinder, *Essential Features of German Art*).[7] The calculative game between "past" {*"Herkunft"*} and "future" {*"Zukunft"*} as enslavement to an uncomprehended present; whereby relativism is apparently supposed to be abolished.

Moreover, {see} *Schelling* himself (see above, p. 3) in the final remark of the treatise.

Nevertheless: not a historiographic and up-to-date explanation of something past, but rather a historical confrontation with what has been {*Gewesenem*} and thus with what first essences {*Wesendem*}.

The aforementioned misgiving subsides; but it can also persist {*bestehen*} – but not for those who under-"stand" {*ver-"stehen"*} otherwise.

---

[7] Wilhelm Pinder, *Wesenszüge deutscher Kunst* (Leipzig: Seemann, 1940).

Preliminary Reflection on the Distinction Between Ground and Existence

§ 6 The Core Section of the Treatise: The Distinction between Essence Insofar as it Exists and Essence Insofar as it is Merely Ground of Existence

We shall initially skip over the introduction and consider the section with which the *primary investigation* begins (357–364). This section, as we have divided it, contains, at its core, the entire treatise, and it does so *in two respects* (see also below, p. 75): *first, as regards content* – insofar as the entire realm of questioning is unfolded, and insofar as what is asked about (the freedom of the human) is outlined. *Then*, however, also as regards the *mode of thinking*: for *how* thinking happens in these investigations comes most acutely to the fore here. Thus, we first practice here that thinking which is also already required in order to think through the introduction appropriately. ("*Dialectics*" – in unconditional thinking, and especially "identity"-thinking.)

Nevertheless, the interpretation of this section will not resolve all of the difficulties, given that we are able to follow it out in thought {*nachdenken*} only in a first attempt; *thus*, once again, the last for comprehension.

This core section is itself organized in turn.

It begins with a paragraph that indicates, as a preliminary remark:

(A) what is being treated: the distinction between "ground" and "existence";[1]

(B) two things are said about this distinction, if we disregard the   12

---

[1] On an accompanying page, Heidegger wrote out the excerpt: "The philosophy of nature of our time has first advanced in science the distinction between essence insofar as it exists and essence insofar as it is merely the ground of existence" (357).

"polemical" side remark which belongs in the context of the introduction.

Regarding A: What is being treated? A distinction, namely the distinction "between essence . . . and essence. . . ." Between two "essences"? Two sorts of essence?

What does essence mean here? Beings; entities {*Wesen*} belonging to nature, to the household, to the state, to the realm of banditry; that which respectively is, with the stress placed on its being.

It is not two essences that are distinguished, but rather *one* essence – that is, *any essence* in a twofold "view"; "view" – but not only that of a viewing observer. What is distinguished cannot, however, be separated; yet what can be separated is, in turn, the *entire* twofold essence each time.

The fact that every essence is distinguished nevertheless has peculiar consequences, so that even disparate and manifold "essences" are each time disparate and manifold in accordance with the *distinction* that determines these respective essences. What does this distinction mean?

Let us first, however, consider what is said about the distinction in a preliminary manner.

Regarding B: What is said about this distinction?

1. That the "philosophy of nature of our time has first advanced" it "in science."

2. The Freedom Treatise "is grounded" on this distinction.

Regarding 1, (a) The "philosophy of nature of our time" = Schelling's "philosophy of nature"; the latter is not a philosophical reflection on the region of "nature" – for instance in Kant's sense (doctrine of categories) – but rather, contra Fichte: nature itself is, in itself, the absolute; "the visible spirit" (subject–object). "Nature" is "the odyssey of spirit." Cognition of "nature" is here knowledge of the absolute. Nature is "identical" with spirit; identity = unity of identity (of identity and nature and identity and spirit) and unity of opposition.

13

$$\left(\frac{\text{Identity}}{\text{Nature} \longleftrightarrow \text{Spirit}} \right)$$

Philosophy of nature – philosophy as a whole from the perspective of another question. What this is supposed to be can be found already on p. 362:

> To show how each succeeding process approaches closer to the essence of nature, until the innermost centrum appears in the

highest division of forces, is the task of a comprehensive philosophy of nature.

(b) In science – which is not the same as "research" in today's sense, but rather the unconditional knowledge of the absolute; within this knowledge (doctrine of science), which aims at the unconditional, the latter is interrogated, and that means experienced, differently – (everything first becomes clear on account of the treatise itself).

Regarding 2. The Freedom Treatise "is grounded" on this distinction. The Freedom Treatise shows the center and ground of the "system of freedom." A "system" – in itself – cannot be invented {*erfunden*} but only "discovered" {*"gefunden"*}; not a human construct, but the jointure of the absolute, which is spirit, as spirit of love; love is the enabling of freedom; the *knowing will*, which binds ground and existence in the absolute, recognizes their opposition and overcomes it in the unity of their essential justice.

Now to the distinction itself and its discussion: initially incomprehensible without further ado; no clear evidence of its occurrence.

Likewise *strange* is the manner in which it is treated – *God* and *the creation of the world* and *the human*; *God, just as though this were the clearest of all.* Indeed. The basic manner of metaphysical absolute thinking: the non-sensuous construction of everything in God.

Misgivings: (a) from a Kantian perspective, (b) from a perspective of ecclesiastical faith – proofs of God, (c) for contemporaries: where everything disintegrates into the indeterminate ("fate" – "providence" – "Lord God").

Which questions initially come up here: the arbitrariness and boundlessness of speculation; mere assertions; where is a guiding thread? Attempt to get closer by way of what is familiar to us. When we attempt to bring clarity of our own accord. "Ground" – "existence": commonplace philosophical concepts; and especially "philosophy of existence" (see "On the History of the Concept of Existence").[2]

§ 7 The Organization of the Preliminary Reflection

We shall begin our elucidation of the core section, and especially the elucidation of the distinction between "ground" and "existence," by way of a preliminary reflection. It approaches this distinction from

---

[2] Lecture in the Freiburg Kränzchen on 7 June 1941 (publication planned for the third division {TN: now in vol. 80.2} of the Collected Works).

"without"; yet at the same time we shall attempt to think beyond this distinction into *the* realm in which the confrontation with Schelling and metaphysics in general is carried out.

The preliminary reflection is organized into four parts:

Chapter 1: the conceptual-historical elucidation of "ground" and "existence."

Chapter 2: the root of this distinction (the point of view according to which the distinguished are distinguished).

Chapter 3: the inner necessity of the distinction (from which the distinguishing {*Unter-scheiden*} emerges); ("the principle of opposition," "negativity"; subjectivity).

Chapter 4: the essence of the distinction {*Unterscheidung*} and the particular formulations of the difference {*Unterschied*} in Schelling (not as something set forth in representation and thought, but the representing itself as deliberate self-dividing {*Sich-Scheiden*}; counterturning, circle).

Yet the preliminary reflection nevertheless has the core section in view, indeed with the aim of displacing the interpretation of the treatise straightaway into the realm where everything is decided, and within which the individual steps are alone comprehensible. At the same time, however, the preliminary reflection looks beyond this into the possibility and necessity of an entirely different way of questioning (the question of being). The latter must, however, emerge where the questioning of metaphysics – and Schelling's questioning in particular – have their impetus and ultimate fulfillment, even though there is no living and developed knowledge of it.

The Conceptual–Historical Elucidation of Ground and Existence

§ 8 *Essentia* and *Existentia*

Existence is determined in the sense of the commonplace distinction between *essentia* and *existentia* in metaphysics. In contrast to what-being (*quidditas*), "*existentia*" means this: that what "is" in such and such a manner, in accordance with its substantive content {*Sachhaltigkeit*}, is also "actual." "Actuality" {*"Wirklichkeit"*} means: effectedness and effectiveness {*Gewirktheit und Wirksamkeit*} (*actualitas*), and that means: presencing – "existence" {*"Dasein"*} in the customary sense of what is somehow "present."

Actus purus – the pure omnipresence of God – pure effecting (interpreted on the basis of *creatio*).

The Scholastic explanation of *existentia* as *sistentia extra nihilum et extra causas*;[1] *extra*, that is, *eductum inter entia actualia* – led out and *beyond* among the actual.

The provenance of the distinction – by way of a reinterpretation of Aristotle: *ti estin – hoti estin*; *prōtē ousia* (*ho tis anthrōpos*) and *deutera ousia* (*to eidos tou anthrōpou*), *zōion*.[2] Proper root: *ousia* as *eidos*; and then *ousia* as *en-ergeia* (see treatise on Aristotle, Phys. B,1, 1939/40).[3]

The development of this distinction into the doctrine of "modalities" as an empty playing with concepts, whose provenance is not considered and which cannot be grounded in its essential ground.

---

[1] {TN: 'standing outside of nothingness and outside of causes.'}

[2] {TN: 'what something is – that it is; first substance (this human)' and 'second substance (the form of the human), animal.'}

[3] "On the Essence and Concept of Φύσις in Aristotle's *Physics* B, 1," trans. Thomas Sheehan, in Martin Heidegger, *Pathmarks*, ed. William McNeill (Cambridge: Cambridge University Press, 1998), pp. 183–230.

(Further difference in Kant, *Critique of Pure Reason*, "The Postulates of Empirical Thought in General," and *Critique of the Power of Judgment*, § 76.)

§ 9 "Existence" and "Philosophy of Existence" (K. Jaspers)

A philosophy of this name must place "existence" at the center, indeed must determine the center on the basis of "existence." "Existence" has an emphatic sense here. For, if existence is tantamount to *being* – then the philosophy of existence would be a "comical title," such as "biology of life." What particular and emphatic meaning does existence have here?

Only the work of K. Jaspers is "philosophy of existence," *including the name*. See *Die geistige Situation der Zeit*, 1931, p. 145:

> *Philosophy of existence* is the way of thought by means of which the human seeks to become himself; it makes use of objective knowledge while at the same time going beyond it. This way of thought does not cognize objects, but elucidates and makes actual the being of the thinker. *Brought into a state of suspense* by having transcended the cognitions of the world (as the adoption of a philosophical attitude toward the world) that fixate being, it *appeals* to its own freedom (as the elucidation of existence) and makes space for its own unconditioned activity through *conjuring up* transcendence (as metaphysics).[4]

Here not "able to be presented." Jaspers says (*Existenzphilosophie: Drei Vorlesungen gehalten am Freien Deutschen Hochstift in Frankfurt a. M.*, September 1937, p. 1) that in this philosophy it comes down "to catching sight of actuality at its origin and to grasping it through the way in which I, in thought, deal with myself – in inner action."[5]

The origin is the human himself – as himself. "We are not merely there {*da*}; rather our Dasein is entrusted to us as the site and the body for the actualization of our origin" (ibid.).[6]

---

[4] {TN: Translated under the title *Man in the Modern Age* (literally, *The Spiritual Situation of the Time*), by Karl Jaspers, trans. E. Paul and C. Paul (London: Routledge, 1933), p. 159 (trans. mod.).}

[5] {TN: Karl Jaspers, *Philosophy of Existence*, trans. Richard F. Grabau (Philadelphia: University of Pennsylvania Press, 1971), p. 3 (trans. mod.).}

[6] {TN: Jaspers, *Philosophy of Existence*, p. 4 (trans. mod.).}

Origin – the encompassing self-enactment of the appropriation of actuality for himself by the human.

"Dasein" = the being present at hand of the human as a *living being* {Lebewesen}. In this presence at hand, "existence" – that is, the human in his self-being – is as existing. "As existence, the human who is himself there speaks. He turns to existence as one irreplaceable individual ['I –   19 self'] to another ['you – self']" (ibid., p. 33).[7]

> Existence is the self-being that relates to itself and *thereby* also to transcendence, *by* which it knows that it has been given to itself and *upon* which it is grounded. (Ibid., p. 17)[8]

Instead of transcendence = the transcendent = God. Hence the tripartite division: world – freedom – God. The Kantian architectonic and the basic stance. And yet different: non-binding and related back to the individual self-being, and everything relativized to this.

§ 10 Kierkegaard's Concept of Existence

An essential impetus for the philosophy of existence: *Kierkegaard* (1813–1855).

Still less can we say something sufficient about him and his work. Since 1900, almost concurrently with Nietzsche, *influential in various ways.* The {German} translation of the *Gesammelte Werke* by Diederichs Publishing House. The influence need not be direct; see R. M. Rilke. Kierkegaard is a "religious thinker"; that is, not a theologian and not a "Christian philosopher" (non-concept); Kierkegaard is more theological than any Christian theologian and more unphilosophical than any metaphysician could ever be; lived at once in the world of German Idealism and Romanticism, of the New Testament and Luther. – The mode of his writing: the pseudonyms, the edifying works and the erudite and poetic works. In an emphatic sense – regarding his stance and mode of thinking – incomparable; he must stand on his own; neither theology nor philosophy can include him in their histories.

---

[7] {TN: Jaspers, *Philosophy of Existence*, p. 40 (trans. mod.); Heidegger's interpolations in square brackets.}

[8] Emphases by Martin Heidegger. {TN: Jaspers, *Philosophy of Existence*, 21 (trans. mod.).}

Now only an indication of Kierkegaard's concept of existence is to be given. For this a citation of a passage from his magnum opus *Concluding Unscientific Postscript II* (1846) should suffice.

20   One thinks that existing is no issue, even less an art (after all we
      all exist), but to think abstractly, that is something. But, to exist
      in truth, that is, to permeate one's existence with consciousness,
      at once eternal as though far beyond it and yet present in it, and
      nevertheless in the course of becoming – that is truly difficult.[9]
      [To become "subjective." To be a human (to live). Subject –
      object]

We will attempt to explain this passage according to the principal directions and within the limits of our task:

1. The passage begins with two oppositions (the "but" that appears twice), where in each case one member of the opposition is "to exist" and is tantamount to being-actual, "Dasein," but evidently also already accentuating *human* existing;
   (a) to exist and "to think abstractly";
   (b) to exist and "to exist in truth."

2. The second sentence delimits what "to exist in truth" means. And herein lies the weight of the passage. Of course, the indication of the *first* opposition is also significant, because we immediately recognize from it the level on which the discussion is moving.

Regarding 1. "To exist" and "to think abstractly." Both are opposed to one another insofar as the one is nothing special, namely "to exist" ("We" humans), whereas "to think abstractly" is "something," that is to say, matters a great deal and poses corresponding challenges. How so? What does "to think abstractly" mean here? To think philosophically, not only indeterminately in general, but also in the mode of the highest figure of philosophy at that time, which is here expressly on Kierkegaard's mind: *Hegel's metaphysics*. Kierkegaard indeed develops his basic position through a constant confrontation with Hegel; but he does not attain it only in this way.

21   The opposition between "to exist" and "to think abstractly" means, more precisely: to think and act as an individual human and to think the absolute as a thinker. In a certain way, we all indeed do the former,

[9] Kierkegaard, *Gesammelte Werke*, vol. 7 (Jena: 1925), p. 7. {TN: Søren Kierkegaard, *Concluding Unscientific Postscript to Philosophical Crumbs*, ed. and trans. Alastair Hannay (Cambridge: Cambridge University Press, 2009), p. 258 (trans. mod.)}

and that occurs almost automatically – as "subjects," we are all determined by "*subjectivity*," comporting ourselves consciously toward things and self-consciously toward ourselves. And this subjectivity is precisely "existence" – which indeed each of us has. But: "*to think abstractly*" – that seems to be difficult, and an art.

"To think abstractly" means for Kierkegaard: to disregard the *singular individual*, this here and now, and to think only the universal and thus also to disregard the attempt to think the individual together with the universal; the *difference* between Kierkegaard and Hegel consists *in the manner of determining this "together."* (Hegel, too, and Hegel especially, thinks together. See below p. 18.)

Behind this lies Platonism: the individual here and now is the temporal; the universal is the enduring, the eternal; to think abstractly: to forget the temporal, to lose oneself in the eternal. "Abstraction" explains everything, but it leaves *out* precisely the "existing," *the "first substance" (according to Aristotle).* See *Concluding Unscientific Postscript II*, chap. III, § 1 (*Gesammelte Werke* VII, p. 2):

The suspect nature of abstract thought becomes evident exactly in connection with all existence-questions, where the abstraction removes the difficulty by dropping it and then priding itself on having explained everything. It explains immortality in general and, what do you know?, everything goes excellently inasmuch as immortality becomes identical with eternity, *the* eternity that is essentially the medium of thought. But whether an existing individual human is immortal, which is just the difficulty, this is something that abstract thought does not trouble itself with. It is disinterested. Yet the difficulty with existence is what interests one who exists, and the one who exists is infinitely interested in existing. Abstract thinking thus helps me with my immortality by killing me off as a particular existing individual and then making me immortal, and so helping rather like the doctor in Holberg who with his medicine took the patient's life but then also expelled the fever. The impression one gets, on contemplating an abstract thinker unwilling to clarify to himself, and to admit to, the relation his abstract thought has to his being someone existing, is a comic one however distinguished he may be, because he is on the point of ceasing to be a human. While, as a composite of the finite and the infinite, an actual human has his actuality precisely in keeping these together, infinitely interested in existing, an abstract thinker of this kind is a two-fold being {*Doppelwesen*}, a fantastical one who lives in the pure being of abstract thought and, now and then, a pitiful professorial figure whom the abstract essence sets aside, as one does a walking-stick.[10]

Whoever is familiar with Hegel's philosophy knows that *it* precisely strives for nothing other than to think, *not* abstractly, but rather "concretely." *According to Hegel*, whoever thinks one-sidedly "thinks abstractly"; for example, the countrywoman with her cow Liese also thinks one-sidedly, because she takes it and everything around it to be what is actual. (Yet to what extent – in another respect – can the countrywoman in her relationship with Liese exemplify philosophy?) Only the philosopher, in Hegel's view, thinks concretely, the one who thinks all the essential sides, according to which it is possible in general to think, on the basis of the unity of their belonging and growing together (concretion).

And yet Kierkegaard asserts that Hegel thinks "abstractly" – thus one-sidedly; how can one who thinks the unconditional whole ever think one-sidedly? *Abstract* divided in two: 1. *one-sided* – to think according to a (proximate) direction of consciousness – (Hegel); 2. *off-sided* – to represent what is thought as what is *metaphysically* thought (beingness), detached – (Kierkegaard).

23

We will not now ask whether Kierkegaard does justice to Hegel, or whether, precisely *because* he is all too dependent on Hegel, he does not judge him unfairly. We will ask only about what Kierkegaard opposes to "simply existing" and above all to "abstract thinking" in the second-named opposition. From there it ought to become apparent in what sense even Hegel's concrete thinking, and it precisely, remains "abstract"/one-sided for Kierkegaard.

Regarding 2. To exist and *"to exist in truth."* What this means is marked off in a particularly concise and decisive way by the quoted passage, in the following moments:

(a) to penetrate one's existence consciously; to be distinguished in one's own self-being as such, not merely to represent it in the mode of psychological analysis, but rather "thoughtfully," *conscientiously*, responsibly. With this, Kierkegaard does not wish to neutralize and degrade "knowledge."

See, on this, a note from 1 August 1853 (see Hirsch, *Kierkegaard-Studien I*, 1930, p. 24):[11]

---

[10] Ibid., p. 2. {TN: Kierkegaard, *Concluding Unscientific Postscript to Philosophical Crumbs*, p. 253 (trans. mod.).}

[11] Emanuel Hirsch, *Kierkegaard-Studien*, vol. 1 (Gütersloh: Bertelsmann, 1933).

Certainly I won't deny that I still accept an *imperative of know-ledge* and that through it one can also influence people, but *then it must be taken up alive in me*, and *this* is what I now see as the main point. It is this my soul thirsts for as the African deserts thirst for water. [. . .] That's what I lacked for leading a *completely human life* and not just a life of *knowledge*, to avoid basing my mind's development on – yes, on something that people call objective – something which at any rate isn't my own, and to base it instead on something which is bound up with the deepest roots of my existence, through which I have, as it were, grown into the divine ["concretely" with him, Hegel], clinging fast to it even if the whole world were to fall apart. *This, you see, is what I need, and this is what I strive for.*[12]

24

The conscious penetration into self-consciousness is supposed to come to the root of the latter and consciously to root the penetrator – to let his rootedness be known. Hence

(b) likewise (to penetrate) eternally far beyond it, as it were – eternally beyond one's own existence, that is, to penetrate into the eternal, to come before God – and thus to be eternally beyond temporality – to stand before God.

(c) "and yet present in it [in temporal existence]" – that is, not to lose oneself and dissolve speculatively in the absolute, but rather to hold fast to the infinite difference between time and eternity – to remain in temporality, not to flee from it fantastically; but also not to take this remaining as persisting in what is given, but rather to take it

(d) "nevertheless in the course of becoming" – that is, in temporal action and in going toward the eternal.

In short: to have one's actuality in the "composite" of eternity and becoming, of infinity and finitude, which, however, consists in holding them together; and that means to be a Christian authentically, that is, always *to become* a Christian; to understand oneself as acting before God on the basis of faith in the fact of God's incarnation in Christ – that means, "to exist in truth."

In contrast, Hegel thinks "abstractly" in Kierkegaard's sense for several reasons:

---

[12] {TN: *Kierkegaard's Journals and Notebooks*, vol. 1: *Journals AA–DD*, ed. Niels Jørgen Cappelørn et al. (Princeton: Princeton University Press, 2007), pp. 19–21.}

1. Because, in Kierkegaard's opinion, he forgets the thinking individual and the individual in general and wishes to exist as the absolute himself.

2. Because he *mediates* the difference between time and eternity – does *not* allow this infinite contradiction to persist, but *sublates* it by, in general, sublating the contradiction in everything – instead of recognizing the paradox that the eternal has become a fact in the temporal.

3. The sublation of all contradictions and the apparent overleaping of the individual is connected to the essence of metaphysics – as metaphysics of the unconditional subjectivity of spirit. (Consider, however, the essence of this thinking in general! See *The Philosophy of Right*.)

The opposition in which Kierkegaard stands to Hegel is in truth that between the *faithful Christian in Kierkegaard's sense and the absolute metaphysics of German Idealism*, which for its part is, however, convinced that it has first elevated the truth of Christianity to absolute truth. That is not only Hegel's view, but also Schelling's (theology – in the abstract domain of philosophy; see *Stuttgarter Privatvorlesungen* 1810; see, below, "Recapitulations and Course of the Interpretation," p. 122, on the final remark of the Freedom Treatise).

Seen from Kierkegaard's perspective, his relation to Hegel's philosophy appears *thus*: Hegel says that philosophy places common human understanding "on its head" (that is to say, on reason; it first brings the human who is rational in himself to [speculative] "understanding"), that is, turning him upside down, philosophy brings the human first *to consciousness*, so that the *"head"* – thinking – is the ground and what is sustaining. That is, philosophy does not think one-sidedly, finitely, abstractly, but rather all-sidedly, infinitely, concretely, from its first step on. In contrast, when Kierkegaard, for his part, in turn reverses Hegel and isolates everything in the existence of the individual, he brings the human of speculative metaphysics, who has been placed on his head, back on his "feet."

Certainly – but only at the cost of him renouncing philosophy as such and existing only as a believer; the great misunderstanding when it comes to Kierkegaard, however, is to claim him for a "Christian philosophy."

For Kierkegaard, *"to exist"* means emphatically: "to exist in truth," that is, to be an individual human before God in the truth of the Christian faith. (In actuality, "in" the actual – *to be a Christian* before the absolutely actual.) Becoming revealed.

Kierkegaard does not exist, however, as some unknown faithful Christian who somewhere carries out his daily work and does his job – he has no job and does not want to have one – but rather exists as an author; he thinks and writes and communicates and intervenes in the conflicts of the day; the thinking of his age becomes potent in him, and he thus establishes a unique dwelling for self-reflection in the nineteenth century. He becomes indispensable, regardless of whether one is an adherent, an opponent, or even merely indifferent.

Now, since my own attempts at thinking have often been brought into connection with Kierkegaard; since, moreover, their subsumption under "the philosophy of existence" has simply become self-evident and everything has in advance sunk into the grave of this heading, I must say a few things for the purpose of clarifying the concept of existence in "Being and Time."[13]

§ 11 Kierkegaard, "Philosophy of Existence," and "Being and Time" (1927)

This should, above all, serve to give us a better understanding of the mode of thinking within which the current confrontation with Schelling is moving. We are not aiming here to highlight our "own standpoint," as it were; nor it is a matter of defending an "originality" thought to be under threat. Yet the difficulty remains that we must speak about what is our own. Self-deceptions are inevitable here, even when appreciable time has elapsed since the earlier publication. (With this, I am not saying that "Being and Time" has become a thing of the past for me. Even today, I still have not "gone further," if only because I know ever more clearly that I am not permitted to go "further"; perhaps, however, I have come a bit closer to what was attempted in "Being and Time.") 27

We take "Being and Time" to be the name for a reflection, the necessity of which lies far beyond the activity of an individual, who can neither "invent" this necessity nor master it. We therefore distinguish between the necessity designated by the name "Being and Time" and the "book" bearing this title. ("Being and Time" as a name for an appropriative event {Ereignis} in beyng itself. "Being and Time" as a formula for a reflection within the history of thinking. "Being and Time" as a title of a treatise that attempts to carry out this thinking.) That this book has its flaws – I believe I know something about this

---

[13] {TN: Heidegger places quotation marks around "Sein und Zeit" in order to designate both the book *Sein und Zeit* and the topic "being and time." We have retained this equivocality throughout by placing quotation marks around "Being and Time."}

myself. Here, it's like climbing an unscaled mountain. Because it is steep and at the same time unfamiliar, whoever proceeds sometimes ends up falling. The hiker has suddenly lost his way. Sometimes he even falls without the reader noticing it, since, after all, the pages keep going; here one can even fall several times. But one also shouldn't go on too long or make much ado about this. These remarks already transgress a boundary, which, admittedly, they must do, because we contemporaries barely find our way to the inherently prevailing necessities without such expedients. Nietzsche once said, although with a different intent: only very late does one have the courage for what one actually knows. We permit ourselves to add: within the realm of the thinking that attempts to think being, even that which one "knows" is, however, each time only the presentiment of a light cast on something that reaches out beyond the thinker from far away.

Thus, if we speak in passing of misinterpretations, these should be neither lamented nor excused, and above all they should not be brought forward as an object of cheap refutations. There is much here that may rest on a superficiality of reading and pondering, but even this superficiality has long been a heritage of recent times. Especially the inability to grasp the task that was posed has grounds that reach deep into the essence of traditional philosophy, that is, of metaphysics; and the insight into these grounds is prepared in "Being and Time" itself (the falling prey of Da-sein to beings).

The misinterpretations are supported by the inevitable fact that such an attempt is the least capable of leaping out of its times. It must knowingly, but also largely against its will, speak in the language of the age and think along the path from which it frees itself. For this reason, it designates itself as "phenomenology," as "metaphysics" of Dasein (Kant book),[14] as "fundamental ontology." What is expressed in all these names is the effort to find shelter somewhere in the familiar and to get one's bearings therein. But, everywhere, there is also the knowledge that we are dealing with a preparation for another sort of thinking; we are dealing, not with a "laying of the groundwork" for a planned "system of philosophy," but with a transformation of questioning and thinking.

Hence we can now say more clearly: in absolutely everything, we are not yet or any longer dealing with "philosophy," but with an attempt to think something essential, something essential that has *always* already been named in the history of the West, without, however, *that* being

---

[14] *Kant and the Problem of Metaphysics*, trans. Richard Taft, 5th edn. (Bloomington: Indiana University Press, 1997).

said which has meanwhile become necessary to think, even if the need {*die Not*} from which the necessity {*Notwendigkeit*} emerges has not yet specifically been experienced. (The need of needlessness.)[15]

We draw what has already and continually been named from a quotation from Aristotle: what is to be thought and questioned is the *being* of beings. Yet, at the end of a long history, Nietzsche also says about being that it is the "last wisps of smoke from the evaporating end of reality."[16] The essay "Being and Time" treats of "being." Indeed: not only of being, but of being *and time*.

There is nothing about "existence" here.

But it cannot be either an accident or mere caprice, let alone the ineptitude of my contemporaries, that this essay has fallen under the title "philosophy of existence."

We will ask:

(a) What occasion is there for classifying "Being and Time" as "philosophy of existence"?

(b) What does "existence" mean in "Being and Time" ("existence" and "Da-sein")?

Through this double reflection, it should become clear how the concept of existence in "Being and Time" is related to Kierkegaard and how it is nevertheless determined from a different sort of questioning.

(a) What Occasion is There for Classifying "Being and Time" as "Philosophy of Existence"?

(α) Analytic of Existence

This occasion is evident everywhere:

There is explicit talk of "existence" and, in relation to this, of the "existentials" as those determinations that are supposed to secure the essence of "existence." And this not in passing; rather, an "analytic of existence" is posed as a *task*. On p. 42[17] one reads: "The 'essence' of Dasein lies in its existence." Jaspers' sentence corresponds almost

---

[15] {TN: The German *Not* also has the senses of 'plight,' 'emergency,' 'distress,' thus 'The plight of being without plight,' etc.}

[16] {TN: Friedrich Nietzsche, *Twilight of the Idols*, in Nietzsche, *The Anti-Christ, Ecce Homo, Twilight of the Idols and Other Writings*, ed. Aaron Ridley and Judith Norman, trans. Judith Norman (Cambridge: Cambridge University Press, 2005), p. 168 ("'Reason' in Philosophy," #4).}

[17] {TN: Here and below Heidegger references the German pagination of *Sein und Zeit*, which can also be found in the margins of the published English translations.}

exactly with this: "As existence, the human who is himself there {*da ist*} speaks."[18]

Thus, why should "Being and Time" not be "philosophy of existence," especially when we consider that the "analytic of existence" is
30   synonymous with "fundamental ontology," and ontology as the knowledge of the being of beings is synonymous with philosophy? The "analytic of existence" is the "foundation" of the philosophy that is devised here. Thus, why not "philosophy of existence"?

(β) Existence – As Understood in the Sense of Kierkegaard's Restriction of It

In all of this, "existence" is in fact claimed explicitly as a name for human Dasein, indeed for the latter's self-being; thus, precisely in the sense of *Kierkegaard's* restriction of the generally used concept of *existentia*. Moreover, everyone who reads and knows Kierkegaard sees the dependence on him, such as in the interpretation of "anxiety"; and Kierkegaard deals with "temporality" constantly. Additionally, Kierkegaard is referred to explicitly ("Being and Time," p. 235 note), and a stance is taken with respect to his interpretation of temporality (p. 338 note).

However, one also notices the *differences* from Kierkegaard; and the difference is indeed palpable enough: in "Being and Time" "the Christian element" is omitted; and Kierkegaard is made use of only for an "atheistic philosophy"; that is, Kierkegaard is misunderstood, obviously because the author lacks the necessary "theological" background knowledge. In addition to the exclusion of the Christian element, there is the other misunderstanding: Kierkegaard declares a "system of human Dasein" to be impossible, whereas "Being and Time" strives for such a system, at least according to the opinion of its "interpreters."

(γ) Philosophy of Anxiety, of the Nothing, of Death, of Care . . .

Such a takeover of Kierkegaard, who on this occasion is now suddenly "discovered" to be, and is simultaneously misinterpreted as, a "philos-
31   opher of existence," must yield peculiar consequences: "Being and Time" inevitably becomes an extremely one-sided "philosophy of anxiety," a "philosophy of the nothing," a "philosophy of death," a "philosophy of care," a cluster of gloom and doom that can be explained only by the "psychology" of an "urban" and "uprooted," "self-tormenting" human, who must of course also lack everything "masterful."

---

[18] {TN: Jaspers, *Philosophy of Existence*, p. 40 (trans. mod.).}

These "designations" each time take a prominent and at the same time misinterpreted "theme" to be the whole, without, however, asking where the aim of "the whole" lies and why precisely such matters as "anxiety," "the nothing," and "death" are considered. The fact that the rejections anchored in such designations are unanimous – irrespective of the diversity of the "worldviews" that pipe up in like manner, whether they be secular or ecclesiastical – shows that two things lie hidden in such resistance: on the one hand, the solidarity of a defense whose motives one does not know or consider, especially not with respect to the fact that friend and enemy thus come together in agreement here; on the other hand, the indication of a ground of resistance that has its hold in the fundamental historical position of the modern age in general, and perhaps even of Western history until now, and that therefore does not first determine the rejection but, already before it, the inability to understand.

Thus, neither can this "critique" be perceived in what it specifically brings forth; rather we must consider what, at bottom, governs this critique, without the latter's knowledge. Yet the "critique" knows itself to be secure, since, after all, it believes it speaks in the sense of modern thinking, which strives for an interpretation of the world and of life that one can designate briefly as "anthropology." Since, in the course of modern history, the human, with the unlimited dominance of the free play of all his creative capacities, positions himself ever more clearly and absolutely as the measure and center of all beings, only a doctrine   32
of the human can constitute the formative core of all interpretations of beings as a whole.

(δ) Philosophical Anthropology

From this perspective, we can see why one would conceive of "Being and Time" as an essay in "philosophical anthropology"; for it indeed treats of human Dasein everywhere, and the use of the concept of existence as restricted to the being of the human only strengthens the conception of "Being and Time" as an "anthropology."

Yet, at the same time, the one-sidedness and thus the untenability of this doctrine of the human are also evident. There is, namely, a doctrine of "attunements," and it is said of "attunements" that they are not background music to various human comportments; rather, they thoroughly dominate these comportments from the ground up. This "doctrine of attunements" may pass as "useful" for psychology and psychiatry, if only anxiety were not again invoked immediately as "the" essential attunement, in typical Heideggerian one-sidedness.

It is correct that "Being and Time" deals only with anxiety extensively.

But it is no less certain that the title of § 40, which deals with anxiety, is worded as follows: "The Basic Disposition of Anxiety as *an* Exemplary Disclosedness of Dasein." We do not read that anxiety is "*the*" exemplary disclosedness of Dasein; nor is it being claimed that it is the only one.

Now, if, all the same, in the course of the questioning throughout "Being and Time," only this "one" basic attunement, anxiety, is dealt with extensively, it would nevertheless be reasonable first to ponder the basis for this.

Instead of at least seeking the reason that guides the formulation of the question, one escapes – in keeping with a style that has long been customary of explaining everything – into psychology. The author must be an anxious man lacking in mastery to circle constantly around anxiety. Should one succeed – and why shouldn't one succeed? – in proving that there are also, alongside the depressing attunements, "uplifting" attunements and "feelings of happiness," then this proof, which even draws on "science" for support, would shatter Heidegger's philosophical anthropology, that is, "Being and Time." One can now finally move beyond "Being and Time."

It will indeed be good when the "masterful" opponents and defeaters of "anxiety" finally move on and stop their relentless assault on "Being and Time" with their interpretations.

Now one could certainly be tempted to ask here whether, without their admitting it, an *anxiety in the face of anxiety* is at work in the zealots who appear again and again opposing anxiety, such that the anxious ones who are hounded only by an uncomprehended anxiety are to be sought precisely where one has supposedly long moved beyond anxiety and is simply "masterful" in each everyday affair and with respect to every newspaper article.

If we were to ask such a question, we ourselves would *also* fall back into "psychological-anthropological" explanation, which the analytic of anxiety that is attempted in "Being and Time" precisely contravenes. – Besides, everyone who is thoughtful knows that anxiety belongs to "heroism" and its possibility with the same degree of necessity as the valley to the mountain. Moreover, there is a courage that can even forgo "heroism."

The strange attempts to present "Being and Time" to one's contemporaries as a one-sided "philosophy of existence" and as an outmoded anthropology could have made their job easier. In § 10 of "Being and Time" and in §§ 36–38 of the text *Kant and the Problem of Metaphysics*, there is indeed a crystal-clear dissociation from every sort of philosophical anthropology. Why, then, still refute "Being and Time" as a one-sided – and that means precisely an untrue – anthropology, when "Being and Time" is not an anthropology at all?

Here we come to the decisive point: if "Being and Time" does not wish to be an anthropology, what then is this continued analytic of human Dasein at all supposed to present? This is indeed the question. And, under the pressure of this question, we must finally begin to ponder what else and how else one could, or would have to, or even must question concerning the human and question in general. The imposition to ponder, to actually think *that*, let alone to direct one's reflection toward it for years, exceeds the acceptable measure of recourse of actual thinking. I am also of this opinion. For this reason, it would be good for one finally to let "Being and Time," both the book and the subject matter, rest for an indefinite future.

Now if, on this occasion, we nevertheless ponder several things, then that should initially serve only to clarify the procedure and the stance from which the thinking-through of Schelling's treatise emerges; we thus do not wish, for instance, formally to "refute" the various reactions to "Being and Time." They serve simply as the signs of inevitable phenomena of the modern age, whose excessive calculation of everything and reflectedness in everything precisely prevents it from ever knowing the realm in which its own history is decided.

Meanwhile, we are now able to say certain things about the necessity of being and time more clearly than was possible in the first attempt of the treatise "Being and Time." We will attempt to do so by way of an elucidation of the sentence: "The 'essence' of Dasein lies in its existence" ("Being and Time," p. 42).

The sentence does not assert that the essence of Dasein consists in and is exhausted by its existence. "The 'essence' of Dasein lies in its existence" means: the essence of Dasein conceals itself in existence; in the thinking-through of existence, the essence of Dasein first becomes an essence that is question-*worthy* and that first awakens questioning. The elucidation of the sentence attempted here becomes a clarification and delimitation of the concepts of existence and Da-sein. Here, however, this always means the attempt to reach, in experience, the relation to that which these concepts conceptually grasp. But insofar as a long tradition has fixed the meaning of the words and concepts of existence, Dasein, and essence – indeed, insofar as they have long become ossified in this meaning – the interpretation of the sentence requires that we free ourselves from the meanings that have been given up to now.

35

(b) Rejection of the Classification of "Being and Time" as Philosophy of Existence by Way of an Elucidation of the Concepts of Existence and Da-sein (Elucidations of "Being and Time")

(α) Existence and Dasein as Meaning "Actuality in General" (As Understood in the Traditional Usage of Language)

If we understand the sentence according to the traditional and customary sense of the concepts it uses, namely "existence," "Dasein," and "essence," then it follows that "essence" is the universal generic character under which something is subordinated and classified, and thus demarcated. The "essence" of the tree is the universal that we call "plant," and the latter in turn belongs in the encompassing genus "living essence." The sentence accordingly means: the universal generic character of Dasein is existence. But existence means *existentia*: actuality, presentness, presence {*Präsenz, Anwesenheit*}. And Dasein indeed means the same; the sentence is therefore an empty tautology. The same thing is said twice, and in neither case is it elucidated. One calls this thoughtlessness. And if this sentence {*Satz*} really is supposed to present the basic principle {*Grundsatz*} of "Being and Time," then the explanation we have just provided of this sentence would condemn the entire undertaking.

If, albeit tentatively, we do *not* ascribe such thoughtlessness to the sentence, but for a moment ponder whether there is perhaps still the possibility of another interpretation, then, in accordance with our earlier remarks, the following suggests itself:

"Existence" is understood in Kierkegaard's sense – as a name for human self-being, for the human's self-knowing being-at-home-with-itself {*Bei-sich-selbst-sein*}; in the language of Kierkegaard and modern philosophy: existence = "subjectivity." Then the sentence says: each being that "is *there*," that is to say, each being that is actually present, each in its own way (stone, plant, animal, human, angel, god), has the essence of its Dasein in existence – that means: it is a "subject" and is determined by subjectivity – by a self-representing being-at-home-with-itself; this self-representing can be of different types and different levels: vague and indeterminate in the apparently lifeless, clearer and more distinct in plants, and simply and unconditionally self-knowing in the Dasein of God.

Then, in its basic features, the sentence says what Leibniz, for the first time, thought about beings in a clear and well-grounded manner.

Only, the sentence cannot be thought in this direction either, provided that we hold with some care to what is said in "Being and Time." In § 4, p. 11, one reads: "Sciences, as comportments of the human, have the mode of being of this being (the human). Terminologically, we conceive of this being as *Dasein*." The title "Dasein," which up until then was taken to be the actuality of every being of whatever type, is now also restricted to the human. Only in the domain of the being of the human, even if not in every humanity and perhaps not yet even in any of them, does what is now called "Dasein" show its essence. Spoken in the language of the treatise "Being and Time": "Dasein" is always meant as "human Dasein." To be sure, the animal is also actual, namely in the mode of "living." But the animal is not determined by "Dasein" any more than plant and stone and God are.

Now, the aforementioned sentence is supposed to say what this "Dasein" that is related to the human is, and in what sense this word "Dasein" is being used in a limited scope. If, however, "Dasein" is left indeterminate, and, in keeping with the previous meaning, is nevertheless supposed to hold as the exclusive name for the being of the human, then we end up with a "tautology" again. In "Being and Time," there is often talk of human Dasein; this then means as much as human human being.

The expression "human Dasein" is indeed misleading, even if it has legitimacy within the context of the basic sentence correctly understood since it does contain the impetus to a decisive question. But, for the most part, and straight away, and that means taken unthinkingly, the expression "human Dasein" gives occasion to speak also of animal, plant, and divine Dasein and thus to take the expression "human Dasein" in "Being and Time" as a *species-restriction* of the general determination. "Dasein" then means entirely general actuality or is equated with "life" as the mode of being of all that lives, as in the familiar title *Kampf ums Dasein*;[19] this title is also used for animals and plants, for example in the doctrine of Darwinism, and reveals in an especially clear manner that Dasein means being present at hand, actuality (as a sort of bracing against falling back into the nothing).

(β) Dasein as the Bodily-Psychic-Rational Being-Actual of the Human, and Existence as the Subjectivity of Self-Being (Jaspers)

But "Dasein" can also be used in a sense that is restricted to the human. "Dasein" then means the *bodily-psychic* being-actual of the human, an actuality that does not exhaust the actuality of the human, but is merely the site for the actualization and effecting {*Verwirklichung und Erwirkung*} of authentic actuality, that is, of "existence" – existence

---

[19] {TN: A translation of Darwin's phrase 'struggle for existence,' used in the title of many German books.}

taken in Kierkegaard's sense as the subjectivity of self-being. And it is *in this way* that Jaspers uses the title "Dasein." Dasein = life = *animalitas* and *rationalitas*. The human is not merely Dasein (*animal*) or a living essence endowed with understanding (*animal rationale* – whereby understanding means: self-representation); the human is a living essence endowed with reason, and reason includes responsible, *self-willing* being-at-home-with-oneself and self-being; it includes *personalitas*, "subjectivity" – "existence" in Kierkegaard's sense (see below Recapitulations and Course of the Treatise, p. 124 [Kant]). And rationality as personhood and spirituality (existence) is what is higher and the essential.

Now, if one compares the sentence in "Being and Time" ("the 'essence' of Dasein lies in its existence") with this, then we can see the convergence with what Jaspers says: "We are not merely there; rather our Dasein is entrusted to us as the site and the body for the actualization of our origin."[20] (See above § 9.) Both sentences must after all converge, since both Jaspers and Heidegger are indeed the representatives of the "philosophy of existence."

And yet everything is different. It is necessary to remark here that Jaspers aligned his use of language with that of "Being and Time"; that is, understood the latter in *his* sense and *also* misinterpreted it. The nearest cause for this was provided by the fact that "Being and Time" also understands "existence" in a narrow sense, as pertaining to the human, but – and this is the all-important "but" – *not* and no longer as "subjectivity," but rather as Da-sein, a name that means neither "actuality in general" nor the "actuality of life" in a more restricted sense (*animalitas*, *rationalitas* without *personalitas*). The sentence under discussion says what Dasein is: "The 'essence' of Dasein lies in its existence."

39   *(γ) "Existentiell" and "Existential" Concepts of Existence*
What, then, does existence mean when the word is supposed to be the name for the self-being of the human and yet does not mean simply the "subjectivity" and the "*personalitas*" and the rationality of *homo* as *animal rationale personale*? Now, the fact that the word "existence" continues to be used in "Being and Time," in spite of its distinctness from *existentia* as well as from Kierkegaard's concept of existence, has caused confusion – in spite of the terminological distinction that is immediately introduced between the "existentiell" and "existential" concepts of existence.

---

[20] {TN: Jaspers, *Philosophy of Existence*, p. 4 (trans. mod.).}

The "existentiell" concept of existence (Kierkegaard's and Jaspers' concept) means the self-being self of the human insofar as this self is interested in itself as this being. The "existential" concept of existence means the self-being of the human insofar as it relates, not to the self that is, but to being and to the relation to being. One can, in hindsight, quarrel over whether it was wise to bring fundamentally distinct questions so close together by means of the nomenclature and thereby only to facilitate their confusion. But, in such cases, the choice of words cannot be made only in accordance with the unpredictable behavior of readers, especially not when the thinking through of what is to be thought is at a loss for words at every step, since it is indeed not a matter of reporting on long-known facts simply in another mode of presentation.

Additionally, the understanding of the "concept of existence" as it is used in "Being and Time" is complicated by the fact that the existential concept of existence that conforms to "Being and Time" was first fully developed only in the division that was not made available due to the abandonment of its publication; for, the third division of the first part, "Time and Being," proved to be insufficient during the printing stage. (The decision to abandon publication was made in the last days of December 1926 during a stay in Heidelberg at the home of K. Jaspers, where lively, friendly debates regarding the page proofs of "Being and Time" made it clear to me that the elaboration of this important division (I, 3) that had been achieved at that time would have remained incomprehensible. The decision to abandon publication was reached on the day we received news of R. M. Rilke's death.)[21] However, at the time, I was of the opinion that, over the course of the year, I would be able to say everything more clearly. That was an illusion. So, there came to be in the following years a few publications that were supposed to lead to the proper question in a roundabout way.

So, one will say: now it is understandable why "Being and Time" remained misunderstood, seeing as the author himself withheld the

40

---

[21] Rilke died on 29 December 1926. The news of his death reached Heidegger in the first days of January 1927. Heidegger traveled on 1 January 1927 to Heidelberg to visit Jaspers. See Martin Heidegger's letter to Elisabeth Blochmann from 22 December 1926: "On 1 January, I will travel until the 10th to Heidelberg to visit Jaspers." In Martin Heidegger / Elisabeth Blochmann, *Briefwechsel 1918–1969*, ed. Joachim W. Storck (Marbach am Neckar: Deutsche Schillergesellschaft, 1989), p. 19. See further Martin Heidegger's letters to Karl Jaspers from 26 and 30 December 1926, in *The Heidegger–Jaspers Correspondence (1920–1963)*, ed. Walter Biemel, trans. Gary E. Aylesworth (Amherst, NY: Humanity Books, 2003).

principal thing from us. All the misinterpretations are then excused. Yet here there is no need of excuse, since no one should be accused. Moreover, things are not *so* simple. From the way in which one "occupied" oneself with the published portion, we may infer that even what was still outstanding would have been rightly clarified in accordance with the usual procedures. But that is not easily discerned and not important either. What is essential, however, is that even the fragment gives enough of an indication at any rate for one to hit upon the decisive *question*. And more was not really required.

One has also noted, quite correctly, that in the treatise "Being and Time" the concepts of consciousness and subjectivity never appear as guiding concepts or fundamental determinations of the being of the human when the latter's essence is being determined. Yet one has not thought beyond this observation. Here, too, one immediately had an explanation ready for the absence of the words "consciousness" and "subjectivity," namely that the author writes an idiosyncratic and refined language. If one had said, a searching language, a presentation seeking the word and not finding it, then one would have come closer to the matter. But, above all, one has not thought *through* that which nevertheless pervades the whole, from the beginning paragraphs on, and contains the ground for why, in thinking through the human essence, there is no longer any thought of consciousness and subjectivity, and none at all of *animal rationale*; for the human is grasped on the basis of Dasein. And of Dasein it is said (and moreover with spaced letters for emphasis) ("Being and Time," p. 12):

"*The understanding of being is itself a determinacy of the being of Dasein.*" That means: Da-sein is, in itself, understanding-being {*Sein-Verstehen*}. "Understanding of being" {*"Seinsverständnis"*} is the name for that toward which everything in "Being and Time" is thinking *exclusively*.

(δ) "Understanding of Being" as Decisive Determination of Dasein and Existence in "Being and Time"[22]

According to the explicit coinage of the word {namely, *Seinsverständnis*}, at issue is the understanding of being, not the cognition and awareness, the explaining and "understanding" of beings. In the designation "understanding of being," "understanding" means: projecting, projected projection. And pro-jection implies: opening up and holding open of the open, clearing of the clearing in which what we name

---

[22] See below (θ) The Essence of Da-sein (p. 47 and following).

being (and not beings) and thus are also familiar with under this name is *openly manifest* as *being.* "Projection" does not mean here "mere plan" in contrast with actual accomplishment; projection means rather unclosing, of which perhaps a planning is in each case only one possible consequence.

With the distinction of Dasein through the understanding of being, 42 human Dasein is now (§ 4) – and with conscious reference to the dominant tradition – initially conceived as the one that understands itself in its being. This still sounds as though simply "*subjectivity*" were meant. In the sense of the interpretation of the being of the human through subjectivity, the human is conscious not only of things, but also of the being that he himself is; he has self-consciousness. Here self-consciousness is not an addition to being conscious of things, but this consciousness of things is determined by self-consciousness.

According to the introductory presentation, the understanding of being relates initially to the being {*Sein*} that human Dasein itself is. But already in this way something other than self-consciousness is being thought. For self-consciousness means: to represent the self as a being (existentiell). In contrast, "Da-sein" means that which understands itself in its *being.* Dasein is the name for the existential "essence" of the human. But – what is this being {*Sein*}, wherein Dasein understands itself?

The first determination of Da-sein is developed in the First Division, Second Chapter (p. 52 and following): "Being-in-the-world in General as the Basic Constitution of Dasein." "Being-in-the-world" is the "*basic constitution*" and thus that which also comprises the "essence" of Dasein, that which grounds the inner possibility of Dasein, irrespective of whether Dasein is "actual" or not.

However, one has taken the determination of that basic constitution entirely differently, precisely *as* it is familiar to one without thinking. "Human Dasein" – as being-in-the-world: naturally, the human is actually there in the world; he appears there – just like animals and plants; he is present at hand in this world and a "temporal" being, which is why in what follows there must also be so much talk of "temporality." The human is present at hand in the world, and one day he will disappear from this world, and that is death; for which reason death is also dealt with in what follows.

That the human is present at hand in the world, one says, is not a 43 unique discovery, but one-sidedness. In saying that human Dasein is being-in-the-world, the being of the human is arbitrarily restricted to this-sidedness, and the beyond is simply denied. But "being-in-the-world" indeed does not mean: to appear among the miscellaneous manifoldness of beings (called "world") precisely "also" as a being (Dasein in the sense of being present at hand); rather, being-in-the-world means: first and in each case to "have" beings as such and as a whole open in their wholeness and to comport oneself to that which is and can be encountered in this openness. Having the world is, however, already the essential *consequence* of standing-in in such openness, that is, of being-in-the-world. For this being-in-the-world, it is precisely not necessary that *the world* as *such* (the openness of beings as a whole and as such) be *knowingly* "had" and as it were specifically represented as an object.

Now, the simple and decisive consideration is the following: if the understanding of being belongs to Da-sein – the understanding of being in which Dasein understands its own being – if, however, Dasein itself is distinguished as being-in-the world, then Da-sein, by understanding "its own being," that is, being-in-the-world, stands in the projection of the being of beings as a whole. The understanding of being does not only mean that the human understands himself in his own being, that, in addition and alongside, he also understands the being of the remaining beings; rather, it means that he understands being in general and beforehand, and that from this understanding of being in general, he can first comport himself to beings that he himself is not as well as to the being that he himself is.

To state this essential matter once again, which is simple and for that very reason so difficult to comprehend for the long-confused perspective of thinking: the human, as Da-sein, is not displaced into an open like a pair of shoes is placed before the door of a room; rather, the human, as Da-sein, *is* the wandering exposedness into the open, whose openness and clearing is called the world.

44   Here, too, it was thus necessary, in proceeding from the customary concept of world, according to which the world is only the summation of all beings, first to attempt to make the essence of world, as the openness of being, understandable, that is, to displace the human specifically into the projection of world, or better, to let the already worlding displacement into the projection upon world be experienced.

Here the reflection intentionally proceeded from beings, which had hardly been thoughtfully considered in their mode of being and were not at all comprehensible through the traditional doctrine of the thing; these beings are called "equipment." Now, instead of recognizing the guiding question – that everything aims at grasping the essence of "world" – one held oneself only to *what* is here interpreted with respect to its world-character – precisely to equipment.

Now one brings up the same misgivings about one-sidedness and says: just as Heidegger is familiar only with anxiety among the attunements, so he arbitrarily restricts the "world" to equipment; for Heidegger, the world consists only of cooking pots, pitchforks, and lampshades; he has no relation to "higher culture" and none at all to "nature"; for indeed none of that appears in "Being and Time."

Yet the proper ground for this misinterpretation does not at all lie in the mere superficiality of "reading," but rather in the fact that one takes it to be self-evident that the author wishes to establish a "system of world" here, whereas something else entirely is being asked about.

The human can be experienced as an "inner-worldly" being (the human stands there next to the tree). And yet the being of the human is nevertheless determined by Da-sein as being-in-the-world. Being-in-the-world is not synonymous with the inner-worldliness of beings of every sort, but rather is the distinguishing characteristic of the being of the human, conceived as Da-sein.

The two sentences, "The understanding of being is itself a determinacy of the being of Dasein" and "The 'essence' of Dasein lies in its existence," say at bottom the same thing. From which emerges the   45
insight: what in "Being and Time" is named by the traditional title "existence" is, to be sure, related to the self-being of the human, but this self-being is no longer taken as subjectivity; rather, the being of the human as Dasein is grasped with respect to the *understanding of being* which is caught sight of for the first time.

This implies that the concept of existence in "Being and Time" emerges from a questioning that is completely foreign to the "philosophy of existence," but is also unknown to Kierkegaard, indeed in general lies outside of the thinking of metaphysics and the whole of philosophy up to that point. This other questioning does allow one to interpret metaphysics hitherto in a more originary manner (see the Kant book), but not the other way around.

And yet the reflection on Dasein, which is distinguished by the understanding of being, is not carried out without a historical reflection. Both belong together. The supposed obsession with a "new" philosophy in "Being and Time" is in truth the *rootedness* {Bodenständigkeit} in its oldest inception.

A historical reflection, guided by the questioning in "Being and Time," on how the being of beings is now understood in the understanding of being, yields the following insight: ever since Plato and Aristotle, being has univocally been determined as *ousia*, beingness; and *ousia* implies: presence, presencing. *Ousia* is more precisely the sustaining word for the opposition of *parousia* and *apousia*, presence and absence. In Plato (see for example the *Theaetetus*) and in Aristotle, the word *ousia* is still used both as an everyday word and as a name for the philosophical fundamental concept. As an everyday word, *ousia* means wealth, goods and chattel, that which is at all times available, because it presences {*anwest*} as lying fixed – still today we call a farm an *Anwesen*.

Now, if the Greeks had at that time been so thoughtless as to judge everything according to the wording, then they would have had to say: see, Plato and Aristotle interpret the whole of beings in view of *ousia*, of wealth, estate – a highly one-sided conception of the world. We have no witnesses for such a misinterpretation. Another reason it did not come up was because the Greeks intuited that a word in language can, beyond its customary everyday meaning, harbor within itself a saying power that, when it is released into the open, makes the word an essential word. The latter then perhaps harbors within itself *a fortiori* something still concealed. Perhaps this is also the case with the words "Dasein," "existence," "care," "world," "history," "time," "being" – perhaps . . .

Ousia means more precisely: the presence of something in its outward look (*eidos* – *idea*). Beings are, that is, are presencing, and *because* they presence, they can be encountered, found lying before one {*vor-gefunden*}, fixed as present at hand {*vor-handen*}. Hence, according to this interpretation of beings as what presences, that which "constantly" presences is what *is* in the highest sense, that is to say, the *aei on*.[23]

With a bit of pondering, we can see from this that presence and constancy are the distinguishing determinations of beings as such.

Just one single – but also decisive and simple – step is now needed in order to recognize the following: "presence" and "constancy" are indeed manifest *determinations of time*: "presence" concerns "the present"; "constancy" means "at every time." Admittedly, to the extent that this is manifest, it becomes ever more obscure *in what sense* "determination of time" and "time" are to be thought here. The proper standing, *aei on*, the constantly present that knows no absence, the eternal, is however precisely *not* "in time" – and nevertheless is thoroughly determined "in terms of time." Or will one deny that presence and constancy are related to "time"?

Only one thing becomes clear from such reflection: being, as constant presencing, is understood on the basis of time, whereby the essence of time and its claim to become the realm of projection for the

---

[23] {TN: 'eternal being.'}

understanding of being remain obscure. The question concerning the 47
understanding of being and the sense of being thereby attains its clarity
and fullness. It asks: what does it mean that being is projected upon
time and understood on the basis of time? What does it mean that time
in general is the open and the realm of projection for being? What does
this all mean? What is happening here, and what has long been going
on? Have we ever given thought to what is properly taking place here
{*sich ereignet*}? A questioning becomes necessary, which is abbreviated
in the title: "Being and Time."

Since then, it has slowly and roughly become known that *ousia*
"properly" meant presence; one repeats that and suddenly acts as
though that had always been well known and self-evident. Yet one
overlooks that even the Greeks themselves were *never* aware of how
exclusively, precisely, they understood being on the basis of time. Thus,
we must be the first ones to ask, where does this Greek projection of
being upon time stem from? Where does the Platonic interpretation of
being as *idea* and the Aristotelian as *energeia* emerge from? [*phusis*] But
also where does the ignorance of the Greek thinkers about this projection of being upon time stem from? What sort of ignorance is this; is it
only an inability to reflect more deeply, or the opposite?

(ε) Dasein, Temporality, and Time

If Dasein is distinguished by the understanding of being, and if the
projection of being claims "time" as openness, then Da-sein must also
already stand in an essential relation to time, that is, be "temporal." The
all-anticipating foresight into the connection between being and time, a
connection that is first to be made clear, is therefore the *sole* – but also
the all-joining and enduring – impetus for the reflection on the "temporality" of Dasein. In this sole connection also lies the impetus for the
reflection on the essence of "time."

Yet Kierkegaard also deals with the "temporality" of the human,
indeed, constantly; and by this he means that the sojourn of the 48
human as a "creature" on earth is temporally delimited and that this
temporality is the "narthex" of eternity in the sense of *beatitudo*, of
"eternal blessedness," as understood by Christianity. In the context of
this Christian-theological discussion of "temporality," which is related
to the salvation of the individual immortal soul, Kierkegaard develops
important insights, as he does wherever he directs his thought. I have
learned from this, but by no means as much as I have learned from
Aristotle's treatise on "time" (Phys. Δ, 10–14), which has been decisive
for every Western reflection on time. I have also learned from Plotinus
(Enn. III, 7), likewise from Augustine (Confess. lib. XI, c. 1–31),

likewise from Kant, likewise from Hegel. I am always learning – but always in relation to the *one* question: "Being and Time." That is why the interpretation of the temporality of Da-sein now also arrives at a completely different approach. The very essence of time unveils itself in a more originary way. (See "Being and Time," §§ 65 and 66: marking off the essential determination of time that has been attained from the traditional interpretation of time in Western metaphysics; on the relative justification of the commonplace representation of time see §§ 78–83. Moreover, it must be pointed out that already in §§ 22–24, even "space," with respect to Da-sein, is shifted into a different questioning and thus is preliminarily interpreted with respect to the question concerning the relation of time and space and concerning the ground of their unity, and indeed within the questioning-realm of the question "Being and Time.")

One typically understands the "temporality" of the being of the human as the fact that the "earthly" actuality and the "this-worldly" activity of the human runs its course "in time," begins in a singular moment and ceases in a single moment. The "time" that the human thus "spends" within this interval is, then, his "temporality." To be "temporal" in such a manner is, then, also the actuality of animals, plants, stones, and planets. Their actuality, whether one takes it as a state or process, runs its course within a somewhere-present-at-hand – or even merely represented as such – "dimension" of "time" as a form or ordering and measure of "duration." "Temporality," represented in this way, is called "within-timeness" in "Being and Time."

49

But "the temporality of Dasein" that is thought through in "Being and Time" considers something completely different, thus not the within-timeness of the human – that the activity of the human elapses "in time." Nor does the temporality of Dasein mean merely that the human, while his activity and actuality run their course "in time," also specifically knows and represents time, which would then have as a consequence that he is "differently" "in time." But one then also still stands entirely outside of what is to be gained in asking about the "temporality of Dasein" when one grants that the human is familiar with the "clock" and, in the use of this tool for measuring time, reckons "with his time" and thus has a "consciousness of time" and therefore is "very differently" "in time." Furthermore, this within-timeness of the human is represented in such an indeterminate manner that one could claim the same for animals, as well. Animals get by, admittedly, without a clock; but the swallows indeed fly off "in September" and the titmice begin hatching "in March," and the rooster crows, not "at 10:00 in the evening," but "at 4:00 in the morning."

Yet the question concerning the temporality of Dasein does not at all merely ask whether the human is differently "in time" than the animal and differently than the planets, but whether his relation to time in general is exhausted by being merely this or that way "in time" like everything else, only "very differently."

The human is indeed differently "in time," insofar as he, expressly reckoning with time, knows and represents time as such. Yet why is the human familiar with time *as time*? Not only because he stands differently "in time," but because time specifically is related to the being of the human. Time does not merely attach to him as a property; rather, it determines Da-sein, insofar as the latter has in itself the character of temporalizing. The manner in which time essences as time determines the way in which human being "goes before itself."   50

It "goes before itself" by going ahead of itself in its possibilities and coming to itself in these possibilities. Human being is, *in itself*, coming-to {*zu-künftig*}, and it thereby comes back to its having-been and takes it into the to-come {*Zu-kunft*} and continually gathers, in all that, future {*Zukunft*} and having-been into a present. In relation to Da-sein, time is not a dimension merely placed around it, a dimension that lies ready as a neutral framework in order that a life accompanied by consciousness could unfurl in it like a coil spring. "Human Dasein" is *trans-ported* {ent-rückt} at once into coming and having-been and presencing; the coming and having been and presencing are thereby known and not known in different ways and to various extents. The knowing and not-knowing of that toward which Dasein is at once temporally transported does not first comprise this transport, but rather already presupposes it. Every moment of Da-sein is as this threefold-united transport.

Time "is" time by temporalizing itself ecstatically, and the unity of time is in each case an ecstatic unity. Future, having-been, and present are not stretches of an unwinding succession of now-points that are somewhere present at hand, that are occupied or unoccupied, that half "are" and half "are" not. My being is not transported into the future because I have a representation of the future; rather, I can represent what is futural only because my being as Da-sein essences in the fundamental manner of letting what is coming come to itself, of being transported into the coming. That we can and in many ways do avert our gaze from what is coming, and often even have to turn away for moments, indeed only confirms that this transport into the coming persists and essences throughout our being, *before* all mere consciousness thereof.

Dasein is not "in time," but "*is*" *as* the temporalizing of time itself.

51   The temporalizing of time essentially also comprises what we, with an entirely different ascription of meaning to the word, call "Da-sein" (see (θ), p. 47 and following). This temporalizing does not first result because the human has a conscious relation to time; rather, the human can reckon with time only because the being of the human is determined by temporalization, stands in the ecstatic open of ecstatic time, and therefore comports itself to it *as time.*

"Time," as it is thus initially known and grasped, is "the same" as that in which all beings run their course. For this reason, it also remains erroneous to suppose that "the time" "in" which the human "lives" "appears" to be a different time than that "in" which the planets wander. This time is precisely the same "for" the human and the planets. But this time, as a form of measure "in" which the human and the animal and the planet endure and proceed, springs from the time that temporalizes itself as Da-sein, a Dasein that is, to be sure, the ground of the being of the human, but is not first effected and actualized {*bewirkt und verwirklicht*} by the human.

So, is the time "in which" human and animal, plant and planet are, something "subjective"? No – for with respect to ecstatic temporality the human can precisely no longer be conceived of as a subject. The standing-in in Da-sein is precisely the overcoming of all subjectivity and of every possibility of subjectivism. How should what precisely does *not* spring from a subjectivity ever be "subjective"?

(ζ) Temporality, Da-sein, Existence

The indications of the basic ecstatic feature of time are, however, only the first steps in grasping the essence of time, that is, in inquiring about it from a nexus of questioning that is entirely different and likewise the only essential one. The heretofore traditional interrogation of the essence of time for the whole of Western thinking was established by Aristotle. Here, time is considered as that according to which and in

52   which the temporal point for the arrival and disappearance of a being, as well as the relations between such temporal points, that is, the duration of presence and absence, is determined, that is, measured, that is, numbered. For this reason, the fundamental essence of time for Aristotle is *arithmos*, number; this refers to that *according to which* there is a *numbering* in the reckoning of time.

Kant says essentially the same thing when he says time is the pure form of intuition of inner sense. Time is *megethos*, dimension, form of positional ordering for the measuring calculation of beings in a sequence. Here, "time" is considered to be what occurs alongside space, movement, and the materiality of things.

Yet the reason why time – first in Greek thought and continually ever since – was never recognized in its ecstatic essence, but rather was interpreted differently (namely, as *ousia tis*[24]), is grounded in the projection of being under which Western history stood inceptively and has long stood since. The traditional essence of time shows time as that within which all beings elapse and according to which all duration and presence are measured – even the being that is highest in the traditional sense, the eternal; because of eternity as "*nunc stans*" – what is this other than a determination measured and conceived of on the basis of "time"?

In contrast, the reflection on the essence of time in "Being and Time" receives its sole impetus and questioning direction from the recognition that the being of beings has, of old, been grasped on the basis of time. Through the interpretation of Dasein as temporality it should now become clear that Da-sein – in which, standing, the human is himself – has its essence in the temporalizing of temporality. But, in accordance with the guiding sentence cited earlier, Da-sein includes the understanding of being, that is, the projection of being into an open from which it, as being {*Sein*} (initially as presencing and constancy), is known and becomes knowable. But the reason why this open is – indeed, perhaps even must be – the ecstatic unity of time, can be surmised when we consider that Dasein, and thus the understanding   53 of being, which characterizes its essence, is thoroughly governed by the essence of time and its ecstatic temporalization.

Now, the fundamental sentence, through whose elucidation we are supposed to become more acquainted with the concept of existence in "Being and Time," says this: "The 'essence' of Dasein lies in its existence." After everything that has been said so far, we must now grasp what existence means, indeed with regard to the 'essence' of Dasein – and only thus.

Da-sein is the ecstatic temporalization of time and is determined by the projection of being, that is to say, it is in itself the one projecting – namely, projecting being upon time. And, within the ambit of questioning in "Being and Time," ex-sistence names precisely this: that Da-sein stands out (ex-sists), ecstatically transported, into the ecstatic openness of time. Ex-sistence is the word for the standing-in in the ecstatic exposedness into the open.

This explicit exposition of the concept of existence, which in all essentials was prepared and prefigured by the interpretation of the

---

[24] {TN: 'a certain substance.'}

ecstatic essence of time, was reserved for the unpublished third division of the first part of "Being and Time." But even without this exposition, one can, with a bit of pondering, reach the following *at least as a question*: if Dasein is ec-static in its temporality, and if the "Analytic of Existence" lays everything on making this ecstatic essence of "time" visible, won't then the essence of ex-sistence perhaps be connected with the *ek-stasis* of time? Ek-sistence is indeed only the Latin word for the Greek *ek-stasis*. [If one is so indignant about the mere "word philosophy" in "Being and Time," why hasn't one ever thought this supposed mere thinking in words through to the end and in its unity? The answer is simple: one merely hangs on the traditional concepts of the word and does not find the resolve ever actually to free oneself, not even for a moment, for a "subject matter" hitherto unfamiliar.]

54   In the lecture courses after 1927, and above all in the lecture "On the Essence of Truth" (1930),[25] which is unpublished but was delivered several times, the concept of existence was developed in the sense of the exposedness into the open of beings, an exposedness that understands being. The word "existence" is thereby conceived of ecstatically, according to "Being and Time," and thus essentially otherwise than in the Scholastic explanation of *ex-sistentia*. What is meant is not that something actual is taken out of previous non-actuality (the nothing) and placed into its actuality; rather the exposedness into the open, the standing-in in the ecstatic unity of transport, is the way in which Dasein alone essences as that in which the being of the human is grounded.

If an opposition to the customary concept of existence is at all allowed, then it would be necessary to say: not a being taken "*out*" of the nothing in the sense of a transference from the non-actual into the actual, but rather the ecstatic placedness into the open of being and thus precisely *into* the nothing, if indeed the nothing belongs to the essence of being.

(Although the word "ex-sistence" – with respect to the ecstatic character of Da-sein – is able to name Da-sein's essence in a well-fitting manner, ever since the public became aware of the "philosophy of existence" [K. Jaspers, *Die geistige Situation der Zeit*, 1931 – see pp. 23 and following and 144 and following] I struck the word "existence" from the lexicon of the thinking circumscribed by the question of "Being and Time." Instead, the apparently opposite name "persistent steadfastness" {*Inständigkeit*} is used. This implies two things: standing-in {*Innestehen*} in the ecstatic openness of "time"; yet this

---

[25] Now in a translation by John Sallis in Martin Heidegger, *Pathmarks*, ed. William McNeill (Cambridge: Cambridge University Press, 1998), pp. 136–154.

standing-in is at the same time persistently steadfast {*inständig*} in the sense of "incessantly remaining in the essential relation to the being of beings"; the "persistent steadfastness in being" is named "care." But even this word is so burdened by everyday language that every other 55 use remains surrounded by misinterpretations. "Care" in "Being and Time" means the persistently steadfast guarding and preservation of the truth of being, never the concern about beings. What is true of care is also true of other fundamental words that are named in the "Analytic of Dasein.")

(η) Anxiety, Death, Guilt, and the Nothing within the Realm of Questioning in "Being and Time"

Everyone who is even somewhat familiar with "Being and Time," in view of what has been said up to now, would be justified in replying as follows: what in the end must be granted must be granted, namely, that in "Being and Time" thinking goes beyond the questions that the title "Being and Time" indicates. The reflection indeed directs itself to the being of *each* being and to the being of beings as a whole, not only to the being of the human and least of all to "existence" in the narrow, Kierkegaardian sense; indeed, not only to *existentia* in the traditional metaphysical meaning either.

If the questioning thus aims at being and *not* at the isolated being, the human, then why do the extensive discussions of anxiety, death, guilt, and the nothing press so conspicuously into the foreground? The answer to this is: the enumerated themes are dealt with only because the *one* question "Being and Time" is posed everywhere, even where it is not at all always being dealt with specifically, and where it seems as though everything were aiming only at a "philosophical anthropology" or a "philosophy of existence."

Of what sort the *one* question of "Being and Time" is and where the "provisional aim" of this treatise is located can be found succinctly and clearly in the preface, on page 1. There it is said, even with spaced letters for emphasis: the question goes toward the "meaning of being." This already implies, above all, that the question does not go toward beings or toward the "meaning of beings." And what "meaning" 56 means is discussed in detail in § 32: "meaning" is, according to "Being and Time," the realm of projection for understanding. Insofar as it is a matter of understanding in the sense of the understanding of being, what is being asked about with the "meaning of being" is the open, from which something like being is at all understandable, in such a way that the words "being" and "is" and their variant forms are not mere sounds and noises, but each time name something which we understand straight away, without considering it specifically, let alone grasping it explicitly.

Then, in § 44, "Dasein, Disclosedness, and Truth," the essence of truth is dealt with, apparently once again arbitrarily and without the right context, and the inceptive determination of the essence of truth within Western thinking is thereby retrieved: that essence of truth that had meanwhile been buried and that also can never again be renewed in its inceptive shape. According to this, truth is *a-lētheia*, unconcealment of beings. After the indication of *this* determination of truth, the openness, the clearing in which "something" shows and bestirs itself and is therefore also knowable and known, is for the first time claimed in "Being and Time" as the still-unveiled essence of truth. "Truth" is not something that first emerges as a relation through a meeting of a representing subject and an object, and that dawns when this relation of *adaequatio* obtains; rather, the meeting of subject and object (and vice versa) is possible only in an open that is already essencing in itself, an open whose openness has its own essential origin into which all of philosophy up to that point had never inquired.

The question concerning the "meaning of being," that is, concerning the realm of projection, the open, in which "being" in general (not just a being) unveils itself to an understanding, is the question concerning the "truth of being." Because "time," insofar as it is grasped ecstatically in its essence, proves to be this open of the projection of being, "time" is the provisional aim toward which "Being and Time" is reaching out in its questioning from the beginning. Here, the name "time" is the *first name* for the truth of being. And reflection {*Besinnung*} is the sole thinking that is directed toward the "meaning {*Sinn*} of being." Everywhere, it is being and its truth that are borne in mind {*im Sinn*}, not beings and their essence.

The knowledge is dawning on us that, already at the inception of Western thinking, being is projected on the basis of time, a projection that, however, remains veiled to itself. Admittedly, this knowledge of the concealed time-character of being at the inception of Western thinking is not confined to the paltry finding that presence and constancy, thus something temporal, are being thought of in the essence or even in the "word" *ousia*. Rather, the inception of Western thinking (Anaximander, Heraclitus, Parmenides) is experienced more inceptively in its fullness, together with the contemporaneous poetizing and all acting and shaping, by dismantling all the retrospective transferences of subsequent metaphysical interpretations. This is the sense of "destructuring {*Destruktion*}," which is the path into the inceptive and has nothing to do with shattering to pieces or annihilation.

Yet, along with this knowledge of the inception, something else, which is no less essential, irrupts into the reflection, something of which every historiographer of the history of philosophy will say right away that is universally known: namely, from early on, with the questioning of what beings are, that which is not also presses forward into the domain of questioning. With respect to being, this means: being is constantly followed by the nothing, like its shadow, almost. Being and nothing belong together. A simple reflection can already provide an intimation of this belongingness and essential relatedness of beyng and the nothing: nowhere do we find the being of beings as itself a being among others. Measured against what is in each case a being, being shows up as ungraspable, precisely as a non-being, as a "nothing"; therefore it is indeed also always possible for us easily to find a being and show it; if, in contrast, we attempt to grasp being, then we reach into the void, into what "is" *not* a being, into the nothing; being essences like the nothing. And yet: what would a being be without being? 58

But it is one thing to have a merely historiographical, scholarly knowledge that the question concerning beings for the most part also concerns that which is not; it is another thing to reflect, in a questioning manner, on what veils itself in the fact that being and nothing go together and where the ground for this lies. This reflection on the essential unity of being and nothing therefore seeks first of all to gain an essential relation of the humanity of Western history to being, which is thoroughly shadowed by the nothing, or alternatively to experience *truly* the *loss of this relation*. It is a matter of persistent steadfastness in the truth *of being*. It is a matter of overcoming the indifference that takes the "is" and "being" to be a God-given self-evidence. Thus, what must be attempted is to bring being itself and the essential and thorough shadowing of being by the nothing into the projection. Thus, what must be attempted is to experience the understanding of being in an uninhibited way and according to the expanses of projection that in an exemplary sense hold the nothing and what pertains to the nothing in the open.

Because in "Being and Time" there is the question concerning the meaning of being, which is essentially related to the nothing, for this reason and *only* for this reason is there treatment of anxiety, death, guilt, and the nothing. The choice of these realms of reflection does not spring from an "anthropology" or a "philosophy of existence" and "philosophy of life" that is stricken with a unique predilection for the gloomy and "negative" and "destructive" and "nihilistic." The questioning concerning anxiety and so forth springs from the experience of the question-worthiness of being, in view of its overshadowing by the nothing. Whether such a questioning, which is subjected to the essential claim {*Wesensanspruch*} of being, and only to this, can then correctly or incorrectly be called "individualistic" and "subjectivist" merits no special discussion.

59 We ought rather to be mindful of the fact that a reflection on anxiety, death, and the nothing that is led by the question of being does not bring into consideration much of what could otherwise be said about anxiety and death. To ask solely about being, and thus to put aside everything that beings offer for consideration in ever new ways and according to constantly changing points of view, this is indeed the highest one-sidedness. But this subtle one-sidedness is a distinctive characteristic of all thinking which thinks being. Where, on the contrary, only beings, and supposedly only beings, are investigated, one may strive for what the sciences call an "exhaustive monograph"; for example, an exhaustive monograph on ants or the "Congress of Vienna" or else "the human" or else "death" or else "anxiety." In such "monographs," which admittedly are already outdated before they appear – since, indeed, already during printing new "material" comes to light – everything is dealt with, only not what is essential. If this came into view, then the essence that was glimpsed would strike down the claim to an "exhaustive" treatment in the first place; for, the essential is essentially inexhaustible. That means: not only is the human never done with his understanding, but the essential itself has its grandeur in constantly remaining question-worthy, quite independently from the narrowness of the human capacity for knowledge. The discussion of anxiety and death and the nothing and guilt and everything else is highly one-sided – directed only to the one "side" of the question that the title "Being and Time" names.

(Now, the fact that this one-sided discussion is also imperfect in its mode of treatment is something the author of "Being and Time" can himself most likely provide some instruction about, if about anything at all. Besides the "limitations" that everyone has, the difficulty of remaining constantly in the one-sidedness of essential questioning is at work here. Yet the usual understanding believes that being "one-sided" is easy and a matter of course. But that is a deception.)

60 Seldom does it come about that we gather questioning into the One and the essential, and that the latter are held in their simple relations, which is to say here: to think Da-sein in its "essence" over the course of the question concerning the truth of being.

(θ) The "Essence" of Da-sein

"Ek-sistence," within the questioning realm of "Being and Time," means: standing-in, indeed the ecstatically transported standing-in, in the open in which, in general, that which we call "being" is projected and from which it is knowable and known. With this standing-in of the human in the truth of being, the human is *he* himself, from out of the unitary ground of all his assets and perils, claimed as he himself and thus according to his self-being. But, in "Being and Time," the essence of the selfhood of the human is determined, not from I-hood, not as personhood, and not at all as the "subjectivity" of a subject, but from the persistent steadfastness in the projection of being, that is, from Da-sein.

If we now once more think through the fundamental sentence that we have taken as a guiding thread, namely, "The 'essence' of Da-sein lies in its existence," then the following results: the "existence" that is thought in the sense of "Being and Time" is brought into view only because the question goes toward Da-sein. And Da-sein is asked about because the "meaning of being" is asked about. Not as though Da-sein were the sought-for meaning (that is, the realm of projection) of being. Da-sein is rather the way in which the open, the clearing, essences, in which "being," as cleared, opens itself to human understanding. Da-sein essences in "its existence" – in accordance with the persistent steadfastness in the ecstatic openness of being, a persistent steadfastness that is proper to it, to Dasein, alone and that distinguishes it, Dasein, alone. "Existence" is thus the *more fulfilled* essence of *ekstasis*.

The word "*Da*" {there, here}, the "*Da*," means precisely this clearing for *Sein* {being}. The essence of Da-sein is *to be* this "*Da*." The human takes this on, namely, to be the *Da*, insofar as he exists (see "Being and Time," p. 133). The word Da-sein is admittedly used here in an entirely different meaning than the typical one.

A distinct emphasis can give a certain indication of the difference between the use of the word heretofore and the meaning of "Da-sein" in "Being and Time." What is meant is not "*Da*sein" in the sense of the presence of a thing or of the human that is here and there and "*da*"; rather, what is being thought is "Da-*sein*," that the clearing for being in general essences and is. The word "*da*" is not the name for a location, whether it be in particular or in general; rather, the "*Da*" names the clearing within which a spatio-temporal ordering of positions and in general space and time in the ordinary sense can be posited.

Da-sein, understood in this way, is called "human," not because it is grounded in the being of the human and is something "human," something measured according to the human, but because, at the most,

61

"the" human is specifically assigned to Da-sein, in order to become persistent steadfastness in Da-sein. "The human" – that is, a historical humanity, for which reason there is also a treatment of historicality {*Geschichtlichkeit*} in "Being and Time" in sections 72–77 (from out of the persistent steadfastness taken over from the destinal {*geschicklichen*} experience of being). But not every historical humanity is specifically assigned to the persistent steadfastness of Dasein; as a result of the forgetting of being, which is to be thought in terms of the destiny of being, there has not yet been such a humanity in history up to this point; for, all of Western history, and the modern history of the world in general, is grounded in metaphysics. But a humanity to come is delivered over to Da-sein.

Thus, for Western history, what we have here called "Da-sein" has up to now remained unable to be experienced, because Western humanity has, of old, conceived of and interpreted itself and beings as a whole in the sense of *the* truth that we in short designate with the name "metaphysics."

The word "Da-sein" is therefore *untranslatable*, also in the sense
62   in which it is thought in "Being and Time." The customary sense of *Dasein* = actuality = presence can be translated as *présence* or "reality." (See, for example, the French translation of "Dasein" in "Being and Time" as "*réalité humaine*"; it obscures everything in every respect.) But in truth Plato's fundamental word *idea* has also never been able to be translated. Every translation is reinterpretation and, *if* it becomes ossified, likewise misinterpretation.

Because Da-sein is not a property and not an accessory "of" the human as he happens to appear, but rather because, at most, the human to come can in each case find a ground of his essence in Da-sein, the talk of "human Dasein" in "Being and Time" remains susceptible to misunderstanding. The name Da-sein must simply be used because it names what never coincides with the being of the human, but rather is of a "higher" essence than the human, if there can be any talk of "higher" and "lower" here. Nevertheless, only the human, and indeed the historical human and the human to come, and he alone on the basis of essential decisions, has a necessary essential relation to Da-sein (see "On the Essence of Ground":[26] the Dasein in the human).

That, in "Being and Time," something is thought in advance which in a certain respect is accessible to reflection and yet, in turn, cannot be made experienceable at will; that, here, thinking passes through

[26] Trans. William McNeill in Heidegger, *Pathmarks*, pp. 97–135.

historical decisions; that this thinking is so little "abstract" that anxiety in the face of it seizes hold of the customary scorners of the "abstract" – all of this and still more besides complicates and encumbers the knowledge of Dasein and makes the experience of its essence rare; for, this essential experience does not, indeed, depend on any acuity of mere pondering, let alone on a contrived zeal for philosophy. The essential experience of Da-sein, *which* the clearing of being essences *as*, is determined by being itself, as is the way *in which* being and *whether* 63 being delivers itself over to the realm of truth of a historical humanity or withdraws.

Thinking out beyond into the essence of Da-sein, within the reflection on that which is alone worthy of thought for essential thinking, namely, being and its "meaning" – this inquiry into the essence of Da-sein that is thus guided can only ever prepare the experience of this essence, so that the historical human will someday be ready, *should* a transformation of his relation to being be accomplished. What is thus indicated is that, in spite of all the essential distinctness of Da-sein vis-à-vis the being of the human, the human in Da-sein can become only so persistently steadfast that the human as human finds his way into the relation to Da-sein; that is, can in a certain way take this on and preserve it and be it in his essential manner.

Da-sein is not anything that a humanity could ever take on without decision; rather, for every human, Da-sein is in each case first his own; according to § 9, Da-sein is "in each case mine." For the belonging to Dasein and, that is to say, at the same time, to the truth of being, the decisiveness of the individual human self is claimed. Self-being, that is to say, here the persistent steadfastness in the truth of being, requires the relinquishment {*Entäußerung*} not only of everything related to the I, but of every sort of merely human activity and making, indeed the relinquishment of *any sort* of predominance of *any* being, even a god, over being. What is required for the persistent steadfastness in Da-sein is therefore in each case that the ownmost self of the individual human be brought into decisiveness.

Now, if one does not at all think through the questioning in "Being and Time" in advance, and if one understands "Dasein" precisely in the customary sense of actuality and does not concern oneself at all with what is being dealt with, then, for example, the following response comes about (see Nic. Hartmann, *Zur Grundlegung der Ontologie*, Berlin and Leipzig 1935, p. 43 and following):

In his metaphysics, Aristotle limited the problem of being far too 64 quickly to specific secondary questions and reformulated them in terms of determinate categories – as substance, form, matter, potency, and act. Prior to all the specification that first arises in his treatment of the problem – not to mention in the solution – he determined the problem itself in a way that is exemplary and has unexplored potential even today.

Chapter 2: Flawed Approach of one Contemporary Investigation
(a) Fallacy in the Modified Question of Being

Martin Heidegger has disputed this. In place of the question about "what is, insofar as it is," he puts the question concerning the "meaning of being." He claims that an ontology is blind as long as it does not clarify this question; the old ontology has to undergo destructuring, a new beginning must be initiated. It has to be achieved through "Dasein," which in his terms is immediately limited to the existence {*Dasein*} of the human. Human Dasein has a privilege over other beings since it is the being who understands its own being. All understanding of being is rooted in it, and ontology must be based on the existential analysis of this "Dasein."

The consequence of this approach is that everything that is, is from the start understood as relative to the human. It is in each case his own. All further determinations then result from this relativization to the "I" of the human: the world, in which I am, is "in each case mine," and could very well be, for each, another world; in the same way truth is "in each case mine." [On the above, see Martin Heidegger, *Sein und Zeit*, Halle 1927; in particular the Introduction, as well as the beginning of Part 1. {Hartmann's note}.]

The question about "what is insofar as it is" is eliminated in this way. What is meant is only what is as it persists for me, is given to me, is understood by me. The fundamental ontological question has already been answered by a blanket decision, indeed by the mere formulation of the question. Even if we wanted to agree with the findings for metaphysical reasons, these would still not be the sort of results that arise from ontological analysis, but are the kind introduced by means of a skewed formulation of the question in order to then draw them from the analysis afterwards as if they were a result.

The situation is not ameliorated by the fact that it is not the epistemological relation, but the life-relation and "Dasein"-relation of humankind to the world that is laid at the basis of the analysis. The relativity of what is to the human is and remains the same, irrespective of how we construe the details of its givenness. The real fallacy in the approach is that being and the understanding of being are brought too close together; being and the givenness of being are virtually conflated. This is why all further distinctions that result from the "existential"-analysis are essentially aspects of givenness, and the whole analysis constitutes an analysis of givenness. However, there would be no objection if, at each stage, the given as such were distinguished from its mode of givenness, and then at least retroactively the question of being would be reclaimed. However, this is exactly what is missing. The modes of givenness are presented as ontological modalities.

Much will be said in what follows in criticism of this position. We could save ourselves the trouble of getting into the critique if the position dealt with the question of being in general. This question is basically bypassed by it, and so it is not even, at bottom, open for discussion. The analysis does not only deal with what is theoretically most universal, however. The Heideggerian existential analysis develops a specific interpretation of spiritual being. What this boils down to is the evisceration and invalidation of everything supra-individually spiritual, all objective spirit, from the ground up, by the one-sidedness of the phenomenological description. The individual and his private decision alone matter, everything common, conventional, and traditional is excluded as inauthentic and ungenuine.[27]

The last sentence, of course, looks particularly good after 1933. Now, this is written, not, for instance, by some inhibited primary school teacher who is "tinkering with philosophy" by accident, but Nicolai Hartmann, whom we are justified in considering one of the first-rate philosophy scholars of the world. And he does not write this on just any occasion where "Being and Time" is mentioned on the side, but in a "laying the foundations of ontology." This specimen of misunderstanding has been quoted so that it doesn't seem as though I were seeing only specters when I speak of misunderstandings. But perhaps they are in fact specters. Perhaps the highest philosophical scholarship also remains separated by an abyss from what philosophy *is* and what it demands. And it is only this that we wish to learn to intuit on the path of actual work, which, admittedly, and however correct it may be, is but a necessary and never sufficient condition for us one day to become properly assigned {*übereignet*} to being.

66

---

[27] Nicolai Hartmann, *Ontology: Laying the Foundations*, trans. Keith R. Peterson (Berlin: Walter de Gruyter, 2019), pp. 54–56 (trans. mod.).

The persistent steadfastness in Da-sein is, according to its possibilities, determined by the respective manner in which it maintains the relation to being. Now, for the most part, the human comports himself to beings without ever thinking of being. To be sure, the relation to being is also not then broken off; for, were being *purely and simply* veiled, then the human would not even be able to comport himself to beings as if he were familiar "only" with them and would thereby forget being. Yet, in the forgetting of being, Da-sein has "fallen prey" to beings and fixates solely on them. In such fixation (insistence), Dasein is alienated from its ownmost {*eigensten*} essence, which is to let the projection and openness of being prevail; in such a fixation, Dasein is *not* able to appropriate {*sich . . . eigen*} itself, it is inauthentic {*uneigentlich*}. Yet Dasein is authentic when it belongs to the truth of being in such a way that being is given precedence over beings.

One has also failed to grasp this distinction between the authenticity and inauthenticity of Dasein from the guiding question of "Being
67   and Time," from the question concerning the truth of being; instead, in accordance with the conception of "existence" in Kierkegaard's and Jaspers' sense, one has been hasty with this distinction and understood it in simple moral-anthropological terms. But this distinction between the authenticity and inauthenticity of Da-sein also remains related to the essence of being and is determined in view of that which everywhere stands in view: the understanding of being.

(1) Understanding of Being, and Being

Now, even when one has not hesitated to classify "Being and Time" as "philosophy of existence," "philosophy of life," and "philosophical anthropology," one was not entirely able to overlook the fact that "Being and Time" asks about the understanding of being, and thus the fact that the question of being, or according to the common title "ontology," takes precedence in everything. Only, one has thereby precisely used the emphasis on the "understanding of being" as a foothold in order to prove that here no "ontology" is possible, to say nothing of attempting a "fundamental ontology," that instead everything from the beginning on must sink into a "subjectivism." For, if there is something that is "objective," thus *not* "subjective," then surely it is being. However, as long as "Being and Time" asks only about the *understanding* of being, then being must, after all, be thought always only in relation to human understanding and human "subjectivity" and can never be represented as being "in itself." In keeping with this consideration, which is grounded in "profundity" – the consideration, namely, that being, and being first and foremost, is something "objective" – one will ultimately persuade oneself of the prevalent "subjectivism" in "Being and Time."

The question as to whether the interpretation of being as the "most objective" of everything objective does not abandon being to subjectivity in a most fundamental and hopeless way, will only be mentioned here and not further pursued. With respect to the "subjectivism" that supposedly lies in the fact that being is brought into relation with the understanding of being, let us note only this: a "subjectivism" is evidently possible only where in general the human is thought beforehand as a subject and the "understanding" is taken as a sort of "subjective" representation. But how could this be, when in "Being and Time" the interpretation of the human as a subject is overcome in advance, and indeed overcome precisely through the insight into the understanding of being as the essence of Da-sein, in which a being-human is grounded? Understanding of being means: projection of being into the open, wherein it has its truth. Understanding of being means: persistent steadfastness in this open and being determined {*bestimmt*} with persistent steadfastness, and this means thoroughly attuned {*durchstimmt*}, by that which revealingly opens itself up in this open, by being. Understanding of being nowhere means that being is a construct of human opinion and exhausts itself in what is meant in this opinion and in being nothing else besides, or in Kantian terms, in being the objectivity of the object that is represented in the subject.

Yet, even if one does not wish to venture so far from the deep-seated "subjective" views about the human as a bodily-psychic-spiritual subject, in order at least to consider which questions are touched on with the determination of understanding as projection, one could nevertheless consider something else: it is said of the projection of being – a projection that distinguishes the essence of Da-sein, and thus of Da-sein itself – that this projection {*Entwurf*} is one that is thrown {*geworfen*}. This implies that "being" does not first "*become*" being by a human projection – in the sense that the human subject "imagines" a view about being – rather the pro-jection places itself into the open in such a way that it is thereby a thrown pro-jection, that is, is determined and attuned by that *which* it projects, and by that *toward which* it must project. Being itself, and only this, can determine the projection of being upon its truth and the essence thereof.

Da-sein, which is distinguished by the relation to being, receives the determination of its "essence" from being itself, and indeed not only insofar as the decision in general as to what Da-sein is (therefore its what-being and "essence") is reached on the basis of being. Rather, the "concept," the essentiality of the essence, is also first of all determined on the basis of being; for, essence – understood verbally – is indeed only the manner in which something is. Every concept of essence springs from a projection of being. But because "Being and Time" in general asks about the truth of being, here, too, the traditional concept of "essentiality" (*essentia*) becomes questionable, a concept which indeed goes back to the traditional interpretation of being as *idea* and *koinon*. Therefore, in the wording of the fundamental sentence, "The 'essence' of Dasein lies in its existence," the term *essence* is put in quotation marks. (The understanding {*Verstehen*} of being is the projection thrown by being into its truth. It is not being that belongs to a human subject; rather, under-standing {*Ver-stehen*},[28] as essencing of openness, belongs to the essence of being.) To inquire into the essence of the understanding of being means, not to relate being to the "subject," but to know being from the ground of its truth, a ground that is being itself.

Only here do we attain a first perspective in which it becomes apparent that Da-sein and the thrown projection of being that determines its "essence" are nowhere to be placed in the zones, regions of questioning, and experiential realms that have lent and still lend their truth and their imprint to metaphysics and its deviations, for example every "worldview." The question concerning the "meaning of being" is an essentially different question from the traditional question concerning the being of beings, a questioning for which "being" must indeed necessarily remain what is most unquestioned and simply unworthy of questioning.

For this reason, when one speaks of the "question of being," let alone claims to interrogate and even answer it, one must know beforehand what one is questioning and plans to inquire into; for, ever since "Being and Time," the title "question of being" has become ambiguous. "Question of being" can mean: to question the being of beings; in this way one questions in the manner of ontology and metaphysics.

70   "Question of being" can, however, also mean questioning the truth of being, the realm of projection in which something like being in general is cleared and comes into the open; then one is no longer questioning in the manner of ontology; rather – measured against "ontology" – one is questioning in a more originary manner than this; and, to the extent that here the aim can still remain first to ground the ground for ontology and to give it a foundation, this questioning can be called a "fundamental-ontological" one.

Proceeding in this way, one can elucidate the question in "Being and

---

[28] {TN: The *ver-* may indicate a transition into the state of standing.}

Time" by contrasting it with the traditional question about "being," that is, about the beingness (*ousia*) of beings. But this elucidation is essentially insufficient, since it indeed determines what is more originary – the question concerning the meaning of being – only from the perspective of what has sprung forth – the discussion of the being of beings – and thus precisely does *not* determine it itself from its ownmost origin and inception. Yet, for this step, or better, leap, we are still not sufficiently prepared and also still not untethered in the right way from the tradition – and thus still not free with respect to it – so that we would be in a position from which to esteem the prior history of truth correctly and genuinely in the necessity of its fundamental features.

Rather, to conclude this elucidation of the concept of existence in "Being and Time," we must point to a decision that first poses itself on the basis of the entirely different questioning of the question of being but that, at the same time, clarifies the latter in its necessity.

(κ) Being and the Human – Anthropomorphism

In the question concerning the "meaning of being," however, and indeed only *through the questioning* concerning being, this (namely, being) must be transported into the relation to the one who questions, thus to the human after all. Indeed, this relation between being and the human also, then, inevitably comes to light in that which is called the "understanding of being." If, therefore, nothing can ever be said about being, if indeed something cannot even be questioned about being without reference to the relation of being to the human, then precisely "the human" moves into the vicinity of the question of being; indeed the human is constantly already encountered in this vicinity, whether or not one has thereby reached a preliminary decision about the relation between being and the human. Because here, in the question of being, the human, be it only as the questioner, is not to be circumvented, the doctrine of the human, that is to say, "anthropology," must after all have the decisive word. 71

This consideration appears to be conclusive. And yet it entirely goes astray. Assuming that the question of being would require, already as a question, that one pose and answer it within the vicinity of the question concerning the human, then the human himself, and that surely means human *being*, must therefore be sufficiently determined in advance. Yet in this determination of human being, however extensively it is laid out and however much it calls on all the sciences, poetry, and doctrines of faith for help in deciphering the human essence, by human *being* one is indeed already thinking not only the *being* of the human but *being in general*. One thereby inevitably and constantly thinks {*denkt*} being and yet does not consider {*bedenkt*} it. On the contrary – knowledge about the human becomes ever more scientific, because the technology of human breeding and regulation has been displaced into the unconditional, no longer allowing for any recess, and promising completeness to science. At the same time, however, the question concerning being thereby becomes ever more a matter of indifference, ever more inconceivable, and therefore ever more null for all calculative thinking. Because all beings have become unconditionally controllable, one, for instance, not only holds the question concerning being to be decided; one must also plainly pass over this question in general as meaningless. With the inflation of anthropology, whether it be *völkisch*-political or "American," the self-deception regarding the simplest ranking of essential questions grows *ad infinitum*.

72   Thus, before all consideration of this being that we call the human, a reflection on being itself must be accomplished in advance. Yet how should this reflection be possible? Being and the being of beings are after all brought right away into the relation to the human. Moreover, a look at the history of the interpretation of beings by metaphysics shows that beings are in many ways conceived according to the image of the human: the cosmos and the ground of the cosmos, God, *theos*, is a human who is thought beyond himself, into and toward the gigantic and unconditional. The human himself is the "microcosmos" – that being wherein all determinations of beings meet in miniature and on the basis of which beings must then be interpreted. All beings indeed borrow their essential shape ("morph") from the human. All interpretation of beings is a single anthropomorphy. And this is why it is anthropology in fact that truly has the decisive word about beings as a whole and about being itself.

With a bit of pondering we notice right away that, in such considerations, an either–or is in play, one which ultimately pushes all questioning concerning the *being* of beings back to the question concerning the *human*: either, one poses the question concerning beings as such on the basis of the human, who after all is supposedly "in the center" of beings; or one poses the question concerning the being of beings purely on the basis of being, in order then to learn right away that here being already stands in relation to the human, which is why it is advisable to question right away and only on the basis of the human. With this either–or (either on the basis of the human or on the basis of being) what is decisive – what is, however, each time already thought together with anything else – remains everywhere unasked, and this is the relation of being to the human. The question remains unasked as to whether precisely this relation as such cannot come to be experienced in a more originary manner; whether the relation of being to the human, experienced in a different way, does not compel one to an entirely different sort of questioning concerning being *and* the human. (But when we question in this different manner, it then becomes clear that the "problem of anthropology" and the "problem" of "anthropomorphism" are completely transformed. The supposed "problems" are then first brought into relation to a genuine question-worthiness.) 73

This indication of the question concerning the "anthropomorphy" of beings (and that means of being) was necessary, because, behind this question – which up to now has never been asked in a thorough and sufficient way but rather has only been disguised – an undecided and barely suspected decision lies concealed. The doctrine of the "analogy of beings" within Western metaphysics, for example, disguises the question of "anthropomorphy." With its help, one resolves questions that one does not at all pose, and cannot even venture to pose, unless the entire building were first to collapse, the building in which one has made oneself at home beforehand.

A superficial knowledge of Schelling's Freedom Treatise already shows not only that the "analogy of being" plays a role for it, but that an "anthropomorphism" is at work, and indeed not behind the thinker's back, but with his complete knowledge.

The attempt to elucidate the concept of existence in "Being and Time" has at a single blow led us into the one and only question of essential thinking. This indicates in what respect "existence" is to be understood here.

As a transition into the elucidation of the other guiding concept of Schelling's distinction between "ground and existence," let us now briefly summarize the delimitations of the various concepts of existence. (See "Recapitulations and Course of Interpretation," pp. 124–129.)

Existence:

1. *Existentia* = *actualitas* = actuality of each actual thing.

2. Christianity of the individual human (Kierkegaard); being a Christian is always becoming a Christian; faith – sin.

3. Self-being of personality from out of the communication with others in the relation to "transcendence."

4. The ecstatic persistent steadfastness in the open of the truth of being (relation to being as inclusion in the clearing; beyng essences as the clearing). 74

1. Arises from the metaphysical question concerning the beingness of beings (*idea – eidos – ousia*; *prōtē ousia*; *tode ti estin*[29]),

2. presupposes 1, insofar as the actuality of the human is meant, but it restricts *existentia* to the human and grasps the latter as

3. subjectivity – self-being (autonomy);

4. arises from a questioning concerning the truth of being that leaps beyond all metaphysics.

These various "concepts of existence" are *historical*, that is: not past views and opinions, but, fused together, essencing now and futurally.

Two examples for the use of the concept of existence:

1. Goethe's words in the well-known letter to Schiller (27 August 1794): "For my birth-day, which falls in this week, no more agreeable present could have come to me than your letter [from 23 August 1794], in which, with a friendly hand, you give the sum of my existence {*Existenz*}, and through your sympathy, encourage me to a more assiduous and active use of my powers."[30] (Existence: of that I am, and of what I am thus being – my actual acting and presencing {*Anwesen*} ["Dasein" in the traditional sense]; what, with this prior actuality, has come out, and wherein it consists; "course of his spirit" and essence of genius.)

2. Schiller (7 September 1794): "With pleasure I accept your kind invitation to Weimar, but with the earnest request, that in no particular of your household arrangements will you make any change with reference to me. . . . Pardon these preliminaries, which I must first settle, in order to make my stay {*Existenz*} with you even possible. I will request the poor liberty of being permitted to be an invalid in your house."[31] (Existence = stay – presence)

§ 12 Preliminary Interpretation of Schelling's Concept of Existence

From the context of these conceptual-historical reflections on the concept of existence, a preliminary interpretation of Schelling's concept of existence (see Chapter 4, below) can be presented:

1. Schelling's concept of existence concerns the self-being of what is and thus thinks selfhood in the sense of "subjectivity," that is, of "egoity" (see below p. 64).

---

[29] {TN: 'first substance; is this particular (thing).'}

[30] *Correspondence between Schiller and Goethe from 1794 to 1805*, trans. George H. Calvert (New York and London: Wiley and Putnam, 1845), p. 7.

[31] Ibid., pp. 13–14 (trans. mod.).

2. Nonetheless, Schelling's concept of existence is not restricted to the human but concerns, precisely as does the traditional concept of *existentia*, every "essence," that is, every being. This signals that Schelling thus thinks every being in a certain way as "subject" in the sense of selfhood and subjectivity.

3. Considered historically, Schelling's concept of existence assumes an intermediate position between the traditional concept of *existentia* and the restricted concept of existence in Kierkegaard and in the "philosophy of existence"; Kierkegaard thinks the human in the sense of the "subjectivity" that German Idealism unfolded conceptually.

4. Schelling's concept of existence, which remains wholly within Western and likewise modern metaphysics, is to be thought without any reference to the concept of existence in "Being and Time."

Nevertheless, there is an echo of Kierkegaard and the philosophy of existence in the concept of existence in "Being and Time":

1. insofar as existence is also restricted to the human, that is, Da-sein in "Being and Time," 76

2. insofar as self-being becomes essential; however: the human is understood on the basis of the understanding of being, and this understanding essences in Da-sein; self-being is thought only on this basis: persistent steadfastness in the clearing of being, in relation to this, not to beings, as *I myself.*

§ 13 The Inceptive Impetuses Determining the Essence of Ground and Their Historical Transformation

Here, in contrast to the previous consideration, let us not mention the doctrines of individual thinkers and the distinct, philosophical fundamental positions; rather, let us mention the inceptive, historical impetuses that determine the essence of ground within Western metaphysics (see "On the Essence of Ground").[32] What we call ground is polysemous: the polysemy shows up more readily in whatever we call "groundless."

1. For example, we call a path "groundless," by which we mean that it does not provide a firm support for walking; it is without firm soil; ground = support, soil; *basis* (*bainō*): 1. stride and gait, 2. what one is walking on, 3. the manner of walking, cadence.

2. We call "groundless" an appearance that befalls us seemingly

---

[32] Trans. William McNeill in Heidegger, *Pathmarks*, pp. 97–135.

without cause; of which we do not know the "primal cause" {*"Ur-sache"*}, that is, that thing to which something familiar is supposed to be traced back; ground = cause, that which precedes something actual as something effected, the effective; but also what triggers the effect or conditions the triggering, the occasion.

3. We call "groundless" a demand that arises without right or entitlement; ground = entitlement, right, legal entitlement, justification; (truth and justice).

77   *Ground*: in each case that to which a producing {*Herstellung*}, a setting-up {*Auf-stellung*}, a standing and going, an "explanation" (a going-through), an appeal goes back; that which somehow lies behind, but behind in such a way that it at the same time precedes and prevails in advance and is effective beforehand.

To this corresponds the Greek name for what we call, ambiguously enough, "ground": *archē* – that whereby something inceptively commences, the *inceptive* and therefore the oldest, the firstling. Yet at the same time this word means as much as *sovereignty* – that which reaches out beyond everything and simultaneously holds it under itself; the character of sovereignty pertains to every inception in the proper sense, and every genuine sovereignty is inceptive. Both, inception and sovereignty, resonate as one in the Greek word *archē*.

The essence of *archē* receives its conceptually articulated character first in Aristotle, in whose thought the entire preceding tradition *gathers* itself in a distinct manner, prefiguring the future history of metaphysics: *pasōn men oun koinon tōn archōn to prōton einai hothen ē estin ē gignetai ē gignōsketai.* The *first* {*das Erste*}, *whence* being, emergence, apprehendedness, that is, the first, whence *presencing*. (Met. Δ 1, 1013 a 17 and following) The "primal" {*Das "Ur"*} – the "en-" {*das "Er"*}.

The *archē geneseōs*, and that means *kinēseōs*,[33] assumes a leading role among these modes of *archē*. This corresponds to the Greek interpretation of beings in the sense of *phusis*, of emerging into presencing. The fact *that* something like movement – in Greek: *metabolē*, the changeover from something to something – lies in *phusis* was not first recognized by Aristotle, although he was the first to grasp sufficiently and comprehensively the essence of movement and movedness in the sense of the Greek concept of being, that is, on the basis of *ousia*. (Aristotle does not interpret being as movement, but movedness shows itself to him explicitly as the highest mode of presencing (*energeia-entelecheia*);

---

[33] {TN: 'source of generation . . . of movement.'}

in this way the Platonic determination of *ousia*, or more precisely its lack of determination, first acquires a determinacy, admittedly with a modified reception of the *idea* in the characterization of beings accord- 78 ing to *hulē* and *morphē/eidos*. *Kinēsis*, interpreted as *energeia*, is the *ousia* of *dunaton hēi dunaton*.[34] The interpretation of *archē* from out of the *aitiai* determined on the basis of "*phusis*" – *aitiai* that then retroactively delimit the essence of *archē* – is testimony to the *phusis*-essence of *einai*; but it is also at the same time testimony to the precedence of *phusei onta*[35] – which are conceived on the basis of *technē* – as that which proximally and continually presences.)

In connection with the interpretation of beings on the basis of *phusei onta* with respect to their being as movedness, the determination of *archē* as *archē geneseōs* takes on a leading role. It is a matter of *anagein eis tas archas* the *phusikē metabolē*[36] according to its modifications (Phys. B). Four types of *archē* are thereby distinguished, and that means here: that, *dia ti* (whereby), in each case in a different respect, something emerging is such an emerging thing and is that which has emerged, and that means that which, standing in itself, is present and constant. In the writings that have come down to us, Aristotle nowhere provides a rigorous and explicit grounding for the fourfold character of this *dia ti* or the *aitia*. To be sure, Met. A 3–7 attempts to make the tetrad intelligible on the basis of the previous question concerning beings, but in so doing the preceding history is interpreted entirely according to the measures of Aristotelian thinking, not from out of itself. This grounding nevertheless remains undeveloped in the Greek–Platonic projection of beings upon beingness in the sense of *idea* (*eidos – technē – poiēsis – ergon*) *phusis/noein*.

An enumerative elucidation of the fourfold *aitia* should suffice here (Phys. B 3; Met. A 3–7, 2).

1. *to ex hou gignetai ti enuparchontos* – that, from out of which, as from out of something underlying and present therein, something emerges {ent*steht*} and accordingly also *per*sists {be*steht*}; bronze for the statue; silver for the bowl; wood for the ship; (*to hupokeimenon*).

2. *to eidos kai to paradeigma* – the outward look and therefore that which shows and immediately gives to see, *what* something is supposed to become and be and is: the outward look of such a thing as a bowl; the outward look of such a thing as a ship; (*to ti ēn einai*[37]).

---

[34] {TN: 'potential as potential.'}
[35] {TN: 'beings by nature.'}
[36] {TN: 'leading the natural change back to its sources.'}
[37] {TN: literally, 'the what it was to be.'}

79   3. *to hothen hē archē tēs metabolēs* – that from which the *change*over
{*Um*schlag} of what is initially present into what looks this or that
way takes its point of departure; *the impact* {*Anschlag*} (the impetus
and the thrusting), which tips the scales {*den Ausschlag gibt*} for the
changeover; *poiēsis* as *metabolē*.

4. *to hou heneka* – that for the sake of which the changeover occurs;
that which "it" *comes down to* in the emerging, that whereby the emerging finds its end (*telos*); that which is *finished* in such and such a way,
because it is somehow suitable (*agathon*); ship, bow; and indeed as that
which has been taken in advance, *proaireton*; – *ergon*.

The four primal causes always contain that from which something
has its finished completeness and suitable presencing; essentially, all
four are related to the *ousia* of an *on* (*on* qua *ergon*). Later, these four
aitiai then entered into the doctrine of Scholastic metaphysics as *causa
materialis, formalis, efficiens*, and *finalis*,[38] and then were flattened
out into the distinction between "form and content" (see Frankfurt
Lectures 1936–1937).[39]

If this delimitation and classification is simply accepted in itself on
the basis of a commonplace intelligibility, then nothing of the Greek
projection of being remains to be recognized; and if Aristotelian
philosophy and Greek metaphysics as a whole are interpreted in
accordance with its guidelines, then one can everywhere provide sup-
porting evidence for this – and yet everything is reinterpreted. This
reinterpretation has its justification and correctness; for indeed all *non*-
inceptive questioning, thinking, calculating, and teaching necessarily
require a reinterpreted "history" (past). All *non*-inceptive questioning
is driven on by anxiety in the face of what is proper to the inception;
whence the idolization of "progress" in all possible guises. The reinterpretation of history is supposed to make the inception ineffectual, but
80   at the same time available as an object to which one can appeal and
with which one can draw attention to oneself.

For the conceptual-historical clarification that is necessary here, only
this one thing is now of importance: the first mentioned mode of *aitia*
– *to hupokeimonen* – is at the same time, in a wider interpretation that

---

[38] {TN: 'material, formal, efficient, and final cause.'}

[39] See "The Origin of the Work of Art," trans. Albert Hofstadter, in Martin
Heidegger, *Basic Writings*, ed. David Farrell Krell (New York: HarperCollins,
1993), pp. 143–212; as well as "On the Origin of the Work of Art: First Version,"
in *The Heidegger Reader*, ed. Günter Figal, trans. Jerome Veith (Bloomington:
Indiana University Press, 2009), pp. 130–150.

is directed elsewhere, the essence of the *on* itself (that is, of *ousia*); *to enuparchon.*

What shows itself in the outward look and presence of something, the manifold of what shows itself, has in each case coalesced, *sumbebēkota*, in each being in a peculiar way, indeed in such a way that all this has set itself up in what already lies there and lies at the basis of what remains, for example, a tree and what is proper to it, its properties; different in each case. The tree itself is *hupokeimonen* for the properties and, therefore, at the same time, that which also lies at the basis of that to which everything is attributed and of which everything is pre-dicated (*kataphasis*) in the addressing and discussion of beings. The tree is thus at the same time *sub-jectum* for the "predicates"; and it is this because it is in itself that which lies at the basis for the properties – *hupostasis, substans.*

The later guiding concept of metaphysics, "*substantia*," thus comprises an interpretation of *ousia* that has a particular orientation; *ousia* never means *substantia* without further ado; rather, *ousia* becomes *substans* on the basis of an emphatic regard for what was previously already present in all its properties, that is, in Greek terms: in that which otherwise, in a still usual manner, also emerges – *sumbainei* – in presence. (*Accidens*, just as little as *substantia*, cannot yield the Greek unless one thinks – alongside and beforehand – *ousia* in the correct interpretation.)

Every proper being, that is, everything that presences of its own accord, is *subjectum*; in this concept of substance, thought in a Greek manner, there is nothing of the "I" or consciousness or selfhood. Just as every being, insofar as it is, presences and exists, so is every being a *subjectum*, that is, that which already lies beforehand and at the basis of the properties: *ground.*

It is to this subjectum that one must each time go back in the propositional statement – "*logos*" – if this saying is to be one that is grounded and groundable. *Logos* means here (already no longer thought in an originary manner): to hold and pass off something for something; *reor – reō*, I say – *ratio*: "to bring to account," give an account, give the ground, ground, explain, make understandable, understanding, reason; but also what is *given* when one gives an account, *the ground*; *ratio sufficiens*; *logos* qua *legomenon kath' hauto*.[40] (Hence the idiom: it is "logical"; what is never to be proven through formal "logic," but what corresponds to the calculation – *what is "factored in."*)

81

---

[40] {TN: 'sufficient reason,' 'something said according to itself.'}

Everywhere where knowing, experiencing, and thinking seeks the true, it goes toward something that is constant and that remains, something that underlies everything; that is to say, in the sense of traditional metaphysics since Plato and Aristotle, the *hupokeimenon*, that is, *subjectum*.

At the beginning of modern metaphysics, the essence of the truth of knowing is transformed into certainty, *certitudo*, which the human, of his own accord, can secure all by himself (here is not the place to present why and how this is the case). Therefore, knowing must now seek a *subjectum certum*.[41] The *ego cogito* shows itself as this *subjectum certum* for Descartes; for in the thinking and doubting and searching for a *subjectum certum*, the I – which is thinking there – is already always what is *presently available*. Thus, the *ego* must be the *subjectum*; and here, the *ego cogito*, the *res cogitans*, is, for all certainty and in the context of all knowing, the *exemplary subjectum*, the *subjectum* in the sense of self-representing representation of something.

The essence of *this exemplary* subject (*subjectum* as *ego*) then becomes in Leibniz the essence of *subjectivity in general* ("egoity" as subjectivity), that is, it becomes the essence of the being of each being in itself and from out of itself. Aristotle's *energeia* is then reinterpreted in the sense of this "subjectivity" (*vis*) and robbed of its Greek essence, and the monadological interpretation is at the same time historically justified. Ever since then, in modern metaphysics – *with respect to its essential feature* – every being is a subject, that is, somehow related to itself, determined by self-being (even in Kant: thing in itself, freedom; the intelligible). In Schelling, too, this self-being characterizes the essence of "existence" (see above § 12).

But where is there any room left here for the determination of beings as ground? Ground is indeed *hupokeimenon*, that which underlies, that which lies before, basis, *subjectum*.

Perhaps Schelling's characterization of beings as "ground" also arises from the modern interpretation of beingness as subjectivity. This, however, is for the moment not yet clear. It cannot be clear, because, up to now, we have generally still taken Schelling's distinction from without, according, as it were, to the isolated, distinguished "pieces," "existence" and "ground." Yet vis-à-vis ground, Schelling himself says more precisely: merely ground of existence, and correspondingly it must also be said: existence of ground and upon ground.

Schelling's distinction aims precisely to show the belongingness of

82

---

[41] {TN: 'subject that is certain.'}

ground and existence in every "essence," that is, every being. That means: the distinction comprises the jointure in every being.

And here the decisive question arises: in what way is every being as such so joined? Wherein does the distinction in ground and existence have its root?

Chapter 2

The Root of Schelling's Distinction between Ground and Existence

In what way are we going to encounter the root of the distinction? By means of a simple reflection. If every being, insofar as it is a being, is determined by the aforementioned distinction, then this distinction must have its root in beings as such, that is, in their being. Thus, the next question arises: how does Schelling determine the essence of being? Assuming we are right to recognize the Freedom Treatise as the *peak of the metaphysics* of German Idealism, we may also be allowed to suspect, then, that in this treatise Schelling expresses himself on the essence of the being of all beings and thereby answers the Aristotelian question: *ti to on?*[1]

In the introduction to the treatise we find a passage that, based on the way it is formulated and delimited, clearly wishes to be held as a claim about the essence of beings as such. After an important discussion, the following sentences – explicitly marked off by a dash (350 end) – ensue: "In the final and highest jurisdiction, there is no other being {*Sein*} at all than willing. Willing is primal being and to this [willing] alone all predicates of it [primal being] apply: groundlessness, eternity, independence from time, self-affirmation. All of philosophy strives only to find this highest expression." (Being as will.)

Our task is:

1. the elucidation of this essential determination of being (§ 14),

2. the demonstration that the distinction is rooted in being as it is determined in this way (§ 15).

---

[1] {TN: 'what is being/that which is?'}

§ 14 Elucidation of the Essential Determination of Being as Willing   84

If we begin our elucidation of the passage with the last sentence, then it immediately becomes apparent that this sentence is only an abbreviated and definitive paraphrase of Aristotle's remark: *kai dē kai to palai te kai nun kai aei zētoumenon kai aei aporoumenon, ti to on*[2] (Met. Z 1, 10028 b 2–4).

The definitive character consists in the fact that the *aei aporoumenon*[3] is missing; it must be missing, for the beginning of the passage declares the essence of beings as such to be found and determined to the highest extent; this, however, is not Schelling's private conviction; rather, the claim to this knowledge distinguishes German Idealism as the unconditional idealism of spirit.

"Willing is primal being," that is, willing corresponds to the originary essence of being. Why? Because the predicates that express the essence of being belong to willing in an exemplary sense; the latter alone is fully sufficient for the aforementioned predicates. (Being? Beings {*das Seiende*} grasped ab-solutely, likewise *that* which is {das *Seiende*} as such.)

(a) The Essential Predicates of Being

What are the essential predicates of being? Groundlessness, eternity, independence from time, self-affirmation. [Proceed from self-affirmation. Elucidate on the basis of the final part of *Ages of the World.*]

(α) Ground-lessness

We hesitate. Did we not hear that "ground" belongs to every being as such? Certainly. Thus, the ground-like belongs to being after all. Indeed. But that is not to say being means: to need a ground. Being is in itself what is ground-like, ground-giving, essencing as the ground, and has the character of ground; and precisely because *it* is what is ground-like, ground-giving, it cannot need a ground (un-ground [406]). The   85
ground-like is ground-less (that which grounds, that which essences as basis, does not need a ground), that is: without something to which it could go back as something outside of itself; no more back to, no

---

[2] {TN: 'and indeed both of old and now, always being sought and always leading to perplexity, what is being/that which is?'}

[3] {TN: 'always leading to perplexity.'}

behind-itself, but rather pure presencing itself: *the first*; (but being *and* time?); the ground-like, that is, <u>*subjectum*</u>.

(β) Eternity

aei; *aeternitas* as *nunc stans*? Being means constancy in a single presencing. (Not a mere "continuing on" *ad infinitum* in every direction, *sempiternitas*; endless continuing is the longest while, boundless boredom;[4] in contrast, "eternity"?)

See Schelling, *Ages of the World* (I/8, p. 260 and following; also not: *nunc stans*, but rather the "overcoming of time," that is, *inclusion*!) To what extent are the traditional predicates being used here; to what extent is it a matter of Schelling's interpretation?

(γ) Independence from Time

Does this not mean the same thing as "eternity"? And, above all: is a decision against "Being and Time" not reached in advance here quite unequivocally through metaphysics itself? (See *Die Weltalter* I/8, p. 301 and following.)

"Independence from time" goes beyond an elucidation of eternity and includes *sempiternitas* as well. "Independence from time" means: that which is as such is not torn along in the flow of succession; rather, that which is as such remains untouched by such changes. Being means: *constancy* (as movement) untouched by succession, presencing unaffected by the changes of disappearing and arriving.

Thus, being in the traditional meaning of metaphysics, which meaning is fundamentally posited in "Being and Time" as that of the inceptive projection of beings.

86   "Independence from time" is not *capable* of speaking against "Being and Time," because, in the case of independence from time, "time" is thought of differently; and nowhere in "Being and Time" is it asserted that beings (to say nothing of being) depend on "time" thus understood. (Being is "dependent" on ecstatic time as an essential character of the "truth" of being, but this "truth" belongs to the essencing of beyng itself.)

The aforementioned predicates elucidate the *hupokeimenon*.

(δ) Self-Affirmation

This final predicate points to the *modern* interpretation of being in the sense of the Leibnizian *exigentia essentiae*,[5] which implies: beings are

---

[4] {TN: *Langeweile*, literally 'long while.'}
[5] {TN: 'demand of essence.'}

insofar as beings deliver themselves {*zustellt*} in their essence and *in such delivering represent {vorstellt} themselves, and in representing strive for themselves.* (Positionality {*Ge-stell*})

(b) Justification of the Predicates of Being

From where do we get these predicates that delimit the essence of being, and on what basis are they justified as the authoritative ones?

1. Schelling says nothing about this; he enumerates them as self-evident determinations. And rightly so; for, it belongs to the essence of metaphysics that these predicates of being – being, as so addressed – are self-explanatory; understanding takes its point of departure here and ends here; the addressing {*Ansprechung*} of the being of beings makes and knows no other claim {*Anspruch*}, especially since everywhere only beings are considered in their beingness and being is taken to be decided in its essence.

2. Yet, meanwhile, this self-evidence has been unsettled by "Being and Time" and become what is properly question-worthy for thoughtful questioning. Yet because here the most immediate task is to grasp Schelling's distinction in its root and necessity and thus first to provide a reference point for the correct confrontation, we shall initially remain within the realm of Schelling's thought.

87

(c) In What Way Willing is Sufficient for the Predicates of Being

Here, in relation to the cited passage, it must be asked: in what way is precisely the interpretation of being as willing sufficient for *the* addressing of being, which is required by the predicates? More precisely: in what way does "willing" contain "groundlessness," "eternity," "independence from time," and "self-affirmation"?

1. What does Schelling understand by "willing" and "will"? In the tradition of metaphysical thinking, the essence of willing is determined in a manifold manner, and the *word* is also claimed for many different things. Here one always thinks of *orexis, desiderium, appetitus sensibilis*, striving for, craving, longing (*nisus*!). (But for what? Why is this mostly left indeterminate? Conversely, in Leibniz: *appetitus, universum*: to strive to bring "oneself" into actualization and actuality as such; *boulēsis*.) In striving for: a certain self-feeling, finding oneself in something; becoming oneself, bringing oneself forth; yearning.

Schelling (359): "The understanding [is] properly the will in the will. . . ." (See 414) (Reason! Kant, Hegel, but the will of love.) This initially sounds strange (especially for contemporary ears: "intellect" – "instinct," "character"). But what does understanding mean? The re-presenting of "unity," *logos*, gathering, original synthesis; re-presenting of the universal as such; rule, order, law; see Aristotle, *De anima* Γ 9, 432 b 5: *en te tōi logistikōi gar hē boulēsis ginetai.*[6]

The under-standing {*Ver-stand*}[7] sets the striving into and toward the universal. Understanding is "*logos*" ("the word," Schelling 361) and thus raises the will beyond the level of the merely "divining will" (359). The understanding is the "universal will" (363). See Kant: will = to act according to concepts; acting on the basis of representing something in general (purpose); see *Critique of the Power of Judgment,* § 10 (Leibniz: *appetitus* is *perceptio – apperceptio*). Will is will *of* the understanding (whether as yearning or as spirit).

The understanding: that which properly wills, that which strives to bring itself into actualization and posits this (Idea).[8] For a con-trast see the metaphysical inversion of this essence in *Nietzsche*: will to power; self-willing as legislation and its execution; willing as command, of striving and of being able to strive, of the empowerment of power.

power:

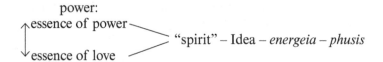

essence of power
essence of love   "spirit" – Idea – *energeia* – *phusis*

2. In what way is willing, grasped in this way, sufficient for the authoritative predicates of being? Schelling has not explicitly shown this. To the contrary, he expresses something different: being is "becoming" (life) (358 and following, 403 and following), and he thereby dis-tinguishes "mere" being (385) and being-"in-itself" (347). In-itself: only "the eternal, what rests in itself, the will . . ." (347) is purely from itself and through itself and in itself counter-turning {*gegenwendig*}.

---

[6] {TN: 'for in the rational (part of the soul) there is will.'}

[7] {TN: above, we noted that the *ver*- may indicate a transition into the state of standing.}

[8] {TN: Here and below, Heidegger writes *Idea* rather than the Greek or the typical German *Idee*. To distinguish them, we have translated *Idea* as 'Idea' (capi-talized) and *Idee* as 'idea,' and have transliterated the Greek as '*idea*' (italicized).}

groundlessness: (a) the being that does not need another ground outside itself (present of its own accord and constant)

eternity: (b) prior to everything – already (striving to attain {*Er-strebnis*} [from – toward])

independence from: (c) not after one another, but "at the same
time   time" – precisely as becoming; independence from "consequence" and succession.

self-affirmation: (d) willing-oneself; (being-which-is {*Seiend-sein*}; the "existential" {*das "Existenzielle"*}) (*Ages of the World*). ("Becoming" in what sense? To bring oneself to oneself and thus precisely "being" {*"Sein"*}).

(d) Being in its Highest and Ultimate Jurisdiction 89

In this interpretation of being as will, in what way does "being" assert itself "in the highest and ultimate jurisdiction"?

1. From where does the authority over what beings are stem in the first place? From being! But how so? From that which most is? And this from where?

2. Why here the "highest" and "ultimate" jurisdiction {*Instanz*}?

(a) the highest – because now, in every respect, presencing and constancy (all "instances" {*Instanzen*} of beings; subject–object), not only what is present at hand as something objective, but "subject," I-hood and for the latter. That which is in *and for* itself; that which neither is nor is not, that which is beyond what is;[9]

(b) the ultimate – because nothing more beyond this; the unconditional and at the same time im-mediate, the ab-solute, the First in all; "certainty." (The only thing left is what Nietzsche then brings about, the inversion.)

---

[9] {TN: 'Das An-*und-für*-sich-Seiende; das weder Seiende noch Nicht-Seiende, das Überseiende.'}

§ 15 Being as Willing as the Root of the Distinction between
Ground and Existence

In what way is being, thus determined as willing in the highest degree, the root of the distinction?

"Root" is supposed to mean: the distinction stems from willing, and what is distinguished has the character of "will" (see below).

The highest being {*Seiende*}, what properly exists, is spirit; but: spirit is the spirit *of love*. Love is the highest, since it is love – "there"; present: 1. before this the ground and before the existing as the separated, 2. but not yet *as* love (406). The un-ground, absolute indifference; the lack of predicate is the only predicate – and yet not the null nothing. The unground divides into two equally eternal inceptions.

Therefore, the distinction must unfold in view of the "will"; therefore, Schelling speaks also of the "will of the ground" and the "will of the understanding."

90

The will is ground, because, as striving (yearning), it goes back to itself and closes itself up within itself; thus, basis for . . .; because fleeing {*Ent-fliehen*} and thus precisely summoning, "urging," "attracting" the other.

The will is understanding, because it goes toward actuality, unity (*universum*), presence, and indeed belongs to what the ground is; selfhood.

The will is <u>subjectum</u> especially, 1. as *hupokeimenon*; but willful, striving (*ex hou*);[10] "basis"; 2. as egoity, consciousness, spirit (*eis ho*),[11] "word," *logos*.

In being as willing, the subjectum-character of beings came to be unfolded in every respect. If beingness in all metaphysics (Greek and modern) is *subjectum*, if primal being is, however, willing, then willing must be the proper *subjectum*, indeed in the unconditional mode: of self-willing. (Hence: denying oneself, closing up, and bringing oneself to oneself.) Love is proper willing, that which properly is. The distinction arises here because it is essentially inherent.

---

[10] {TN: 'from which.'}
[11] {TN: 'into which.'}

The Inner Necessity of Schelling's Distinction between Ground and Existence

But is the distinction, then, necessary, and in what sense are we to grasp this necessity? The distinction is "a very real" one, and not "merely logical, or one called on as a heuristic aid" (407 and following). This distinction is not, for instance, to be grasped only as though it had to be thought by us, as though "we" could not make do without it in our thinking and "system." Rather, being itself as willing necessitates it; that which is as such divides, distinguishes itself; discord, op-position, willed and brought forth by being itself; (see 403 and following, 358, 375, 380 note, 400, 406 and following).

Only in "becoming" do beings first become sensible to "themselves." "Becoming": op-positionality of ground and existence; what presupposes is what is presupposed and vice versa.

Will – properly: to come to oneself, to gather oneself together, to will oneself, self-being, spirit, *love* (406) (see § 15); to come to oneself, to reveal oneself, thus to distinguish.

Love – as letting the ground be effective; as the against-which of the ground, love itself can and must be so that a unifying One and unity and love itself will be; unity, *as* unity, *unification*. *Centrum* (381): the purest essence of all essence; *ens entium, ens summum; causa realis, ratio vera*!! (Leibniz).[1] See Hegel's "negativity"; Schelling, *Stuttgarter Privatvorlesungen*, "The principle of opposition."

---

[1] {TN: 'the being of beings, highest being, real cause, true reason.'}

Chapter 4

The Various Formulations of Schelling's Distinction between Ground and Existence

(a) "mere ground of existence" and "existence" (in the sense of existing) (357),
(b) "basis" and "what exists" (395),
(c) "ground of existence" and "that which exists" (373),
(d) will of the ground and will of love (375),
(e) existence and what exists,
(f) being {Sein} ("object") beings {Seiendes} ("subject"),[a]
(e) and (f) after the freedom treatise.

Reciprocal relation between two things that are distinguished in an equally essential way, and on the basis of an in-distinguishable thing, but dividing in itself and from itself for the sake of the most original and complete unity.

The formulations (e) and (f) initially seem strange, and yet they are the ones that are actually adequate: being {Sein} = the being {das Seiende} that has not yet come out of itself but that closes up in itself. "Being {Seyn} is ipseity, ownness; dissociation; but love is the nothing of ownness, love does not seek its own and therefore cannot be that which is {seyend seyn}, not even of its own accord" (The Ages of the World I/8, p. 210).[1] Beyng: going back to itself; not "expanding," not "giving itself"; what obfuscates; the No; drawing itself together, attracting.

"Beings": what undertakes to be a being. Being a being {Seiendsein}:

---

[a] There is no figuration of the unity of the un-ground, and that means: "of what is beyond that which is" {"des Überseyenden"}. [Note between two spirals sketched by Heidegger.]

[1] {TN: F. W. J. Schelling, The Ages of the World, trans. Jason M. Wirth (Albany: State University of New York Press, 2000), pp. 5–6 (trans. mod.).}

"the existential" {*"das Existenzielle"*} (see *The Ages of the World* I/8, p. 260).

Here it becomes abundantly clear: 94

1. how everything is thought on the basis of the being that most is {*Seiend-Seiendsten*}, from the *summum ens, theion, akrotaton on*;[2]

2. everywhere only beings as beings; and being is that which is properly achieved by what most is and is correspondingly thought of all beings;

3. this thinking does not escape the positing of the *on* as *hupokeimenon*. See the later doctrine of potencies: A^1, A^2, A^3, A^4.

Metaphysically – onto-theologically – however, in the highest fulfillment.

The core section (357–364) "elucidates," in its way, the distinction clarified just now. Namely, in such a way that one is led to this distinction on the basis of beings, and indeed: 1. on the basis of God as the highest being, 2. on the basis of creation – as process of transfiguration, 3. on the basis of the human. God, world, human: *metaphysica specialis*.

Yet "beings" are thus already interpreted in the sense of the distinction; thus, what is found is only what has already been placed inside it; therefore, a "circle"! Yes: but of what sort? Here, what does it mean to place inside? Is this one of Mr. Schelling's views? Or? And in what sense "place inside"?

System as essential jointure of beings as such. Thus, comprehend their unity first? How? "Intuition" and construction. The essence of "construction":

1. the prior guideline {*Vor-gabe*} of the un-conditional;

2. underlying this is the "distinction" between beingness and beings, and indeed also *in* Schelling's distinction itself;

3. how the essence of all metaphysics becomes visible from here; *on akrotaton (theion), on koinotaton, on analogon*.[3] How the essence of metaphysics is connected to this; see Nietzsche-essay. The "real" idealism – "idealism"; "Idea" and "life," "becoming," "being"; the negative as real counterforce.

---

[2] {TN: 'the highest being, the divine, the highest being.'}
[3] {TN: 'utmost being (divinity), commonest being, being by analogy.'}

95   **§ 16 The Proper Aim of the Interpretation of the Freedom Treatise:**
Reaching the Fundamental Position of the Metaphysics of German
Idealism. Evil and the System

The difficulty for the understanding (confrontation) does not lie in *what* is discussed there; for these are questions and doctrines well known from the tradition of metaphysics. The difficulty lies in the *mode of treatment*; whereby the latter admittedly should not be taken as the "formal" side of a method, into whose husk and shell only a well-known "content" is poured and stirred up differently in it.

Here, mode of treatment means the *fundamental position* from which one questions and according to which what *is without question* is determined; the manner of proceeding is regulated by this fundamental position which constitutes what is properly to be known and what the mode of "truth" ("certainty") is.

The fundamental position is itself determined by the guiding projection of beings upon being as the beingness of beings as a whole. (Essence and origin of this projection lie in obscurity, because up to now metaphysics was explained and could be explained only by metaphysics.)

Initially, the customary title of the treatise would be rather cumbersome for the first task, which is to reach the *fundamental position*.

We call this treatise, in short, the "Freedom Treatise," and we do so with a certain degree of justification based on the title. But it actually treats of the essence of evil, and only because it treats of this does it treat of human freedom. For, in the essence of the human, evil *is* properly the extreme opposition and uprising of the spirit *against* the absolute (tearing oneself away from the universal will, the against-it, the will replacing it in the "against"). Evil "*is*" as *freedom*; for the latter "is" the capacity for good *and* evil. The good "is" evil and evil "is" the good.

96   But why is evil treated of at all? Because it is the innermost and furthermost discord in beings. But why exactly discord?

Evil is thought because the *unity* of the jointure of beings as a whole must appear at the same time and most sharply in this most extreme and proper discord as dis-jointure. (The most extreme freedom *against* the absolute within the whole of beings.) And it comes down to this: beings and their jointure (fundamental jointure); that is why the question of pantheism is linked to the question of freedom (Introduction), and indeed as a question concerning the system. "System" is the name for the *essence* of beings as a whole and as such, that is, for the beingness of beings; the systematic is the being of beings, because being is now subjectivity. To think this is the essence and task of metaphysics.

But metaphysics is not a discipline; rather, since Plato, it has been the fundamental grasping of the *truth* of beings as a whole. Meanwhile, truth has become certainty (subjectivity).

Our proper aim is directed at the metaphysics of German Idealism, in which Western metaphysics is fulfilled in a certain respect (Schelling's treatise within this metaphysics). It is for this reason that, in interpreting this treatise, we have posed the all-anticipating question concerning the *beingness* of beings; for this reason, we first treated of the "distinction between ground and existence."

§ 17 Transition from the Preliminary Reflection to the Interpretation of the Core Section of the Treatise and of the Latter Itself

1. *Reminder of the task*: grasp the metaphysics of German Idealism as a fulfillment of metaphysics; the position of Schelling's treatise within this metaphysics; "system of freedom"; system of beings themselves; being as systasis; system and question of pantheism; metaphysics: the truth about beings as a whole: the beingness (being) of beings. Thus, ask beforehand: how does Schelling grasp being?   97

2. *The trajectory up to now*. Illumination of the being of beings by means of the clarification of the distinction between ground and existence; do not go over the trajectory in detail.

1st chapter: elucidation of the concepts of existence and ground.

2nd chapter: origin of the distinction.

3rd chapter: necessity of the distinction.

4th chapter: the various formulations of the distinction in Schelling. Hold fast to the main issue in what follows:

(a) Being is willing (see "being is willing," p. 81 and following).

(b) Being is differentiatedness, unifying division; becoming. The "distinction" as a character of being itself; being essences as distinguishing; that which, dividing, unites, and this "essence" has the basic feature of the *idea*, of appearing; to reveal itself, to go out into manifoldness and thus first let unity essence. Important for the interpretation of the core section; compare what is said there about the "word"; self-representing; re-presenting and negativity.

(c) In what way, then: the exceptional character of the metaphysics of German Idealism, Schelling's distinction and Hegel's "negativity."

(d) In what way we find here a fulfillment of Western metaphysics.

(α) Beings as "subjectum": 1. *hupokeimenon – ousia*. 2. I-hood, selfhood.

(β) In the distinction both are not only taken up, but taken back and sublated into a unity of division: ground of existence and existence "of" the ground.

Supplement to the clarification of being by way of a reference to the "copula"; see pp. 79–80.

98   However, with the question concerning the determination of the being of beings, the complete essence of metaphysics has not yet been traversed, and thus the fulfillment is not yet to be evaluated either.

3. *Metaphysics according to the complete concept.*
     Being of beings:
     (a) beings have the priority
     (α) in what way is this at all the case and in what way at the beginning: *idea – koinon*; *agathon* as *aitia – intellectus divinus,*
     (β) in what way in the *Critique of Pure Reason*: "experience" – double sense,
     (γ) in what way in German Idealism: as the absolute; the absolute as the first, the certain; see Descartes.
     This clarifies the basic jointure of the essence of metaphysics:
     (b) the *theological* essence of all metaphysics,
     (c) the *ontological* essence of metaphysics,
     (d) the *analogical* essence of metaphysics.
     See the medieval conception of metaphysics: *metaphysica* as *scientia regulatrix*; it contains and orders knowledge because it goes – and insofar as it does so – toward the *maxime intelligibilia*:
     1. *ex ordine intelligendi*:[4] (*intelligere* goes toward the *causae*; metaphysics deals with the *prima causa* for everything else; *Deus*, and thus only on this basis, *creatum*).
     2. *ex comparatione intellectus ad sensum*:[5] metaphysics goes toward the universal, not toward the particular; it deals with *ens commune* (*via resolutionis – magis communia post minus communia*).[6]
     3. *ex ipsa cognitione intellectus* (gen. *objectivus*);[7] *intellectus divinus* is the proper *substantia separata*, the proper being {*Seiende*} in itself.

4. *Copula* (see lecture course from Summer Semester 1936).[8]

---

     [4] {TN: 'from the order of the understanding.'}
     [5] {TN: 'from the comparison between the understanding and the senses.'}
     [6] {TN: 'by way of resolution – more common things after less common things.'}
     [7] {TN: 'from knowledge itself of the understanding (object genitive).'}
     [8] Heidegger, *Schelling's Treatise on the Essence of Human Freedom*, pp. 74–83 ("Pantheism and the Ontological Question. [Identity, Dialectic of the 'Is']").

Being – is self-distinguishing and, therein, a belonging-together and therefore, and in this way, "identity."

Being is predominantly said in the "is"; therefore, it is important to   99
gain an understanding about this "little linking word" "is"; this is why the copula is treated of on p. 341, and indeed in connection with the question of pantheism.

Do not think the "is" "abstractly," one-sidedly, for example: "is constituted," "is present at hand," but rather always in the sense of the "distinction" and its manner of essencing.

The elucidation of the possible senses of the copula: *A is b.*

1. b is what A is – everything placed on A.

2. A is what b is – everything placed on b. Here either A or b is what, of itself, gives the measure, what grounds the "equality."

3. A and b belong together in a unity of being, a unity that does not emerge from both as a sum, but rather persists for both and enables them.

4. The A (or the respective S) takes on being the P, but in such a way that it is at the same time dependent on the latter. *The good is evil* – not in every respect, but: 1. sublates it in itself, without eliminating it; 2. but is in need precisely of evil, in order to be the good. See, on this, Hegel, *Phenomenology of Spirit*, Preface, on the speculative proposition (the "counterthrust").

5. *The distinction in ground for existence and existence* ("of" ground).

The distinction as such pertains to every "essence," that is, every being as such. *Primal being is willing.*

Western metaphysics: truth about beings as such.

Where does this interpretation of being (not viewed historiographically) come from? Being is conceived here as "*existentia*" in the broader sense; *existentia* as *actualitas*, *actu esse*;[9] since Descartes the *actus*   100
is *cogitare, ego cogito, repraesentare* (see 6): to represent oneself to oneself and thus to present oneself; *exigentia essentiae*;[10] *principium existentiae*[11] is *perfectio*; *essentiae gradus*;[12] *appetitus* – a representing striving – will (Leibniz).

The distinction is "a very real" one (407), and not "merely logical"; present in the essence of being itself, therefore will of the ground and

---

[9] {TN: 'being in act.'}
[10] {TN: 'demand of essence.'}
[11] {TN: 'principle of existence.'}
[12] {TN: 'degree of essence.'}

will of the understanding. Re-presenting unfolding of the unity of what is manifold and opposed → "universum."

Every will is un-willingness {Wider-wille} *in the sense of counter-willing* {Gegen-willens}, *that is, willing-against, craving. Willing: counterturning in itself* (contradiction).

Spirit: the selfhood of the will of the understanding; spirit is spirit (breath) of "love."

6. *Being (*existentia, *actuality) as subjectivity (subjectity),*[13] *that is, re-presenting.*

Kant (Logic lecture course, introduction V) says: what representation is, "cannot be explained at all. For we would always have to explain *what representation is* by means of yet another representation."[14]

Is that an argument? And what does it mean to explain? Clarifying, not "leading back" and deriving; but unfolding in its own essence. Is what is clear in re-presenting perhaps in no way obvious and distinctly construed?

Kant's argument is only the modern mirror image of the fundamental conviction of metaphysics: being is taken to "be" self-evident, being "is" . . .

Re-presenting implies: 1. "striving" out beyond oneself (negativity), 2. distinguishing – "dividing" – negativity (changeover), 3. "becoming" (not as "succession" and "activity," but rather in essence; from-to, changeover, transition), 4. bringing to oneself – re-presenting oneself – revealing.

101   All four determinations, together with the *repraesentare* of unity (presencing of the manifold in gatheredness), delimit the essence of

---

[13] {TN: a Heideggerian neologism, sometimes written here as *Subjektität* ('subjektity'), sometimes as *Subjectität* ('subjectity'). In his lectures on Nietzsche, Heidegger explains how it differs from *Subjektivität* ('subjectivity') as follows: "The common name subjectivity immediately and all too stubbornly burdens thinking with erroneous opinions which interpret every relation of being to the human, or even to his I-hood, as a destruction of objective being [...]. *The name subiectity* [Subiectität] *should emphasize the fact that being is determined in terms of the* subiectum, *but not necessarily by an I.* Moreover, the term contains at the same time a reference to the *hupokeimenon*, and thus to the beginning of metaphysics." Martin Heidegger, *Nietzsche*, Gesamtausgabe, vol. 2, ed. Brigitte Schillbach (Frankfurt am Main: Vittorio Klostermann, 1997), p. 451 / *The End of Philosophy*, trans. Joan Stambaugh (Chicago: University of Chicago Press, 1973), p. 46 (trans. mod.).}

[14] Immanuel Kant, *The Jäsche Logic*, in *Lectures on Logic*, trans. J. Michael Young (Cambridge: Cambridge University Press, 1992), p. 545.

"willing." Hence, willing as the title for the modern interpretation of being in the sense of *existentia*.

Hence, the essence of being includes "phenomenology," the history of self-revealing – as the becoming of itself. The phenomenology "of" spirit is to be understood in the same way as the talk of the "harmony of the spheres"; "phenomenology" not as a heading for a "science" that arrives belatedly on the scene.

Will – as *will to power*; see 7: Schelling and Nietzsche. The present age – has not taken up Nietzsche's doctrine, but rather the reverse: Nietzsche fore-told and thus showed in advance the truth into which modern history moves, because it already comes from it.

7. *Schelling – Nietzsche* (see pp. 69–70).

Being is willing (*perceptio – appetitus*); as is the case in the tradition of theological metaphysics, "actus" lies behind it; *actus* as the Roman reinterpretation of *energeia*; *en-ergeia – entelecheia* (see the Leibnizian interpretation of the latter as *vis activa primitiva*[15]) – *ousia* – of *kinou-mena – kinounta* – as the proper *onta* (*phusei*);[16] *ousia* and *idea*.

Every willing wills itself, but does so in different ways. In willing as self-willing there lie two fundamental possibilities of essential unfolding:

1. *self*-willing as coming-to-oneself and thus self-revealing and appearing before oneself ("absolute idea"); the understanding as will in the willing; unconditional subjectivity as *"love"* (no longer willing anything that is proper to one);

2. self-*willing* as going out beyond oneself; overpowering and command; "will to power"; the command as will in the willing; "over-powering"; unconditional subjectivity as "power."

(A) Unconditional subjectivity in each case; how that is so is to be shown only from the essence of re-presenting; re-presentation and negativity.

(B) But the contrary and discordant – "struggle," "contradiction" –   102
is essentially in "love" and "power."

(C) Schelling: willing the nothing – serene intimacy {*gelassene Innigkeit*}, pure willing. Nietzsche: willing the same time and again: eternal return.

(D) The will of love – (letting the ground be effective); willing nothing, not something that is proper to one and not what is someone else's, nor oneself; will to power and overpowering.

---

[15] {TN: 'primitive active force.'}
[16] {TN: 'beings (by nature).'}

(E) The will as spirit and love includes, as unity, system; for the "will to power": no system (see accordingly Kierkegaard: no system of "Dasein," but "organization" or "church").

8. *Hegel – Schelling – Nietzsche.*

Hegel: will of knowing (recognizing) – (desire).

Schelling: will of love (understanding – universal will); letting the ground be effective; willing nothing more.

Nietzsche: will to power (overpowering; sublation of the distinction between the sensuous and the non-sensuous); only willing – as willing.

"Will" as willing-one-self; self-being, in each case different – true.

Will and subjectity: see the transitional reflection on Hegel (pp. 142–151), a few indications from the Preface to the *Phenomenology of Spirit.*

9. *The core section of the Freedom Treatise (357–364) as "elucidation" of the distinction between ground and existence* (see above, p. 75).

The investigation "grounds itself" on this distinction. This investigation is however an advance into the middle of the system. System itself: see pp. 85–87.

The distinction is "elucidated"; see Schelling pp. 358 and following (see below, pp. 85–87). Different "reflections" (see § 22) are supposed to lead into this same distinction as a grounding distinction. Different reflections on beings – namely: I. God, II. the world (creation), III. the human.

103

What does leading into mean? Beings are brought forward insofar as they are thoroughly governed by this distinction, that is to say, determined in their beingness by it. Are we only bringing in "examples" here? If not, what does this procedure imply?

The distinction aims at the construction of the essence of the human within the whole of beings. This construction is supposed to present the human as that being which is God in an exceptional sense: *the human "is" God.*

The human as the central essence, the being that "is" in the center. The bond through which God takes the creaturely nature *into himself,* through which God "is" this nature. The question of anthropomorphism must be discussed by taking this concept of the human – who "is" God – as a point of departure; only in this way does it lead into the question concerning the truth of being.

"Being" – here, everywhere, and in a decided manner as existence of the ground: "*subjectity*"; the human who *is in this manner*, as one who constructs; "philosophy"; "anthropomorphy"; "circle."

10. *The distinction between ground and existence as the essential determination of "existence" in the sense of subjectity.*

In order to grasp the "distinction" truly, we ought not to accept it "immediately"; rather, we must think it in a "real" manner, that is, as the reality of the real in the sense of the *being* of beings (that is, on the basis of the existence of the ground, that is, to grasp its *being*-a-distinction *from out of itself*; as dis-tinction, will, will of the understanding, existence).

Thus, in the essence of the distinction, one must distinguish between:

1. what is distinguished – the elements of the opposition and their difference,

2. the binding of what is bound together – elevation and transfiguration of the ground into existence; the latter begets the ground; but also the generation of existence from out of the ground – ground *of* existence,

3. and that which binds, exceptionally characterized as the *one* element, namely existence (the prevalence of existence; see, though in a different manner, already Leibniz!).   104

The distinction is the *bond* that contains the opposition in itself (lets the ground be effective) and at the same time transfigures and binds it as one of the things bound; that which is self-binding!

Existence always polysemous: "side" 1. and 2. and 3. In the distinction, existence has *priority* in the sense of *superiority* in the *actus*!

Nevertheless, at the same time a circle: the difference includes (1) – that which is opposed, and because this belongs together with the difference, it is also compatible. But there is incompatibility when the ground as such (being as such) wills to be existence, that is, when it rises up into that which itself is {*zum Seienden selbst*} (the perversion and its rising up).

Evil is what comparatively *is not* {*Nicht-seiende*} (that is, being {*Sein*}), which towers up into what is and suppresses what truly is (see Schelling, *Stuttgarter Privatvorlesungen* I/7, p. 459).

An Interpretation of the Core Section, "The Elucidation of the Distinction" Between Ground and Existence

§ 18 The "Elucidation of the Distinction" as the Presentation of Beings as a Whole (God, World, Human)

Three parts (on the surface): God (Chapter 1), world (Chapter 2), the human (Chapter 3). Beings as a whole in their fundamental articulation.

The distinction: *being* {Sein}. To consider *beings in their being* in a uniform and absolute manner.

The "elucidation" of the distinction: so that the latter comes to light in its full essence more plainly, more clearly, and more purely; not a simple confirmation of empty formulas and their applicability.

The essence of the distinction (essence of being as "will"); its fullness: the dis-tinguishing {*Unter-scheiden*} itself – the dividing {*Scheiden*} – that which can be separated – that which cannot be separated.

The "elucidation": as presenting forth – not of the distinction in beings, but rather the presenting forth of beings as such in the distinction and in that as which the distinction properly essences and why it does so – in the absolute.

Thus: the absolute – God Himself (Chapter 1). Then, between the first and second chapters, our consideration of the privilege of the absolute (§ 23); the extent to which, over its course, our interpretation of the "elucidation" each time radiates out into the whole → the various concepts of nature.

The "elucidation of the distinction" is the presentation of beings as a whole in light of *this distinction*. Thus, the "elucidation" encompasses – at once as one, and in a coinage that is proper to it and conjoined from out of the construction – the whole of modern metaphysics, that is to   106 say, theology, cosmology, and psychology. (Consider the opposite order in Kant's transcendental dialectic!)

The essential here is the *unity* in the absolute.

The being of "nature" (that is, of creation) is its *life-process*; the latter is, as process, *the creation of the world* (*conservatio est perpetua creatio*).[1] World creation is, however, "*the personalization of God*" – so that he "becomes" He Himself.

But world creation achieves its purpose in the human: the human is the "eternal difference {*Differenz*} with God," as the point where spirit arises as such; and this "*in* the midst of nature beyond nature."

Nature: the presentation of the absolute in what is not (in being); (God himself deifies nature).

Creation: not out of nothing, but out of what is not; beginning of creation: is the overcoming of divine egoism, that is, ownness, that is, "ipse-ity" (and, at the same time, also love).

The distinction is "*that which has been intuited*" {"Angeschaute"} *in advance*, and indeed in a such a way that being is intuited in what most is {*Seiendsten*}, namely, in the absolute. In the presentation of beings, the "*distinction*" becomes "clear." (Circle?!)

1. The distinction is not derived, not "clarified" on the basis of something still more clear; it is itself what is most clear (see what is said about primal being and willing: the *highest jurisdiction* under which being is judged; see above § 14 and § 15).

2. But that which most is, the absolute, in which the distinction presents itself, is also not first proven and demonstrated as what is ultimate in hindsight; rather, it is that which is unprovable, that which is in no need of proof. Therefore, what is most comprehensible is that the absolute is that which is, pure and simple.

Why is it that that which most is, is more comprehensible than that nothing is? Yet the *nihil* seems to be "easier" ("nothing is of its own accord, as it were"); by contrast, what is most difficult (namely for making and producing, which thinks finitely and entirely only from out of itself!) is to produce "something."

For the comprehending of the being of beings, that is, for the thinking of willing, what is more comprehensible is: that the will, as will, wills itself; for even when it wills nothing, it still wills itself: it wills the will. For the will, not willing is incomprehensible and the most difficult; not willing means giving itself up by renouncing itself (see below, pp. 99–100).

[1] {TN: 'preservation is continual creation.'}

The confrontation with the positing of the distinction, that is to say, with the projection of beings as a whole upon beingness as it is thus determined: beyng-historical.

3. The absolute and the system. The system in God's understanding; the understanding is the will in the will, thus: the system as the primal will of the absolute.

The Reflection that Takes God as a Starting Point

(a) The direct elucidation on the basis of the being of God as the absolute; nature "in" God and "He Himself" (existence). (§ 19)

(b) The analogical elucidation: an elucidation of the elucidation; show the absolute – which is to be presented – in that in which it presents itself: in nature as "that which is not"; correspondence as answer to the word – here, correspondence not as a form of "reflection," but rather as the essence of *being itself*; "analogy" and "system" (see Chapters 2 and 3); "analogy" on the basis of the essence of the distinction (see § 18). (§ 20)

(c) The circle as that from out of which everything becomes; the relation between what is distinguished (nature and existence); the priority. (§ 21)

(d) Back to God; "God has in himself . . ." (§ 22)

The privilege of the "theological" as the privilege of the unconditional. The unconditional as what is certain, purely and simply; truth as certainty – intellectual intuition – intuition and construction; the "element" of the presentation.

§ 19 The Direct Elucidation: The Presentation of the Being of Beings "in" God. Philosophy as Unconditional Knowledge of the Absolute in Contrast to Theology and Mathematics. The Various Senses of the Word "Nature"

The "elucidation" is a "philosophical" elucidation *for* philosophy; so not, for instance, an elucidation for an understanding that would, at whim, press itself to the fore.

The essence of philosophy within the absolute metaphysics of spirit (see the essence of philosophy and its name); presentation of beings in   110 their being on the basis of the non-sensuous *intuition of the absolute* (see p. 92); to grasp everything as *"being* {seiend} *'in' God"*; the "in" not as immanence, however, which presupposes being {*Sein*} in the sense of being present at hand (of one inside the other); "being" as existence of the ground.

Philosophy as unconditional knowledge (truth already decided as certainty). Therefore, to bring philosophy in its unconditionality into relief in accordance with two aspects which have been decisive for it within the history of metaphysics: theology and mathematics. (This sheds light on the importance of the reference to the Preface of *The Phenomenology of Spirit*.)

1. The goal Hegel "set" himself (*Phenomenology of Spirit*, Preface, II, 6):[1] "to bring philosophy closer to the form of science, to the goal where it can lay aside the name *'love* of *knowledge'* and be *actual knowledge*."

The end of metaphysics, in the sense of its fulfillment, is thus announced by:

(a) philosophy laying aside its name, becoming "absolute knowledge" (German Idealism),

(b) philosophy *relinquishing* the "system" (Nietzsche); will to power, "organization," "total." Nietzsche "wills" no system because he knows himself to be in the system of all possible systems (as modes of insuring stocks), in the unconditionality of the will to power. (Kierkegaard is not to be mentioned here because he does not belong in the history of philosophy, and because his struggle against the "system" has another sense.)

Actual knowledge, that is, an absolutely self-knowing knowledge as the actuality of the actual itself (not, for instance, as merely a mode of "grasping" the absolute); (*philosophia* – in its Platonic character! Christian;) no longer to *strive* from the conditional toward the unconditional – as though the latter were something never reached but constantly searched for – rather the *unconditional* is the beginning and end (point of departure and element), and all "becoming" "is" within the unconditional as the essencing of in-finity. The fact that Hegel at the same time places all the emphasis on "work" is not opposed to the overcoming of *philia*; the latter is the expression of finite representation.

2. We must understand the following demand accordingly, namely, the demand that "the cognizing of absolute actuality become entirely

111

---

[1] *Sämtliche Werke*, vol. 2, p. 14 (II, 6).

clear to itself about its nature" (ibid. II, 14). This does not mean deploying an "epistemological theory" – a prior sharpening of the knife before we can cut correctly – rather it means that the nature of the cognizing of absolute actuality is precisely the essence of this actuality, the "being" {*"Sein"*} of the absolute itself (beingness = subjectivity); the "element," the ether.

(This also does away with the common misinterpretation of the *Phenomenology of Spirit*! – not some "epistemological doctrine" of absolute metaphysics.) (See now also the interpretation of the "Introduction" to the *Phenomenology of Spirit*, 1942.)[2]

(a) Philosophy and Theology

The history of the essence of truth makes clear the extent to which "theology" and "mathematics" play the necessary role of a guiding thread within metaphysics.

Truth: *alētheia* and *idea tou agathou*[3] – *causa* (theology).

Truth: *veritas – certitudo – intuitus – deductio* (mathematics).

Since Plato and Aristotle, the question concerning the *on*, that is, its *archē* as *aitia*, is the question concerning the *theion*, and, therefore, *prōtē philosophia epistēmē theologikē*;[4] the modification by Christianity that occurs there.

Precisely in what is proper to it, philosophy is thus theology, being   112
subordinated to it; accordingly, theology is, at the same time, the limit for the possible unconditionality of absolute metaphysics.

Consequently, philosophy and theology are conceived of differently by Hegel and Schelling: see *Phenomenology of Spirit*: "religion" is not yet absolute knowledge. Similarly in Schelling (for example: *Stuttgarter Privatvorlesungen*, I/7, p. 423): philosophy is related to theology; but theology is "more just an abstraction of philosophy"; "in a way, it takes God as a particular object, whereas philosophy at the same time considers God as the highest explanatory ground of all things, thereby extending the idea of God even beyond other objects." "The unconditional is the element in which every demonstration is possible."

---

[2] Martin Heidegger, "Elucidation of the 'Introduction to Hegel's 'Phenomenology of Spirit' (1942)," in Heidegger, *Hegel*, trans. Joseph Arel and Niels Feuerhahn (Bloomington: Indiana University Press, 2015).

[3] {TN: 'idea of the good.'}

[4] {TN: 'first philosophy is theological knowledge.'}

(b) Philosophy and Mathematics

In the beginning of modern metaphysics, the essence of truth trans-forms itself into certainty. Mathematics is a model of unconditionally conclusive "demonstration" (*mathesis universalis*).[5] It is then a matter of course to raise metaphysics *ordine geometrico*[6] into knowledge in a scientific manner.

But the mathematical, that is, magnitude, is not a possible element of the "absolute distinction" (that is to say, of the negation of the nega-tion, of unconditional subjectity). The "principle of magnitude" is the "non-conceptual distinction." (vol. 2, p. 44 [II, 36]) "Time – the existing {*daseyende*} concept itself." (ibid.) (Here, merely the simple apartness {*Auseinander*} of one by one {*Nacheinander*} – in the not-yet-now and no-longer-now; a double negation indeed, but only as an existing one {*daseiende*} and not as a negation that comes to itself, not "the pure unrest of life" (vol. 2, p. 44 [II, 36]).) So here, no element of the absolute in the mathematical; metaphysics unable to be determined on this basis; see *Phenomenology of Spirit*, Preface, p. 40 and following [II, 32 and following], especially p. 44 [36].

113   ### *(c) The Concept of the Absolute in Schelling and Hegel*

See below § 23; the unconditional priority of the certainty (and that means, at the same time, beingness) of the absolute.

1. *That which detaches itself* from the bond in the relation, a bond that is one-sided in each case – *absolvere*.

2. That which detaches itself as *that which brings itself to itself* and thus fulfills itself. That which absolves itself (becoming revealed to itself); revealability not as an addendum – qua retroactive consciousness – but rather as *the* fundamental aspect of *self-being*.

3. That which absolves itself as that which exculpates itself {*Sichfreisprechende*} into freedom {*Freiheit*} (concept) and thus recon-ciles; oppositions not extinguished but sublated as revealed; absolution, reconciliation as mediation into the allness of the all.

4. Absolution as the in-finity of the finite, the wholeness of the whole; absolution: liberation into freedom pure and simple; two co-eternal inceptions; the "all in all."

5. *Essentially* pervasive for absoluteness: "becoming" – as *selfhood* and sublation; *tollere, elevare, conservare*.

---

[5] {TN: 'universal learning.'}
[6] {TN: 'in geometrical order.'}

(d) The Various Senses of the Word "Nature" within the "Elucidation"

1. "It is *nature* – in God." "It": God, insofar as he is ground. "Nature" (although echoing Boehme) here grasped on the basis of subjectity and by going through the Kantian-Fichtean determination; "nature" = the non-I (Fichte); I as self and spirit or (Schelling): be*ings* {*Sei*ende} in distinction to non-beings. "Nature" as the *idealist*-metaphysical name for "ground"; non-I – "positively" – "contraction." "Nature" = the world – before the eternal act of creation?

2. Gravity and light "in nature." Here "nature" means: creation (that which is created and indeed non-human creation; the realm of the *non-historical* in creation). This created nature is the presentation of the absolute in what is not; but this "nature" is already not only ground 114 on account of its being {*seiend*} – divided – but it is already, in a way, "existing" – light. But "light" is itself still closed off, because here spirit has not yet dawned, because it is not yet that which exists in its proper sense. Therefore, "nature" is not yet "*actu*" – but neither is it pure being {*Sein*} ("essence") in distinction to beings; rather, it is already a *being* {*ein* Seiende}– as that which is not {*das Nicht-Seiende*}.

"Essence" {*"Wesen"*} likewise polysemous: (1) *essence,* insofar as it exists and insofar as it is the ground of existence, that is, the *respective "being"* {"Seiende"}; (2) *"pure essence"* – as being ground, pure and simple; essence = "being," pure and simple; (3) essence as *what* something is – *quidditas*, the what-concept; (4) essence as the "essential" – that which exists.

Gravity "*only*" "*follows*" from the "nature" of absolute identity. ("Nature" here means *ground*, and indeed God as ground, insofar as he is at the same time the one involved in formation {*der Mitbildende*}; this explains the "only.") "To follow" – as a manner of becoming revealed, that is, of *being* revealed in the sense of existing. Gravity "is" – according to a certain empowering intensification (potency) – "nature" in God.

3. "Nature" in general: (1) nature in God; (what does not exist); (2) the absolute in the presentation of non-beings, beyond (this side of) "spirit" – absolutely; (that which in a certain way exists). "Nature" in general: the deepened concept that Schelling's philosophy of nature already had in view but did not fully master before fully establishing the "distinction." The "polemical" in the concept of "nature" – initially against Fichte, but also "transcendental philosophy."

4. Points 1–3 name specifically Schellingian coinages of the concept of nature – the "nature" of absolute identity. In addition, Schelling still uses the term in its commonplace meaning, in the sense of the "nature

of things" (359), "nature" = the what- and how-being of something, the "nature" of the subject matter (going back to *phusis* = *ousia*); *natura* – in the sense of "that which is" *naturā suā*.[7]

115   For the sake of contrast, useful to refer to Kant's concept of nature: "*formaliter*": "the existence {*Dasein*} of things, insofar as it is *determined in accordance with universal laws*." In the determinations of "*existence*," conforming with laws is essential (in distinction to "essence"); "existence" here = actuality = the possibility of sensuous experience – objectivity (*Prolegomena*, § 14); "*materialiter*": "the epitome of all objects of experience" (*Prolegomena*, § 16). See *First Metaphysical Foundations of Natural Science*.

5. The various concepts of "nature" refer, at the same time, to the character of "potency" of the absolute. In what way? The concept of "potency" (self-reveal, *repraesentare*; "relation to existence," the respective transformations of the latter): (1) to be capable of – *possibilitas* – *essentia* – *nisus* – *conatus* – to be able (the "more," over and beyond itself); (2) *essentiae gradus*[8] (*perfectio*) (as a *principium essentiae*;[9] Leibniz); intensification and its ground, "high and low"; (the mathematical concept – "superiority," see § 21); self-intensification as revelation of essence. *Perfectio*: "completion," in each case in accordance with the degree of dividedness and of coming-to-itself of beings each time determined by the distinction; (3) self-relation.

The formal work in Schelling's *doctrine of potencies*: the threefold of potency, each time recurring in this threefoldness, in each "potency"; potencies as "periods" of the God's self-revelation. See below § 24, where the connection between nature in God (nature inceptively without rule) and nature as creature is first addressed.

(1a) *Concept of nature*. (*Correction*: emphasis of the sentence not on "follow" but on "only.")[10]

(1b) The antecedence – as essence of the *will itself* – of "being" in itself; priority, circular; (subjectity, § 21).

---

[7] {TN: 'in its nature.'}

[8] {TN: '*degree* of essence.'}

[9] {TN: 'principle of essence.'}

[10] Allusion to the sentence: "For this very reason gravity is neither pure essence nor even the actual being of absolute identity, but follows only from its nature" (358). This correction resulted from a criticism in a letter from Ms. Bröcker-Oltmanns, who regularly attended the seminar. This letter is enclosed with the manuscript and is dated 4 July 1941. It bears Heidegger's handwritten remark: "This correction is altogether convincing. 6 July 1941 / regarding p. 59 {of the manuscript}."

(2) *The precedence of the absolute*, (a) the fundamental position of speculative thought, § 23, (b) anthropomorphism (see (3)). 116

(3) Elucidation of the distinction by means of a reflection on *creation* (its essence); the human – the proper creature.

(4) The distinction – (as the will of love); in-separability and separability (type of unity) of principles.

§ 20 The Analogical Elucidation: Presentation of the Correspondence Between the Stations of the Being of the Absolute

The *analogy* of the relation between gravity and light with that between the ground in God and God's existence is a relation of relations; but not able to be grasped in the mode of the *analogia proportionalitatis*.[11] The analogy here is not a simple "image"; rather that which is "intuitively pictured" is here, in a corresponding manner, a being, and only as such is it mentioned here. The relation of correspondence is that between two "distinctions," that is, stations of the being of the absolute. And the correspondence {*Entsprechung*} lies in the presenting forth, in that the gravity–light relation is not an accessory manner of depicting things, but rather the being of gravity is what it is in the sense of the *revealing* of "being" (that is, of the will of love). The relation understood in the sense of *this* distinction therefore *cor-responds* {ent-spricht}, complies with, and is sufficient for absolute identity in its own manner.

Gravity – light: on the basis of the projection of being in general and precisely not according to accidental "poetic" views; more knowing than science, which works with random "models." (See the historical connection between Leibniz's concept of *vis* and dynamics in physics.)

The interpretation lies in the projected direction of the interpretation of being as "will" – and this is more fundamental than every scientifically exact observation. What present-day physics "knows" about gravity is not more, but essentially "less," inasmuch as it is relegated to 117 the arbitrariness of the projection of a discipline.

The "analogy" in the sense of "phenomenology": as a manner of self-appearing, and that means, of "being."

The correspondence prevails essentially in the very distinction between what is distinguished, and it is only first to that – to this

---

[11] {TN: 'analogy of proportionality.'}

correspondence at the level of being {*seinshaften*} – that beings correspond; the "*analogia entis*."[12]

§ 21 The Circularity of the Distinction Between Ground and Existence

The circle as that "from which everything becomes"; "becoming," thus characterized in a specific manner ("will"), is the essence of being, and this in its essential unity; as distinction, it is that from which being essences. (The distinction as the essential origin of "becoming.")

Now the "elucidation" of the distinction by means of the more detailed clarification of the "circle"; the circular character of the distinction and the subjektity of being; self-willing.

"Circle": where the beginning is the end and the end the beginning (formalistic).

The *priority* – the "antecedent":

(a) according to time (the origin of time, see *Stuttgarter Privatvorlesungen*, I/7, pp. 428 and following),

(b) according to essence (constitution of the "what"?) – or what is essential; the proper: existence,

(c) according to rank (superiority of existence, see 360, 408); however, priority here relates only to "that antecedence" of light before gravity; but later in general it goes beyond the circle of becoming; this circle possible irrespective of c); (to what extent superiority belongs essentially to the distinction; essence of the "will" and superiority; over and beyond the self, selfhood; see 359, end: "the higher," which has

118   raised itself from eternal yearning for the eternal act of self-revelation); priority – the antecedent – "ahead"; in which respect?

On the a priori, see Kant's *Prolegomena*; not the a priori – in whatbeing, *essentia*; condition of possibility; not as a temporal antecedent, but as being in the sense of will, that is, proper existing. The *prius* is itself circular, and superiority therein nevertheless; "existence" – this is, essentially, superiority (see distinction); prevailing of existence over *non-existence*, see Leibniz.

---

[12] {TN: 'analogy of being.'}

§ 22 Summary of What Was Said about the Distinction in God

Pose a question here: what does it mean that the reflection *that takes its point of departure from God* comes first?

It does not only come first because God is the absolute in the sense of the highest, for the absolute is indeed the all as *that which exists*.

This reflection comes first because the reflection in general remains directed first of all at the absolute. God is first, even *pros hēmas*.[13]

The *reflection* has here, and in what follows, the character of speculation in the sense of the *construction* of beings in the absolute.

Thus, it is necessary to insert here a reflection on the precedence of certainty.

§ 23 Excursus: The Unconditional Precedence of the Certainty (That Is to Say, Concurrently: the Beingness) of the Absolute

See I/7, p. 329; see among other passages I/7, p. 423.

On the concept of the absolute, see above, p. 92.

(*In contrast*, according to Leibniz, *Principes de la nature et de la grâce, fondés en raison*, ed. Gerhardt, VI, pp. 598 and following, no. 7 – but VII, 289; the modified concept of *existentia* – yet there only seems to be an "opposition" between the two "positions.")   119

If the absolute is spirit, the one who exists, unconditional subjektity, then this precedence of the absolute, that is, its certainty, that is, truth, that is, its revealability, that is, its existence, refers to the precedence of the *subjectum* as such.

A recollection can show how, though admittedly in the form of traditional theological metaphysics, the securing of the certainty of the *ego cogito* (*sum cogitans*)[14] already goes together with the *pre-givenness of God*, who himself provides the ultimate securing of certainty (Descartes, Third Meditation). This securing nexus of representing oneself before oneself {*Sich-selbst-Vor-stellens*} is then grasped from itself in its unconditional character by German Idealism. (In between, the clarification by way of Kant's transcendental philosophy.)

The absolute is that which cannot be proven not only *prōton kath' hauto*, but also *pros hēmas*,[15] that is to say, it is in no need of proof, because every proof of beings is in the ether of the absolute. That the

---

[13] {TN: 'for us.'}

[14] {TN: 'I think (am thinking).'}

[15] {TN: 'first according to itself, but also for us.'}

absolute is: this is what is most comprehensible, since to comprehend is to think in the absolute. Certainty.

What is more comprehensible is *that beings (that is, the absolute) are, rather than that "Nothing" is.*

"Nothing": "in itself" in fact "easier," since it needs nothing at all for this; and yet: the most difficult is that Nothing should *be*, since being (essence) is *nisus – exigentia essentiae*.[16]

Philosophy begins with the "confession" that, without the absolute, it would not be present at all (I/7, p. 423). Philosophy cannot, then, already be philosophy "beforehand," and then want in the first instance to prove the absolute in its "existence." Philosophy is *absolute knowledge* – thus knowledge "of" the absolute (objective and subjective genitive).

Philosophy as human effort; certainly – but the human is the "central essence," *the creaturely god.* Philosophy as "spiritual presentation of the universe" of beings as such; the universe is the manifestation of God; philosophy is thus the "ongoing demonstration of God" (I/7, p. 424).

Philosophy is, in the first step, absolute knowledge, also in the sense that it knows of its belonging to the absolute. The absolute as unconditional subjektity. The precedence of the absolute must be grasped in the modern era as the unconditional precedence of subjektity: *the ether and the element of knowledge.*

On page 392, Schelling clearly says that, "in us," God is the *spiritual light* itself, in which everything else becomes clear. The elucidation and its translucence receive their *clarity* from this light.

Initially, the claim of absolute construction appears to be pretentious and fantastical. And yet this claim is the *confession "that everything already is."* Renouncing the curious will-to-explain-first – in the manner of the demiurgical thought of creation (*Deus faber*[17]).

The fundamental position in the becoming of beings themselves; the stroke of magic (387); "divine magic" (391): "the immediate presence of beings in consciousness and to cognition," the knowledge of what is before all question-worthiness; the relation to that which one does not at all first question. (One does not ask one's neighbor whether the sun is shining, that is, one does not run next door to some being in order first to prove what properly is and find it confirmed.)

If God *is* in *us* the light of representation, how do matters stand with the anthropomorphizing of beings? What does it mean, then, to bring

---

[16] {TN: 'exertion – demand of essence.'}
[17] {TN: 'God the maker.'}

something closer to us in a human manner? Nothing other than: to think beings *absolutely*.

In contrast, Kant: "It is fanaticism to have, or even desire to have, an experience – or even a perception referring to it – of the existence {*Daseyn*} and of an effect that can only originate from God" (Kant, *Opus postumum* I, ed. Artur Buchenau, I/74, Berlin/Leipzig 1936). Kant's concepts of "being," "existence" { *"Dasein"*}, "*Existenz*," "objectivity" {*Gegenständlichkeit*}, "Objektivität."

The absolute, however, is: "spiritual," "personal," "living," and not "mechanical" (Spinoza).   121

What is the relation to Leibniz? Precedence of "existence," given *existentia: essentiae exigentia*;[18] the principle of reason; see the *24 Theses*.[19] *Quid "est" potius? Ens aut nihil?* What do *"est"* and *esse* mean?[20] The realm of decision of this question and the manner of questioning?

And if beings are preferable, then must not the being which is in an unconditional way be the most preferable, insofar as this being essences in each being (thought on the basis of unconditional subjektity)?

The absolute is then not only *to prōton kath' hauto*, but also *pros hēmas*.[21] That which is in no need of proof or demonstration, about which and in which we are in agreement. What is most comprehensible is that God "is." See the concept of existence, below § 26.

When does the nothing appear as what is easier and more intelligible? If beings are held to be what is more difficult, and that means more laborious, which requires a making of sorts; if beingness means being produced; doing nothing is easier than undertaking and accomplishing something (for those who are essentially lazy and easygoing, that is, those who do not will).

But what if being, in itself, is: willing, self-willing? Then the nothing is what is more difficult as *non*-willing (see Nietzsche: still preferable to *will nothing* – and thus still to will); to prefer absolute nihilism, since here there is still the opportunity for the will to will, that is, overpowering.

If being = willing, what is most intelligible is that which most is. If being = presence, presence-at-hand, which first requires assistance and is not "of its own accord" (spontaneous, and essentially so), then beings are what most require explanation. (Proofs of God)

---

[18] {TN: 'existence: demand of essence.'}
[19] See the supplement, pp. 162–167.
[20] {TN: 'Which is preferable? Beings or nothing? What do "is" and to be mean?'}
[21] {TN: 'the first according to itself, but also for us.'}

How has unconditional metaphysics unfolded in the meantime? Today this theological philosophy seems to us strange and fanciful. Is our thought more sober? Really?

122   We think in a still more "absolute" way than this absolute metaphysics; in a still more "subjective" way; with still "more will." Intensification in the absolute – namely, into the *counter-essence*; *will as will to power*; will to power and the necessity of the overman.

The metaphysics of the unconditional will to power is expressed in three short phrases, concluding an editorial that appeared in a June issue of the weekly newspaper *Das Reich*. As its shortest formulation, a saying from a Berlin taxi driver is quoted there (not as a "joke" but in all the seriousness of agreement and insight into that which is). The saying reads: "*Adolf weeß et, Gott ahnt et und dir jeht's nischt an.*" {Adolf knows it, God senses it, and it's none of your business.}

Here is expressed the unconditional fulfillment of Western *metaphysica specialis*. These three phrases are the most authentic, Berlinese interpretation of Nietzsche's *Thus Spoke Zarathustra*; they outweigh everything written in the Nietzsche literature.

The Reflection that Takes its Point of Departure from Things[a]

Reflection {*Be-trachtung*}:[1] not merely staring at what is present-at-hand, but rather presenting forth of beings as such, that is, in their being: "things" – that which has been created in a broad sense (the human as the proper creature, see on this Chapter 3).

Now bring the distinction before the non-sensuous eye *as that* which constitutes *the being of things*. Things – per se – that which in a way is, in its own right; creation; the created (in its "becoming"-created; formation through the imagination {*Ein-bildung*}).[2]

---

[a] (From the end of p. 358: "A reflection {*Betrachtung*} starting out from things leads to the same distinction . . ." up to the middle of p. 362: ". . . philosophy of nature.")

[1] {TN: *Trachten*, like *streben*, means 'to strive.' From the Latin *tractare*, meaning, among other things, 'to tug.'}

[2] {TN: *Einbildung*, in German, refers primarily to the imaginative faculty, but Heidegger, following Schelling, understands it literally, as a creative 'building into,' 'im-pression,' or 'in-forming,' which is proper to the divine imagination. (Note that the noun *Bild* means 'image.') As Schelling writes in the Freedom Treatise (349 and 362): "the divine imagination [*Imagination*], which is the cause of differentiation [*Spezifikation*] of beings in the world [*Weltwesen*], is not like its human counterpart in that the latter grants merely ideal actuality to created beings [*Schöpfungen*]. The representations [*Repräsentationen*] of the divinity can be independent beings [*Wesen*] only; for what is the limiting element in our representations [*Vorstellungen*] other than exactly that we see what is not independent? God looks at [*schaut . . . an*] things in themselves. [...] Since [...] the understanding, or the light placed in inceptive nature, arouses the yearning that is striving back into itself to separate the forces (for the surrender of darkness), while emphasizing precisely in this separation the unity closed up within the separated elements – the hidden glimpse of light – something comprehensible and individuated first emerges in this manner and, indeed, not through external representation [*Vorstellen*] but rather through genuine *im-pression* [Ein-Bildung], since that which arises in nature is impressed

Things that are: 1. *divided from God* (*no immanence* – as being onti-
cally nearby and together, like apples in a crate or the "internal organs"
in the body); 2. *nevertheless not "outside"* (thus "in God"; not "beside"
God, so that God would not constitute being); 3. (1. and 2.): dependent
"on" God – "before" God.

These indications and the rejection of "immanence" should determine the manner of the being "of things" (of creation) (that is, first,
refer to the question-worthiness and prepare the manner in which these
created beings present themselves in the absolute, that is, in the distinction).

Things as that which is, namely, as becoming and "becoming in
God"; but not insofar as he exists. The existing, absolute God is the free
one, pure and simple. Things are *not* able to be in *him* nor in his manner,
for, as creation, they are *dependent*, but precisely dependent *on* God =
on the *ground* in God – and "before" God; and, therefore, they are not
that which properly exists, that is, spiritual.

§ 24 The Ground in God as "Originary Yearning"

The ground in God: "yearning" { *"Sehnsucht"* }, "the first stirring of
divine existence {*Dasein*}"; the will to come to oneself; the ground of
that which is without rule (the ungraspable state in nature); the craving
{*Sucht*} for the eternal *one*: to *bring oneself forth*; the craving – toward
[existence]; the yearning is not the existing self.

The eternal ground in God – addressed as "yearning," thought in
a human way; thus, in a human way, the "eternal ground" is brought
nearer; but not thereby anthropomorphized and degraded. Quite the
contrary: in this way, the "ground" is elevated to its absolute essence;
rather than a causal mechanism, the *personality* of the human as a
guiding thread (not a mechanical but a "living" God). And besides:
how is the human in general grasped here? (See below: central-essence.)

"Originary yearning" (360); the eternal ground is also will, but will
without understanding, as *without* under-standing {*ver-stand*loser} but
already will, which directs itself toward the understanding (360); (what
is initially without rule, the ungraspable).

But then the attempt: to think the ground *before* the *eternal* act of
self-revelation ("the world" prior to creation; that which simply is not
but is not Nothing!); eternity prior to the eternity of creation.

[*hineingebildet*] into her or, still more correctly, through awakening, since the understanding brings to the fore the unity or idea concealed in the separated ground."}

After the eternal act: the eternal ground is already *raised up*, through the higher one that has raised itself up from it; "is, namely, in the world" (359); whence the world?

(a) World as we glimpse it: "creature."

(b) World prior to creation: is the eternal ground in God; see above, pp. 93–95; nature as inceptively without rule: "the element" or "instrument" of the *understanding* (the wherein and whereby – in each case in accordance with the degree of potency).

Inceptive nature is "the ground for God's existence." Therein the glimpsing – representing – Idea; "unity."

Originary yearning and, corresponding to it, "an inner reflexive representation"; in the *appetitus* a re-presenting is engendered, that which is re-presented can only be God himself.   125

In this inner reflection, the ground, the ground's will, the yearning as such, is "grasped"; the *craving for itself, but as re-presented; yearning as "glimpse of life,"* life that *glimpses* and *essence of life*. In this way, the proto-type {*Vor-bild*} of the human is formed {*er-bildet*}. (In what way? What is the human?)

What is loved, willed, in this glimpse of *life* is that the division between ground and existence would come to be and that *the world would be*. (See 363.) To love the world: that is, to let the ground be effective and, in this way, to enable the *division* and thereby the highest *unity* and "freedom" in the creature. The human *as God in the creature* (God–human).

§ 25 Creation as Formation through the Imagination; the Creature as "Image"

The first view {Anblick} of oneself; the image as "likeness": here, God essencing entirely in his ground, raised up in the image. *To give oneself a view of oneself* – "image"; the "image" {*"Bild"*} – to form {*bilden*}.

1. Glimpsed {*er-blickt*}:[3] "life," something that exists,

2. The glimpsing itself, representing, existing (see below § 27)

Form through the imagination {*Ein-bilden*} = come to oneself = exist. Formation through the imagination as the fundamental essence of creation and of the natural process; imagination and potentiation.

---

[3] {TN: possibly, 'brought into being (*er-*) through a glimpse (*Blick*).'}

All that matters in Chapter 2 is the being of things – *the being of creation*.

This being as "becoming"; "becoming" as self-willing, willing-oneself-as . . . Creation here is not a making, but rather a letting-become, an inner letting-"become" (and indeed a letting-"oneself"-become).

1. *Formation through the imagination*: what creating (letting-become) aims at.

2. *The proper creature* is that which, divided from God, specifically stands in itself before God and yet in God – the human. It is not that which is most dependent, but rather that which is freest within creation; "human freedom" and the image-likeness to the absolute. "God's" proper creature: that which God, as he himself, lets become.

126

If creation is formation through the imagination, then being an "*image*" – that is, being-*glimpsed* {*Er*-blickt*sein*}, and indeed as that which itself glimpses (re-presenting, understanding) – is essential for the *creature*. The *glimpsed glimpsing in the eternal yearning* (the most extreme division of the centra). *Formation through the imagination* as "working of the understanding."

Division: "unity" – "*universum*" effected only in the division.

(a) To form imaginatively into {*Hin-ein-Bilden*} "nature": "ground," and to form this out into itself {*Herausbilden*};

(b) Formation {*Er-bilden*} of what is each time one, individual (*monas*) in the *uni*ty of the absolute (awakening of the "Idea");

(c) The progressing (potential) reaching-back into the depths of ground, because depth increases with height; not to eliminate darkness but rather place it into the light;

(d) Transfiguration: not dissolution (evaporation), but rather let darkness appear as darkness in the light;

(e) Dividing and uniting; the word, "logos"; propositional statement, "concept."

Formation through the imagination: the re-presentational exposing of the unity that is internally placed.

(Unity – as bond)

                        "soul"

(Unity – as centrum)

The Reflection that Takes its Point of Departure from the Human

§ 26 The Necessity of Creation and the Essence of the Human as the Proper Creature in which God Himself Reveals Himself[a]

Why creation at all? Creation is the self-revelation of God in another, which is divided from him (existence) and yet "in" him.

Why must God *necessarily* reveal himself? (374) Because he is *God*. And he is God only inasmuch as he is the existing God. (A god who did not exist, that is, did not appear and re-present itself, would not be a god.) To exist, though, means: to reveal oneself.

In order to reveal *himself*, such a being, as something created, is required in which he can reveal *himself*, a being which, *as a creature*, is of such an essence that, *in it* – and not only "for" it – *God reveals himself*.

God – as the one who exists – needs the human, and this is why the human is the "first," that which is, in every respect, first formed {*Er-bildete*}, glimpsed. The human is the proper creature.

The creatureliness of the creature, its existing, is determined on the basis of its freedom: as freedom *from* God, *before* God, *in* God ("source of self-movement").

Creating is an *act* (396, 402): letting become in the becoming of the absolute. How, then, imagination {*Einbildung*}? Letting become from out of the independent ground, in such a way that what could *not* be for itself *is for itself* (404). Act: revelation, which follows from the will of love (395).

[a] See above, pp. 98–99.

128   **§ 27 Human Will as "Divine Glimpse of Life" and "Seed of God"**

The human: "image-likeness" of God, "glimpse of life," "seed"; "central essence" ("the two centra"); p. 386: through his act, the human is, "also outside what is created, free and himself an eternal beginning."

The inceptive ground – striving back wholly into itself – pulling toward itself; but since it is ground "for" existence, there lies in it – concealed – the "glimpse of light," the (divine) "glimpse of life"; a glimpsing, re-presenting of unity, formation {*Er-bilden*} of what is each time one (unity – Idea), unified, delimited, comprehensible, singular.

"The understanding" = primal will (363, see 359): "properly, the understanding is the will in the will."

"Universal will": will to the *universum*, to the being of beings as a whole, which wills itself as absolute; love. (Willing is primal being.) Being: what pertains to the understanding in the sense of universal will.

Human will (363): "divine glimpse of life," "*seed – concealed* in the eternal yearning – *of God*." Human will is this seed.

Does this only mean to say what the human will is, or does it mean that the human will makes this seed *existent*, that *this seed is in the manner of existing* and therefore contains in itself two principles that are nevertheless *separate*?

Human will is the *existence* of this seed (will of the understanding), it is God existent in the created. God can glimpse *himself* as existence only in something that is *independent of him* (378). Independence from God is precisely the highest existent correspondence *to* God.

The Concept of "Glimpse of Life"

1. Glimpsing {*Er-blicken*} *of* "life" – (existence); "light" – something re-presented – "unity";

129   2. As the glimpsing {*Er-blicken*} itself, the first existence (the manner in which God first exists in God).

Ground (gravity): pull – (holding-to-oneself)
     Yearning: holding-to-oneself (pull);
     Attending to the *self*: "reflection" {*"Reflexion"*} – re-presenting – view – image; the re-presentation – unity – word.

Image-likeness (378): God can possess *himself* only in the image of something *independent from God* (of an existing being which itself is), and the latter, as such, must be *in him*. *Independence* is precisely a supreme essential correspondence, but only a *correspondence*, and precisely this is not an anthropomorphizing or a coincidence.

"*The human*": "Only in the human, therefore, is the word fully proclaimed which in all other things is held back and incomplete" (363 and following). "Unity" – as represented, produced. The human is the "most complete of all visible creatures"; he *alone* is capable *of evil* (368). "The human is placed on that summit where he has in himself the source of self-movement toward good or evil in equal portions" (374). "Endpoint of nature" (377), "the archetypical and divine human" (377). "The essence of the human is essentially *his own act*" (385).

The human is the beginning of creation – the centrum; the human refers back to it. Therefore, the human is "outside the created," "free and himself an eternal beginning" (386).

The act simultaneous with creation that constitutes the essence of the human himself (387).

Human will as seed "of" God (363). *As seed – for* God? As the seed formed {*er-bildete*} *by God?* Seed – "what arises and to what end"?

"The human will is to be regarded as a bond of living forces" (365) (Soul).

Human will: as "seed" of God, as sun, from out of which unity rises: as existing, creaturely spirit; as seed of what is independent and free in itself.

130

Conclusion

Overview

1. *The distinction* and the essence of freedom and of human freedom in particular (§ 28)
2. *The distinction* in its full essence: being as will. Will of love; love and spirit, soul; will to glorification (399) (§ 29)
3. *The distinction and human essence.* This essence is determined on the basis of the essence of created independence, that is, of the independence that is released from the ground and thus belongs to ground and does not have power over the ground. The essence of the human is determined on the basis of created freedom. Freedom, however, essences *in* the distinction. (§ 30)
4. *The essence of evil* (§ 31)
5. *Evil and the "system"* (§ 32)
6. *The system and the truth (certainty) of beings as a whole* (§ 33)
7. *The truth of beings as a whole and metaphysics*[1]
8. *Metaphysics as o n e course of the history of beyng*
9. *What confrontation* {Auseinander-setzung} *means with respect to metaphysics* (§ 34)

§ 28 The "Distinction" and the Essence of Freedom and of Human Freedom in Particular

The core section of the *Freedom* Treatise treats of the "distinction."
132 What inner connection persists between the distinction and freedom, in particular between *the distinction and human freedom*?
1. The essence of the distinction with respect to freedom;

---

[1] 7. and 8. are not specifically discussed.

2. Freedom as independence (being-for-oneself, that is, self-being);

3. The distinction and the essencing of the "principles."

The distinction between ground and existence entails: possibility of independence (existence), but this in its essential relation to (dependence) ground.

Therefore, with the distinction, the metaphysical possibility of an independence from the absolute is posited, a possibility that is at the same time posited in the absolute. Freedom is grasped as *independence*; yet this concept is, for Schelling, no longer negative, but rather positive in the highest sense, since it signifies the *self*-depending belonging to the absolute. Independence not only *"from,"* as a being-for-itself; rather, the for-itself is, at the same time and first of all, a *being toward God* and *before* God and *"in"* God. Therefore, as a result of this *unavoidability* of belonging, necessity accompanies freedom.

The distinction as the essencing of principles: their inseparability and separability.

In God, the ground and existence are "inseparable," "indissociable," that is, *in* essential unity: God *is* the ground and *is* existence. (In-separability: retain essentially in originary unity.)

The ground belongs to God's essence, which means that this essence (of love) *holds sway* over the ground.

The ground is nothing independent from God, but rather is God: *God is the ground.* The *unity* between the ground and existence is that of the essential originary harmony. *Inseparability* is the essential impossibility of a "disharmony," that is, of a perverted unity. *Separability* is the essential possibility of the perversion of the unity of principles, indeed as "spiritual" perversion.

In the human, ground and existence are *separable*, that is, are not retained in the essential unity determined on the basis of the human essence. *The ground* remains something independent from the human, 133 something that does not come under the power (the will of existence) of the human. (As long as the human attempts to have power over the ground, evil is existent.)

In God and in the human, there is the same *unity* of principles, that is to say, the distinction "actually" essencing as spirit.

In God, the unity of harmony; spirit of love; (excluding all possibility of perversion). In the human, unity as essential possibility of disharmony (perverted unity); this "possibility" is not an empty one but a possibility that essences, in accordance with the assignment to the ground that is independent from the human; independence implies, with respect to the human, that he does not master the ground.

The human – grasped on the basis of the essence of his freedom. The essence of freedom in general; freedom and distinction.

Independence relative to the absolute and in the absolute. Decisive question: 1. Wherein lies the possibility of good and evil, and 2. How does this question come about?

Essence of the human: independent – as spirit; dependent on something independent in him – on "ground." As principle, the ground is separable.

Human freedom; *human will* (independence from – before – *in* God).

Capacity for evil, for that which, in a certain sense, is what is most purely spiritual; capacity for the will of the understanding which, *as* universal will, makes itself into self-will and thus makes the counterwill into the proper.

What the human will is can be determined only *on the basis of existence*, existentielly, that is, on the basis of the fact that it "*is*"; "the seed concealed in the eternal yearning." Why "seed"? The deepest point of inceptive darkness (God's).

Freedom – independence, merely negative? Certainly, but what is insufficiently determined is not in-dependence as such, but rather the fact that independence is precisely not thought through in its full essence; that such an independence is *in* God, that is, not only independence "from" God – as away from – but relative to God. In the human: where the word is fully proclaimed; here, spirit as spirit at home with itself, and indeed as proclaimed-speaking spirit {*ausgesprochensprechender*}.

Freedom as capacity *toward* the good and *toward* evil. The counteraction against the *reaction of ground* lies essentially in the "toward."

The will of the ground reacts each time differently according to whether the *will of the understanding* is a universal will or the will to its perversion; each time according to whether existence determines itself as self-being, as independence, and so relates to the independent ground.

The human as "*final purpose of creation*," "that, whatever could not be for itself, should be for itself insofar as it is raised into existence out of darkness – darkness as a ground independent from God" (404). The human as spirit – created.

§ 29 The "Distinction" in its Full Essence

1. How the distinction essences as the unification of what is distinguished.
   (a) The essential determination is characterized on the basis of

existence and lies in the revelation of unity. (Unity – co-belonging – being.)

(b) The more decisive the division, the more revealed the unity; unity as bond: the living bond as "soul."

2. *The distinction in its pure – absolute – essence.* The distinction is the essence of being as will. *Will* is willing-oneself (that is, one's own essence) and thus existence, thus unity as spirit, *will of the understanding*, unification. Will of the spirit, as absolute will, is *the spirit of love*. In an absolute manner, the distinction is the unifying unity as *the will of love*.

Love is letting the ground be effective, so that there may be a possibility of unification. Love, as will, wills *itself*, but it does *not* will something "for itself." Love wills itself, that is, the revelation of unity; each individual is a being within the whole and simply this.

Love wills the revelation of the absolute, that is, its glorification (399). Here, "glorification" must be grasped in a Greek manner, metaphysically, on the basis of the essence of being.

The *doxa theou*;[2] *dokein* – to come into appearance and shine in its proper essence; presence, presencing {*Präsenz, Anwesung*}, → *phusis*. As *splendor and glory*, the highest and purest appearance as a going-back-into-itself, into the most proper essential repose, not in the erroneous form of the non-essence of declaiming and hyperbole and blustering, which are always only a pretext for having already forgotten. Such "glory" does not essence in itself, but rather is "dependent" and is a construct of that which lacks essence.

3. *The distinction, as unity of "spirit," is not the highest.* "Spirit," as self-depending will of the understanding, of the word, is always "spirit" of . . ., "breath" of . . ., arising from the unity that essences in an originary manner; *but* the possibility of the perversion of unity.

Evil is spiritual, indeed it is "what is most purely spiritual": "for it wages the fiercest war against all *being* {Seyn}, indeed it would like to cancel out {*aufheben*} the ground of creation" (I/7, p. 468). Since the spiritual is evil, spirit cannot be what is highest. (Against Hegel; the ground cannot be canceled out.)

The higher, more essential bond is *the soul*; it is *goodness itself*. *Goodness is the spirit of love.* ("The soul is what is properly divine *in the human*, it is thus the *impersonal*, that which properly is {*das eigentlich Seiende*}, to which the personal must be subjected as that which is not {*Nichtseyendes*}" I/7, p. 468.) (Here it becomes evident that the bond is

135

---

[2] {TN: 'glory of God.'}

what properly is of being {*das eigentlich Seiende des Seins*} and not *one* of the things distinguished, namely, existence.)

"The soul as centrum." (In the Freedom Treatise, the essence of the "soul" is not yet so decisively unfolded.)

§ 30 The "Distinction" and the Essence of the Human

136

Human will "is," as will of spirit, the "*seed*," the possibility of the counter-god, "the deepest point of inceptive darkness."

"The final purpose of creation": "that, whatever could not be for itself, should be for itself insofar as it is raised into existence out of darkness – darkness as a ground independent from God" (I/7, p. 404).

The human exists, is spirit, that is, that created being in which what has risen from the ground is fully awake, that is to say, is understanding *as spirit*. The human is the *word fully proclaimed*, in him spirit reveals itself as spirit, that is, *God as existing actu*. (And *for* this "essence" the absolute is therefore also what is "first" in every respect.)

The human exists as human; thus, the principles must here be separable.

Human will "is" the seed and the possibility of the counter-god. The most spiritual spirit; glimpse of life; glimpse – light – unity – word – "logos."

§ 31 The Essence of Evil

Evil is the will of spirit, which, *as* universal will, transposes itself into self-will as such, so that the latter might be the universal will. Evil is not the mere arousing of selfhood in itself, but rather the ownmost act, highest understanding. This tearing itself away from the universal will does not wander off into the indeterminate; it consists, rather, in transposing itself into self-will, in order to make the latter into the universal will and thereby pervert and replace the human will. Therein consists the *malice* {Bosheit} of evil {*Bösen*}, a malice which is spirituality at its highest.

In evil, the human strives – of his own accord and in a selfish manner, precisely – for what God's love is; for the latter is the originary prevailing over the ground as the prevailing over its own essential condition. Love possesses the ground in essential force. In evil, will wills to be the will of the ground and to possess the ground in its will as universal will. In evil, the human *is* the counter-god.

137

Evil is the exceeding of the ground's potentiality. This lies – as to its possibility – concealed in the absolute ground, *not as* the existing will of the latter.

Evil is real negativity. By means of this treatise on evil, Schelling implicitly wants, at the same time, to bring the negativity unfolded in Hegel's *Phenomenology* beyond the "ideal" and consciousness-bound essence of the distinction between subject and object.

The historical relationship to Plotinus.

"Evil" is the *exceeding* of the ground's potentiality, exceeding toward existence.

"Evil" is "the primal ground of existence to the extent that this ground strives toward actualization in created beings {*Wesen*} and therefore is in fact only the higher potency of the ground that is effective in nature" (378).

". . . Evil [remains] always the human's own choice; the ground cannot make evil as such, and every creature falls due to its own fault" (382).

"The general possibility of evil consists . . . in the fact that the human, instead of making his selfhood [self-will, particular will] into the basis and instrument, can rather strive to elevate it into that which governs [superiority] and into total will and, conversely, to make what is spiritual in himself into a means" (389).

The evil human: the one who, removed from the *centrum* (*centrum* – middle – bond – spirit) wants to be himself the creating will for himself over and above everything. (See p. 390)

Evil and the ground. The ground is condition. Evil: the will to possess the ground completely in the self-willed force of the *actus*.

"The human never gains control over the condition, although in evil he strives to do so; the condition is only lent to him, and is independent from him; hence, his personality and selfhood can never rise to full actuality" (399).

(Whence the sorrow inherent in all finite life.)

"For, aroused selfhood in itself is not evil; but it is so only to the extent that it has completely torn itself away from its opposite, the light or the universal will" (399–400).

"Therefore, only the awakening of life is the will of the ground, not evil immediately and in itself" (400).

(The will of the ground is indeed that there be an independent ground of the good.)

"To the extent that selfhood, in its breaking away, is the principle of evil, the ground does indeed arouse the possible principle of evil, yet not evil itself and not for the sake of evil" (401).

138

"For evil is only evil to the extent that it exceeds potentiality, but, reduced to non-being or the state of potency, it is what it always should be, basis, subordinate, and, as such, no longer in contradiction with God's holiness or love" (405).

§ 32 Evil and the System

1. The concept of system in Schelling's sense.

2. The concept of system and truth as certainty, the self-representing representation of that which is re-presented as the presenting together (*sustasis*) that grasps itself in itself.

3. Truth as certainty and the being of beings; being as "unity."

139   **§ 33 The System and the Truth (Certainty) of Beings as a Whole**

System and subjectity. How the systasis is determined in its essential jointure on the basis of the self-re-presenting of representation and of what it represents in the element of representedness in general.

Presenting-before-oneself {Vor-sich-hinstellen} *and presenting together*. The together as unity in the sense of the "unity" "of" being (the *unity* of presencing that belongs to being itself). Unity of the re-presentedness of self-re-presenting representation: subjectity.

It is not enough to develop the "system" formally on the basis of the prevailing of *mathesis*, for *mathesis* is already the essential consequence of *certitudo*, and the latter belongs together with subjectity as being.

In absolute construction, things are not compared with each other, rather each one is considered *in itself*, that is, in its self-being, existence, *qua* existing, which is to say, each is considered absolutely.

On Schelling's concept of system, p. 399: "In the divine understanding there is a system; yet God himself [']is['] not a system, he is life. . . ." Which is to say: there is no "system" as something foreign to the absolute, in which the system would be first installed in order then to be a system. The system exists in God's understanding (see 337); that is, certainly *not* that there would be *only* a re-presented "schema" and "plan" (no restriction with respect to an actuality of the system), since the understanding is the will in the will; the will is, however, being, existence.

God, that which most is, *the* existing one, the living one. "*The system*" *is the essencing of the absolute will itself*. The manner of actualization of the actual, the manner of existing of what exists.

The absolute is not only the antecedent in itself – *tēi phusei*[3] – in being, but also the ante-cedent for us. It antecedes the human as that toward which the human is already headed – without explicit conceptual knowledge of it.

Now grasp this, however, on the basis of *subjectity*, in a modern and unconditional way, following the way in which the *distinction* is the *will* – as willing – of the absolute. Being as that which most is!

140

§ 34 What Confrontation Means with Respect to Metaphysics

Confrontation {*Aus-einander-setzung*}[4] is the experience of the truth of beings as the experience of an essencing of the truth of being.

The experience of the way in which the history of being prevails throughout ourselves, thus carrying us into unreached abodes in which a decision concerning the grounding of the truth of being must be taken.

Confrontation {*Aus-einander-setzung*} is the displacement into this realm of decision.[5]

―

[3] {TN: 'by nature.'}

[4] {TN: more literally, 'setting (apart) from one another.'}

[5] See also: The Confrontation with the Metaphysics of German Idealism and with Metaphysics in General, pp. 152–155.

Recapitulations and Course of the Interpretation

Recapitulations and course of the interpretation of Schelling's *Philosophical Investigations into the Essence of Human Freedom and the Matters Connected Therewith*

Observe   in the "recapitulations," what has preceded will each time again be more sharply thought through and completed.

Therefore, these recapitulations are not a mere transcript and abridged rendering of what has been respectively dealt with.

The course that has been taken by the interpretation

Recapitulations

Consider   dealing with *the* metaphysics of German Idealism *as such* by way of *one* thinker (Schelling) and just a single treatise from his work.

Claim   the *peak* of the metaphysics of German Idealism → (Nietzsche)

Recapitulation of 14 January

Preliminary Consideration

1. The role of "freedom" in philosophical thought

To what extent is it an "object" for reflection? Not only in general, as one among others, but as determining.

Kant: "the fact of freedom"; "supersensuous fact"
    – the only one; freedom and moral law; "postulates."
    The *only knowable* thing in itself (otherwise only "appear-

ances" are knowable); see *Critique of Judgment* and *Critique*   142
of Practical Reason.

Freedom as "keystone of the system" (*Critique of Practical Reason,*
Preface)

[Why and from where this role of freedom as fundamental fact? Not yet
to be questioned at this point. (Subject.)]

2. *The concepts of freedom attained in the history of thinking*
   (1) spontaneity: "I can," "I am able to" (source of self-movement);
   (2) negative freedom;
   (3) positive freedom (*propensio in bonum*);[1]
   (4) self-legislation (autonomy); categorical imperative, formalism
       (*Critique of Practical Reason* § 7);
   (5) *Libertas indifferentiae*: "freedom of choice": "I can" = everything
       is at my discretion, I only have to choose;
   (6) Freedom as mastery over sensibility (the latter as nature =
       "material of duty" (Fichte)); what is to be overcome;
       [Initially without inner connection; where does it reside? (in sub-
       jectivity)]
       The concatenation of several or all of these concepts of freedom;
       on what ground? (The "problem of the freedom of the will," a
       question of the illusionists in philosophy; ontic explanation of
       freedom by way of psychology, sociology, statistics – or the cor-
       responding denial.)

3. *Schelling's treatise*
   Where and in what manner was it first published?
   F. W. J. Schellings philosophische Schriften. Erster Band – Landshut,
   1809; separately, 1834; then *Sämmtliche Werke* I/7, p. 331 and following;
   the edition I have here from the Philosophische Bibliothek, 1925[2] (an
   array of misprints).

1. *Title*   143
   Preliminary elucidation;
   Observe: "philosophical investigations" – "philosophy"?
                     human freedom (thus there is still another freedom
                     in the absolute)
                     the human – questioned;

---

[1] {TN: 'inclination to the good.'}

[2] Philosophische Bibliothek, no. 197, Leipzig, 1925, ed. Christian Herrmann (the
edition of Heidegger's personal copy).

essence of freedom, from where is it possible – and actual how?

the human capable of freedom as "central essence"; the matters connected therewith;

"connection" and "system";

"system of freedom"

(freedom as center of the system; system – not as something made by the human, but rather as the jointure of beings as a whole).

2. *Outline*   (see § 4)

3. *The foundation*   treats of *evil* {Böse} (the malevolent {*Bösartige*}; not what is morally bad); the malevolent as highest spirit; not "something sensuous";

evil – opposition – negativity; unity – beingness – *hen*;

repulsiveness.

Recapitulation of 21 January

Let us dwell on misgivings! – That may show the extent to which we undertake this task thoughtfully, and not as an arbitrary reading exercise in the history of philosophy.

A further misgiving: whether we do not fall prey to historicism and currentism? (See § 5) – This misgiving is especially important, since it approaches us of its own accord, such that it itself prohibits us from encountering his treatise.

To what extent also all "restoration" and "eschatology" belong to it; likewise: mere "scholasticism"; the illusionists in philosophy; one has one's own truth and does not fundamentally let oneself engage with anything: one takes "philosophy" to be only embellishment.

Schelling's own demand in the final remark of the treatise (415/16); are we not acting in opposition to it by dealing with Schelling?

Beginning of the interpretation:

The interpretation itself runs the risk of tracing the main concepts and every word back to earlier ones and of believing one has thereby explained something. This risk is especially present in a philosophy that knowingly thinks prior thought unconditionally. Thus, the talk of this or that person having "already" said and meant this, of this being already here or there, of Schelling being influenced by this or that. In this way nothing is brought into knowledge, if one stays put with what one has procured as if it were established and clear. However, it is a matter neither of establishing dependencies nor of rescuing an originality, but of experiencing the necessity of decisions that, for their part, are themselves not of our making.

If, therefore – seemingly – historiographical indications are given, then they have another sense – initially the sense that what is named is even more question-worthy than Schelling's words.

Singling out the core section (357–364);

in what way is it the core section? In terms of content and its mode of thinking;

(Identity-thinking of the absolute dialectics of subjectivity).

Core section; first paragraph:

1. Indication of the distinction established by "the philosophy of nature of our time."
   - (a) the distinction itself; "ground" – "existence"; formulaic and   145
     imprecise; well-known philosophical concepts;
   - (b) what does the distinction concern?
     Every "essence," that is, every being in its being.
   - (c) in what way does the philosophy of nature come to this distinction? What is "philosophy of nature"? – Not a subject of Scholastic philosophy, but rather *the* philosophy of absolute thought from *one necessary* point of view; (nature is not one region among others, but an essential shape of the absolute itself);
   - (d) the distinction *introduced* into "science," that is, absolute knowledge;

2. Indication of the role and importance of this distinction.
   The entire Freedom Treatise is "grounded" on it. Yet the treatise treats of the center, or better: from out of the center of "the system of freedom." Here, then, is the governing center of the system and that means, consequently, of the whole of philosophy (that is, of metaphysics).

It is to be supposed, then, that that which this distinction treats of is that which is treated by all of metaphysics. See Aristotle's phrase: *kai dē kai to palai te kai nun kai aei zētoumenon kai aei aporoumenon, ti to on* (*Met.* Z 1, 1028b 2–4).

"And so it is therefore that which of old and now and ever again is sought and which *thereby* ever again leads to impasse, that which we question in the question: what are beings {*das Seiende*}?"

Subsequently, Aristotelian philosophy was inherited and particularly tailored for church doctrine, but what was essential was set aside: (1) seeking, and especially (2) that what is sought for repeatedly puts one in a situation with no way out; Aristotelian doctrine was instead used as a

way out of all difficulties. The repercussions of the medieval Scholastic reinterpretation of Aristotle can still be felt in our time; in saying this
146   not only do we mean the conception of Aristotle controlled by the church, but also the philosophical conception: Werner Jaeger (*Aristotle* [1923]) thinks entirely on the path laid by Scholasticism.

But it is a matter of taking seriously the question itself and consider-ing what it says rightly: *ti to on; on* as participle: *metochē* – "participat-ing" (in *ptōsis* and *chronos*, noun and verb).

What are beings {*das Seiende*} (noun) as being {*Seiend*}, as being-ness {*Seiendheit*} (verb)? – An "essence" in its essentiality, for example, "living essence."

What are beings? What are they? Being {*Seiend*}: being everywhere and each time, that is, determined by beingness, and therefore by "being" {*"Sein"*}; from beings to being; *phusei on; meta . . . ta phusei onta;*[3] what is sought for is what determines beings as such: being {*Sein*}; what is questioned is supposed then to become the answer: "being" answers what beings are.

A hint is thereby given as to the way in which we must attempt to understand the distinction and follow it out in thought {*nach-zudenken*} (see pp. 134–135).
(Here, first the preliminary glimpse of the entire core section).

The core section and Schelling's approach
Strange: Assertions that are not at all demonstrable without further ado; "dictums"; arbitrary "speculation"; and this after Kant!
Which questions impose themselves here? Misgivings; with no guiding thread or solid ground; perhaps a "conceptual fiction"? a "game of thinking"? After Kant's critique of speculative reason? Yet Kant like-wise calls the philosopher the "legislator of reason."

Schelling's procedure: "speculative," analogizing, "dialectical"; what does this all mean?

Let us initially select three[4] paths, more from the periphery:
(A) Elucidation of the concepts of "existence" and "ground" as tra-ditional "metaphysical" concepts (starting from "philosophy of existence" and reference to the traditional use of term);
147   (B) The distinction itself is grounded in *what* it distinguishes: "being"; (willing is primal being;)
Subjectivity ⟵⟶ *erōs – desiderium;*

---

[3] {TN: 'beings/what is by nature; beyond . . . beings by nature.'}
[4] {TN: based on what follows, it seems that this should be 'four.'}

(C) The distinction becomes necessary on the basis of the "opposition" that belongs to being (as subjectivity) ("the principle of opposition" and "negativity");
(D) The essence of the distinction as the essence of a division that becomes (see pp. 9ff.)

Recapitulation of 28 January

Brief reference to the final remark of Schelling's treatise: here it is said:

> The time of merely historiographical faith is past, if the possibility of immediate cognition is given. We have an older revelation than any written one – nature. (415)

These sentences initially give the indication that Schelling himself seems to discourage us from a historiographical reflection and thus from an interpretation of his own writing, which is after all something that, for us, lies in the past. This rejection springs from the appeal to "the possibility of immediate cognition," which is posited as given. Immediate cognition is one that is not mediated by propositions and cognitions on which one relies in order to arrive at further cognition subsequently; immediate cognition is one that apprehends *straight away* what is to be cognized here, namely, what beings are as a whole. Immediate cognition here is not meant in the sense of a particular perception of an isolated object; rather "cognition" here is always cognition of the absolute. For this to happen, the absolute must show itself, open itself up, reveal itself {*öffnen, offenbaren*}. "Older" than any written revelation (the Bible!) is "nature." What does "nature" mean? – The absolute itself. "Older"? – That which precedes, in the sense that it must first have revealed itself (nature "in" God – God himself –), so that another revelation could then be. (Here, transposed into the unconditional, is a variation on the sentence: *gratia supponit naturam*.)[5]

Yet Schelling speaks, however, "only" of the "*possibility* of immediate cognition"; *if* it is given; it *is* given through the new fundamental position of German Idealism vis-à-vis Kant, and indeed precisely by way of Kant. Here, "possibility" in no way means only: not precluded, but rather, positively: the ability and foundation are given, that is, the immediate relation to the absolute.

---

[5] {TN: 'grace builds on nature.'}

"Historiographical faith" and "immediate cognition"
This distinction was initially and correctly interpreted to mean that philosophy should not *"historiographically orient"* itself in order to ground a new philosophy by means of acquaintance with past philosophies. The distinction has, however, a *wider scope* and characterizes the fundamental position of this entire treatise and, for this reason, also that of the metaphysics of German Idealism.

The mention of "older revelation" refers to biblical revelation. Cognition based on this older revelation towers over, therefore, also the truth of Christian faith as a "historiographical" faith, inasmuch as Christian faith is based on the "historiographical" fact – posited by faith – of the incarnation of God in Christ.

The system of philosophy, that is, science, is thus the only true system in the sense of absolute system: the *"system of religion becomes science."* To which corresponds, p. 412, the demand that revealed truths be developed into truths of reason.

And this is in keeping with Hegel's fundamental position in the *Phenomenology of Spirit*, where "religion," as a shape of reason, is subordinated in advance to "absolute knowledge"; absolute knowledge = philosophy.

149   Only from here does Schelling's final remark attain its full scope, but also its inner relation to that which the entire treatise thinks through.

On the characterization of "immediate cognition" in the speculative dialectics of German Idealism
An entry by Hegel from the Jena period (1802–1807):

> The peasant woman lives within the circle of her Liese, who is her best cow; then the black one, the spotted one, and so on; also of Martin, her boy, and Ursula, her girl, etc. To the philosopher, infinity, perception, movement, sensuous laws [for example, Kant's transcendental philosophy!], etc. are things just as familiar. As her dead brother and uncle are to the peasant-wife, so Plato, Spinoza, etc. are to the philosopher. The one has as much actuality as the other, but the latter are immortal.[6]

---

[6] Jon Stewart (ed.), *Miscellaneous Writings of G. W. F. Hegel* (Evanston, Ill.: Northwestern University Press, 2002), p. 246. Cf. Karl Rosenkranz, *Georg Wilhelm Friedrich Hegels Leben* (Darmstadt: Wissenschaftliche Buchgesellschaft, 1963), 537 and following.

Today, the "peasant woman with her Liese" is hardly still a fitting example of the immediate essential relation that Hegel wants to illustrate and that he calls "immediate cognition," namely in the sense of speculative-theological "dialectics" (intellectual intuition). Why not? Because, in the meantime, this life in an immediately familiar and enduring circle has been altogether shattered and has made room for entirely different relations; yet, for example, the relationship between an airplane pilot and his "machine" (which for him is just his "box"); and yet not; the displacement into the pure procedure of the empowering of power (the abandonment of beings by being).

Transition to the interpretation of the core section of the treatise, pp. 357–364, by way of a preliminary reflection
First, a brief indication of what kind of character the core section has   150
for us: strange, "speculative" (following Kant's *Critique*), "dialectical," "analogical," "theological." (But "theology" for Schelling and Hegel is only an "abstraction" of philosophy.)

The preliminary reflection in four chapters; see § 7.

On the first chapter: ground and existence

1. "Existence" and *"existentia"*; *essentia* and *existentia*; *ens actu*;[7] *actualitas*; actuality = *"Dasein"* (the Dasein of God, the Dasein of the human, the Dasein of animal and plant and earth and sea, in the comprehensible sense of ontology, "is there" {*"ist da"*}, or "the chalk is not there" – "but it is there!" Because it is "there," it is *therefore* available); effective effectedness; effectedness – and then?

In this interpretation: *agere* – as *creare*; biblical–theological; but *ens pot. – ens actu*[8] – by the same token *essentia* and *existentia* refer back to Aristotle and Plato.

The modern interpretation of Aristotle and Plato, including Hegel's interpretation, goes back to the interpretation of the Middle Ages. And this interpretation of Plato and Aristotle likewise determines the interpretation of the previous "philosophy" – pre-Platonic, pre-Socratic. The latter is determined on the basis of Aristotle; but an essentially disfigured and un-Greek Aristotle.

This is the best evidence for how difficult it is to free oneself from this tradition.

Jaeger: neo-Kantian, Christian-theological, only not Greek – in spite of *Paideia*.

Bear in mind for the present case that the Greeks have no word at all

---

[7] {TN: 'a being in act.'}
[8] {TN: 'a being in potency – a being in act.'}

for *existentia*; but rather simply *einai* – what is thought under this – ; see the twofold distinction of *ousia* in Aristotle (*ho tis anthrōpos*; *to eidos tou anthrōpou – zōion*);[9] see *Categories*; *actus – actualitas – energeia – en-ergeia*; the latter on the basis of *actus* – Scholastic; after that, though with a metaphysical interpretation: Leibniz.

(Jaeger!) – un-Greek – just as with *ousia* as substance.

But presencing – in the manner of *eidos – essentia*! Utterly concealed by what came later, and thoroughly so by modern philosophy; seen for the first time since "Being and Time"; one now acts as though one had always meant this; that this is only an illusion is shown by the fact that one does not let oneself engage further with what underlies this insight; see below "existence" and "philosophy of existence" and "Being and Time";

2. Existence and philosophy of existence
3. Kierkegaard's concept of existence
4. Kierkegaard, philosophy of existence, and "Being and Time"

Recapitulation of 4 February

The concept of existence in K. Jaspers and Kierkegaard
In Kierkegaard:
Existence indeed in the traditional sense of *actuality*, how something *actually* is; but at the same time restricted to the human; how the human *qua* human actually is, inasmuch as he is *himself*;
Thereby:
the essence (*essentia*) of the human distinguished by *ratio*, *rationalitas*, rationality as personality;

Reason:	self-consciousness, self-determination, relation to self-being; this self as related to itself; see Kant: animality, humankind (rationality), personality, (rational and at the same time capable of accountability); *Religion within the Bounds of Bare Reason*, 1793 (Part I, no. 1);
Self-being:	yet at the same time related to God as the highest being (eternity); understood in a Christian way;
The human:	essentially: a composite of the irreconcilability of time and eternity (understood in a Christian way); the paradox;
"Existence":	self-being; as an individual, "infinite" = to be unconditionally "interested" in this composite; *inter-esse*:[10]

---

[9] {TN: 'this human; the form of the human – animal.'}
[10] {TN: literally, 'being between.'}

151

152

between time and eternity (understood in a Christian way);

self-being;

being-oneself {*Selbst-sein*} as an individual, someone temporal, before God, before the eternal, and that means essentially as a faithful Christian, that is, in an essential relation to the proper paradox of God become human; this relation as faith; (thus the question of whether eternal salvation is to be built on a historiographical truth;)

because existence in general is conceived as self-being, here is thus already the modern concept of the human = "subjectivity."

"Existence": the actualization of a uniformly manifold relationship in which the human as such stands: the relationship to himself as a "being," to God as the highest being, and with this also to "world" as the remaining nonhuman being into which the human is created;

actualization of the manifoldly unitary *self*-relationship to *beings*;

"existence" therefore indeed capturing *existentia*, yet at the same time *restricted* to the being of the human; this "restriction," however, entails precisely the relationship to all beings (metaphysics).

In what way, with the growing inability actually to respond to a thinker, entirely unanticipated blunders must be averted:

Kierkegaard restricts the concept of "existence" to the human; therefore, animals, plants, stones, and planets accordingly do not "exist." And if they do not "exist," that is to say, according to the usual epistemological way of thinking, if they are not "objective," they can only be "subjective." One infers – on the basis of the restriction of the concept of existence, according to which "existence" is supposed to designate only human subjectivity – the non-actuality of beings that are not designated by the term existence. "One" – not some clueless student, but Nic. Hartmann, who in his book *The Problem of Spiritual Being: Investigations into the Foundations of the Philosophy of History and the Human Sciences*,[11] issues the following instruction (p. 84): "In the same

153

---

[11] Nicolai Hartmann, *Das Problem des geistigen Seins: Untersuchungen zur*

way, there is also a lopsided orientation in the Kierkegaardian concept of existence, according to which the world, within which spirit is found, does not exist but rather only persists for spirit – as that which alone is existential {*existenziellen*} – and is thus its world."

Hartmann is speaking of Kierkegaard and has "Being and Time" in mind; by means of a gross misinterpretation of "Being and Time," he also at the same time misunderstands Kierkegaard whose concept of existence – which he does not grasp – he simply equates with that of "Being and Time." Yet Kierkegaard says clearly enough in the cited passage: "We all exist," that is to say, we are, in the ordinary and indeterminate sense, "actual," just as everything else is also "actual."

In contrast to the Kierkegaardian "theory" of existence, which "sins" against the concept of existence (thus a "sin," not a mere mistake), Hartmann offers the following instruction (ibid., p. 84): "A human, and a thing exists. They exist in very different ways, to be sure. But they exist with each other in the one existing world. And the existence itself is the same." How uplifting it must be for a mind corrupted by the "sins" of "Being and Time" to read such things and thus learn that the human and things exist, in other words, that they are actually present at hand!

Indeed, "existence itself" is even "the same" in humans and things. – In what way, however, things and humans are supposed to "exist in different ways," that is what Nic. Hartmann keeps secret with such a presupposition.

154

Transition to clarifying the concept of existence in "Being and Time"
A. In what way is it related to Kierkegaard's concept of existence?
   1. also a name for the being of the human; restricted;
   2. also a name for the *self-being* of the human; emphasized;
      even though everything within "de-Christianization";
      "atheist anthropology";
      and yet!

Recapitulation of 11 February

Preliminary reminder of the essential connection between the "core section" and the "introduction"

Grundlegung der Geschichtsphilosophie und der Geisteswissenschaften (Berlin: De Gruyter, 1933).

Answering the question: in what way is the section that treats of the distinction between ground and existence (357–364) the core section of the Freedom Treatise, which is supposed to be the peak of the metaphysics of German Idealism? The core contains the innermost of what must be thought when one thinks the "system of freedom" and, with "freedom," the innermost centerpoint of the system and the ground of metaphysics.

System of freedom: the whole of beings (the all), conjoined from out of the fundamental relation of the freedom of the human being, and that means of the freedom from God, who is all, before God, and in God. From a first glance at the outline, however, it appeared that the Freedom Treatise only takes evil as its proper "theme." Why is this so? Does the reflection on the center of the system treat of evil because the latter is also related to freedom, or does it treat of freedom because evil is what is properly question-worthy in the system? And why is this what is question-worthy? As what is counter to God, *dustasis* and *apostasis*,[12] the most extreme diremption arising from the insurrection of the "soul's" selfishness – which is seized by spirit – in the intimacy with the ground as the *primal ground* of existence; God does not oppose the will of the ground, since if he did he would annul {*aufhöbe*} the condition of his own existence, that is, personality (I/7, p. 483). God "is" all. (See Preliminary Glimpses and Directives, pp. 138–141.)

155

The question of freedom is, as question of system, the question of pan-theism; freedom *is* the connection with God, it *is* the essential jointure of the "system" (see the title of the treatise). In what way is it the case that: "all is God" or "God is all"? Here the "is" is decisive; the bond – copula; the "is" as the word of the being of beings ("system of metaphysics"). This is what is treated by the introduction.

[the *pan* of *panta* – without the being of beings? No! See on primal being and the distinction between ground and existence. But both: only *next to each other* and themselves *without* truth {*Wahr-heit*} and without the proper difference {*Differenz*}, and thus onto-theological.

Preserve {*wahren*} the unity of beings and save freedom: how else if not by: essencing into God {*in Gott hineinwesen*}? How, then, must the human (the "being") *be*?

Ground – existence
Nature – freedom
Reason that urges unity (necessity)
Feeling that insists on freedom (freedom)

---

[12] {TN: *dustasis*, apparently a neologism based on *dus* ('bad,' see *dystopia*) and *stasis* ('standing'). *Apostasis*: 'standing away from.'}

Essencing into God – yet in such a way that the human is free *from* God, *in* God and *for* God. Divinity of God – how?]

Yet in the part designated as the "core section," a distinction regarding *beings as such*, that is, with respect to the being of beings. In the core section the innermost is thought, which is at the same time the ground of the center of the system: the being of beings as such.

"Existence" and "Dasein" in "Being and Time"
Concepts of existence previously discussed:

1. *existentia*: actuality of every actual thing (what "is" not simply nothing);
2. existence: restricted to the self-being of the human; "subjectivity";
    (a) Christianness of the creaturely human as an individual;
    (b) personality of the rational being {*Vernunftswesens*} (the human) in the midst of the world and with respect to its "transcendence";

The elucidation that comes from without is attempted by way of a discussion of two guiding principles printed in spaced-out letters for emphasis:

1. *"The 'essence' of Dasein lies in its existence"* (p. 42).
2. *"The understanding of being is itself a determinacy of the being of Dasein"* (p. 12).

Regarding 1. In this sentence, all three nouns – Dasein, essence, existence – are meant to have a sense other than the customary one, that is to say, they are to be thought on the basis of a different experience and different questions. But then the attempt to find an "entry" step-by-step remains hopeless; for one would first like to presume that Dasein and essence are given as what is known, and then, through an appropriate consideration, that it would be possible to conclude what existence is. Or, conversely: the essence of existence is delimited and, on that basis, the essence of Dasein is determined. But in either case the reflection turns in a circle. The essence of Dasein is not to be thought without existence, and existence is not to be thought without the essence of Dasein. We only make our way into this circle, which is inevitable, through a leap. Every discussion therefore remains provisional. Yet the leap can be prepared by reflecting on the second sentence.

Regarding 2. Here there is talk of "the understanding of being"; it

	was pointed out that Da-sein understands itself in its own being. This being {*Sein*}, however, remains distinguished by "being-in-the-world."
Example:	Over there a human stands beside a tree. Human and tree are "in the world"; both beings "stand" there; indeed, they stand in the "open." Yet the human "stands" – without having sufficiently taken this up into his essence – in the open as such, so that, in this (unknown) open, what encounters us "is" that which encounters *as* "a being," and the standing is an essentially different one.

To what extent, from without, the abyssal difference between "consciousness" and "being-in-the-world" can be accomplished –; standing in the openness of being (not only of beings); being is understood – projected –

ousia	as the term for *par-* and *apousia*, presence and absence; *the on*;
aei on	as that which properly is, in which the essence of being is fully accomplished; *what is everlastingly present*.

Presence and constancy as "temporal" determinations; but "time" in what sense?

In any case: *being and time*; a question, and, indeed, *the* question concerning the openness of being and the essencing of this openness.

Recapitulation of 18 February

On the clarification of the question indicated by the title "Being and Time"

The concept of existence in "Being and Time" must be thought on the basis of this question.

On time, temporality, Da-sein, being

The question of "Being and Time" can be developed through a "reminder" of the temporal character of the inceptive essence of being, insofar as the latter is determined as *ousia* (more inceptively in *phusis*). More precisely, to speak of "reminder" here is indeed inappropriate; for it is not a matter of calling back to memory something forgotten; that is impossible, since *ousia* previously had not yet at all been thought in its temporal character. This temporal character remained concealed – and has since then remained concealed – and it is still today something strange; because "time" here essences differently, and being in general is held to be unworthy of question. In what way? The interpretation of being as *ousia* was so powerful that even "time" itself was comprehended on the basis of this understanding of being as *ousia tis* (Aristotle, *Physics* Δ 10).

Time as calculated and elapsing; chronos, arithmos – numbering number (Aristotle, *Physics* Δ 11, 219b); *to proteron – husteron* "is" *prōton en tōi topōi*, first in places, related to place; before – behind – *prōton*, that is, apprehended on the basis of presencing;

chronos in Aristotle, *corresponding to* "space," *as*

topos   the "there" and "over there" and "here," the "where," thus the when; "time" in the sense of "there for the time being," "in the time" of an hour, "around the time when"; thus time agreed upon, calculated, and to be counted, time as "dated."

    In both coinages the predominance of *ousia* is apparent, according to which thinking aims at the presencing of "space" and "time" in the modern sense, that is, "place" and "point in time." That said, extension (*megethos*) does not go unrecognized; but not taken as the first (Leibniz, Kant) that becomes restricted, but rather taken as the *apeiron* into which the "where" and "when" disappear – *mē on*.[13]

Temporality as ecstatic temporalization

    Bringing about the essencing {*Erwesung*} of the truth of beyng (in an in-between manner – abyssal);

    neither cyclical nor eschatological;

    not at all a "course," lapsing or elapsing or orbiting {*Verlauf, Ab- und Auslaufen und Umlaufen*}; being and time, both are especially and similarly inaccessible on account of an overly great nearness;

    1. we immediately think past it (overhastiness)

    2. we are satisfied with the indeterminate (fleetingness)

159   3. since all of this is – apparently – ineffectual, un-graspable, and like the nothing (usefulness and performance)

(*Being is the nothing*; this "is" not a being, in the way we know and believe we know beings;)

the difficulty of thinking what is simple;

the difficulty of leaving behind familiarity as the sole measure.

---

[13] {TN: 'non-being.'}

Recapitulation of 25 February

The concept of existence in "Being and Time" springs from the question named in the title. In the unfolding of this question, a reflection on the essence of "time" becomes necessary, which includes a historical confrontation with the previous interpretation of the essence of time.

For this, it is necessary to distinguish:

1. pre-conceptual reckoning with time (time of day, time of year);
2. the *conceptual formulation* – which this enables – of the essence of time thus projected; a pre-concept of being leads the way here, since "time" somehow "is" {*"seiend"*};
   (a) Greek: *chronos* – corresponding to *topos* – reckoned, numbering time; date {*Datum*}, given, present time; time as "dated"; *arithmos kinēseōs kata to proteron kai husteron*[14] (Aristotle, *Physics* Δ, 219b 1f.); *proteron* – *husteron, prōton en topōi*[15] (Aristotle, *Physics* Δ 219a 14f.);
   (b) modern: as dimension and ordering schema for all occurrences and human actions; "time" as "parameter," that is, as that along which points and distances are measured out; "time" as fourth dimension of the "four-dimensional world"; (t)
3. the question concerning time with respect to the peregrination of the individual human soul on earth, a peregrination which is "temporally" limited and experienced in a Christian manner; "temporality" – "eternity";
4. Time as the first name for the realm of projection of the truth of being; "time" is the ecstatic in-between (time-space); not the wherein of beings, but rather the clearing of being itself.

160

The concepts of existence discussed and their reciprocal relation (see p. 73f.)

With regard to metaphysics, necessary to consider: understanding of being and "subjectivity" as "I-hood"; being and the human; anthropomorphy;

The ambiguity of the question of being; metaphysics and "Being and Time"

It seems at first glance that "Being and Time" is, at best, an "addendum" to metaphysics, a kind of anthropological "epistemology" of "ontology," as it were. Should "Being and Time" prove unable to be

---

[14] {TN: 'number of movement according to before and after.'}
[15] {TN: 'before – after, first in place.'}

this, then it would still be the case, at most, that here a more originary metaphysical questioning is attempted, but precisely still a metaphysical questioning.

In truth, however, there is no more metaphysics here, but rather an entirely other inception; yet, for this reason, there persists, all the more, an inceptive relation to the first inception. This is why the inceptive historical recollection is necessary, and therefore also the reason for the occasional designation and interpretation of the approach as "metaphysics"; see the Kant book and *What is Metaphysics?*; being and essentiality of "essence."

For it is indeed also the case that "Being and Time" nowhere corresponds to what one rightly expects from an "ontology," the first step of which, if one can call it that, solely consists in taking the essence of being for granted and unquestionable in advance.

One has also identified "Being and Time," among other things, with Fichte's fundamental position and interpreted it by way of this position, whereas here the most extreme contrast arguably prevails, assuming there is even possibility of comparison. Yet the contrast is already askew, since "Being and Time" does not think in some merely "realistic" way, in contradistinction to Fichte's unconditional "egoistic" idealism.

161

On the subject of this idealism, Schiller writes to Goethe on 28 October 1794, thus around the time when the first *Wissenschaftslehre* appeared:

> According to Fichte's oral remarks – since in his book there was not yet any discussion of this – the *I* is creative, even through its representations, and all reality is only in the I. The world for him is only a ball which the I has thrown and which it catches again in reflection {*Reflexion*}!! Thus, it is said that he actually declared his own divinity, as we were anticipating of late.[16]

According to Fichte, the I throws the world, and according to "Being and Time," it is not only the I but Da-Sein – essencing before all humanity – that is what is thrown.

Recapitulation of 4 March

The conceptual-historical elucidation of the essence of ground

[16] *Correspondence between Schiller and Goethe from 1794 to 1805*, p. 27; Heidegger's emphasis (trans. mod.).

It is guided by a double aim:

1. it is a matter of showing that, and in what way, the essence of ground goes ultimately together with the metaphysical interpretation of beings (*idea, ousia, hupokeimenon, subjectum*);
2. in this way, what is strange in the Schellingian distinction is removed in advance, but the insight into what is peculiar to it is also prepared.

In Greek metaphysics, the guiding term for what we call "ground" is the word *archē* in the twofold sense of inception and sovereignty; in modern philosophy, by contrast, it is the term *ratio* (*principium rationis sufficientis; grande illud principium;*[17] Leibniz).

How does *ratio* (*reor, rheō, rhēsis* – saying, stating, holding an opinion) come to have the sense of "ground"? [*hupokeimenon, legomenon kath' auto,*[18] *logos*]   162

This can be seen only if we grasp the guiding term that includes *all* the metaphysical essential determinations of "ground" and that attests, at the same time, to the univocal indication of the guiding projection of beings.

hupokeimenon   that which lies there already beforehand, what is already present and what is present in advance; [of *poiēsis* and *technē*] the concept is polysemous [*legein – kataphasis, apophasis*], which arises from the Aristotelian interpretation of *archē* and *aitia*; the resulting content of this concept, in no particular order:

    1. *ex hou*: that *from out of which...* [*poioumenon*]
    2. *paradeigma*: that *after which...* [*ergon – phusei on*][19]
    3. *proaireton*: what is taken *in advance*, because it is what delimits in advance (*telos*) [for making, manufacturing]
    4. *kath' hou legetai ti: that upon which* something goes back; (*aitia* – the relation to *phusei onta*;)[20] *archē kinēseōs*[21] in the narrower sense, the later *causa efficiens*, remains curiously undetermined; in Greek thought, it is not at all what is essential, the way it will later be in Christian thought (creation) and modern thought ("technology").

hupokeimenon in Latin translation: *sub-jectum*; every being is, as a

---

[17] {TN: 'principle of sufficient reason; that great beginning.'}
[18] {TN: 'what is said according to itself.'}
[19] {TN: 'a being by nature.'}
[20] {TN: 'beings by nature.'}
[21] {TN: 'source of movement.'}

being, *subjectum* (*sub-stans*). This sentence holds for *all* metaphysics from Plato to Nietzsche. Yet it is also on the basis of this sentence that we can first grasp the way in which "subjectivity" becomes the fundamental metaphysical concept in modern metaphysics, whereby "subjectivity" means "selfhood" – a representing relatedness back to the self.

163   Descartes takes the *first* step toward this determination – based on the transformation of the essence of truth (*veritas* as *certitudo cognitionis humanae*).[22] (Where does this transformation come from? From the history of beyng.)

Leibniz takes the *second* step, which is no less decisive.
1. How does the *ego* come to be the distinguished subjectum (*mens – sive animus*)?[23]
2. How does the essence of the subjectum thereby come to be subjectivity in the sense of *selfhood*? (See Leibniz on *mentes*, Gerhardt VII, p. 291, likewise p. 307; *mentes* as *partes totales.*)

His fundamental metaphysical position designates the proper turning point between the metaphysics that came before and that of German Idealism.

The point is not to explain Schelling's distinction in a historiographical manner; rather, in order to grasp its concealed contents, it is necessary for us to recall briefly certain lines of Leibniz's thinking. This would also be the case even if we did not know that Schelling had already, at age sixteen, read one of Leibniz's major texts, the so-called *Monadology* (written in French in 1714, published in German after Leibniz's death in 1720, in Latin in 1721, original text in 1840).

Recapitulation of 11 March

Why this recalling of Leibniz in the course of this preliminary consideration between the first chapter and Chapters 2 to 4?

In Chapters 2 to 4, discussion of Schelling's *Investigations*; his treatise as peak of the metaphysics of German Idealism; the latter, however, distinguished by the fundamental trait of modern metaphysics; here *hupokeimenon* becomes subjectivity (selfhood); in two main stages: Descartes: *one subjectum* as *ego* (*percipiens, mens*); and Leibniz: *percipere, appercipere* as *subjectum* pure and simple; *monas.*

164   *How the changeover from* hupokeimenon *to subjectivity occurs*

---

[22] {TN: 'certainty of human knowledge.'}
[23] {TN: 'mind – or intelligence.'}

"Recall" briefly – not historiographically, however, but thoughtfully – that all of this bears the modern and therefore current and nearest interpretation of beings; here: the sphere of essential questions and decisions; the reference to Leibniz in view of his determination of "*existentia*";

previously: *essentia* and *existentia* in the sense of *potentia – actus*, possibility (being without contradiction) – actuality;

now: both "concepts" transformed, grasped in a more originary manner; on the basis of the old distinction it looks as though *essentia*, as *possibilitas*, were closer to *existentia* and, conversely, the latter (*existentia*) closer to *essentia*, so that they meet in the "middle," as it were; but in this way everything is awry;

essentia	"is" *possibilitas* (not *potentia*) = *nisus, conatus, praetensio ad existentiam;*[24]

das Mögen in its double sense:

    1. "*es 'mag' sein*" {"it 'may' be"} = it "can" be (is possible)

    2. "*er 'mag' ihn nicht*" {"he doesn't 'like' him"} = inclination toward; "love"

the able being-inclined-to . . . : (striving urge to bring about {*er-strebendes Erdrängnis*})

[potencies]

existentia	is *perfectio* (*gradus essentiae*) or *essentiae exigentia*[25]

(Gerhardt VII, p. 195, note); thereby essentially polysemous (*agere – actio – vis; exactum, actualitas* of the *exactus*);

wrestle from the inclination to that toward which one is inclined – (toward itself); [execution]

journeying out into the "essence," *perfectio*; yet also driving, *per-ficere* – deliver; taking the measure (*per-fectio*), "*exactum*," "exact."

---

[24] {TN: 'stretching forward to existence.'}
[25] {TN: 'perfection (degree of essence) or demand of essence.'}

This clarifies a few principles:

165   "Et ut possibilitas est pricipium Essentiae, ita perfectio seu Essentiae gradus ... principium existentiae." (*De rerum originatione radicali*, Gerhardt VII, p. 304.)[26]

(ibid.: *Mathesis Divina; Mechanismus Metaphysicus*)

... E n s   n e c e s s a r i u m [that is, *id de cuius essentiae est existentia*] est *Existentificans* (Gerhardt VII, p. 289) [*facit ut aliquid existat*].[27]

O m n e   p o s s i b i l e *Existiturire*[28] (ibid.) ("exigit existere";[29] see VII, p. 194, 289).
[*causa? ratio? fons? faciens? origo? efficiens?*]
ens is *exigens* (*exigentia*), *exactum*; *appetitus* – *perceptio*; ("will," "urge");
Subjectum (in the sense of Descartes' *mens sive animus percipiens*[30]) is, in the essential and universal sense, the essence of the *ens*.

Therefore, *mentes* have a special rank among the *entia* – in them, the essence of "being."

See on this VII, p. 289 and following (24 Theses).[31]

Thesis 21:   "Et Mentium maxima habetur ratio, quia per ipsas quam maxima varietas in quam minimo spatio obtinetur."[32]
"And most to be taken into account, as *entia*, are *mentes*, since through them the greatest possible variety in the smallest possible space is held steady, firm, and constant."

---

[26] {TN: "And just as possibility is the foundation of Essence, so perfection or degree of Essence [...] is the foundation of existence." G. W. Leibniz, "On the Ultimate Origination of Things," in *Philosophical Essays*, ed. and trans. Roger Ariew and Daniel Garber (Indianapolis and Cambridge: Hackett, 1989), p. 151 (trans. mod.).}

[27] {TN: "t h e   n e c e s s a r y   B e i n g [that is, that whose essence is existence] is *Existifying* [...] [makes something exist]." This comes from the fourth thesis of an untitled text by Leibniz, which Heidegger refers to as the "24 Theses." Here and below, we have drawn, with occasional modifications, on Lloyd Strickland's translation, available at http://www.leibniz-translations.com/theses.htm.}

[28] {TN: "e v e r y   p o s s i b l e is *existence-seeking*." 6th thesis.}

[29] {TN: "demands to exist."}

[30] {TN: 'perceiving mind or intelligence'}

[31] Reproduced here in the Supplement, pp. 162–167.

[32] {TN: "And the greatest consideration is given to Minds, because through them one obtains the greatest possible variety in the smallest possible space."}

– Here, in *mentes,* is the *highest presence* {Praesenz}
(*spatium* of the "metaphysical point," that is, of the *monas*);
yet now, corresponding to the transformation of the *subjectum, prae-sentia* (*ousia*) has become *repraesentatio* (in a double sense), the representing (striving) presenting-oneself-forth {*Sich-dar-stellen*}; *perceptio,*
but *multorum in uno expressio;*[33] ["ideal" and "real"]
subjectum, existens, ens = *monas,* one thing [unity]; see <u>hen</u>; see   166
"system";

Essence of the unity intended here on the basis of presencing and constancy: *gathering* (*logos*; Heraclitus, Parmenides) into presencing; this is what unifies, retains;
existentia: the pressing toward itself of an essence; "self-assertion" (will); then flattened out and regression in the Leibniz school;
existentia as *complimentum possibilitatis.*[34]

---

[33] {TN: 'perception, but of many in one expression.'}
[34] {TN: 'complement of possibility.}

Appendix

Preliminary Glimpses and Directives

Preliminary Glimpses and Directives of the New Interpretation of Schelling's Freedom Treatise

(The inner connection between the "core section" and the "introduction."

In what way the question of freedom touches on the center of the system. In what way the question of freedom treats of evil and deals with pantheism.)

The inner connection between the "core section" and the "introduction" of the Freedom Treatise (see Recapitulations and Course of the Interpretation, pp. 127–128).

Our aim is: knowledge of the metaphysics of German Idealism by way of a confrontation with Schelling's Freedom Treatise.

Metaphysics asks:

ti to on – what are "beings *qua* beings"
  what are beings in their being
  what is the being of beings
(see Aristotle's sentence, *Metaphysics* Z 1) (the Kant book, conclusion); in short, but also indeterminately: the question concerning "being": meant now as beings in their being, now as the being of beings.

Our path for interpreting the Freedom Treatise at first seems like a detour, inasmuch as the "preliminary consideration" prepares for the interpretation of the "core section." This section treats of the distinction between "ground" and "existence." This distinction concerns every "essence," that is, every being as such. This distinction aims at the being of beings. This distinction concerns that which is asked about in meta-
170 physics and indicates how Schelling's metaphysics asks about the being of beings and determines it. Therefore, this section – which treats of the core content of metaphysics – is the core section. This "core section" belongs to the Freedom Treatise.

The Freedom Treatise treats of freedom as the center of the system. The system is the essence of beings as such and as a whole and thus determines being; in what way is the latter "systematic"?

The system "is the system of freedom." Yet freedom is human freedom; and the question of the system is: how does human freedom belong to the whole of beings, that is, to their "ground"?

"System" arises from the essence of truth in the sense of certainty and from the looming essence of being in the sense of the will to will.

In Western metaphysics, this ground of beings as a whole is called, and is: God, *theos*.

Schelling conceives of freedom not only as independence from nature, but more essentially as independence *from* God, and yet *before* God, that is, in relation to God, that is, "*in*" God. For everything "is" – inasmuch as it "is" – god-like and therefore, in some way, God. *Pan estin theos.*[1]

The system is determined in its unity by this sentence; it names the being of beings as a whole. This is why the introduction to the fundamental question of the system of freedom must discuss this basic principle of the system. This is why the introduction, and therefore the entire treatise, must everywhere treat of "*pantheism*" – this heading as name for a, nay, *the* fundamental metaphysical question that lies concealed in it. In what way?

"All is God" calls for the determination of the all, the determination of God; but it calls above all for the determination of the "is" and, with it, of how "God" "is" all, and how all "is" God. Yet the "is" names being.

The "is" is considered to be a linking word (copula) in the propositional statement; the propositional statement, "*logos*," as the fundamental form of thinking; to think, *noein*, as the fundamental relation to being (*ousia, idea*).

To ask about "pantheism," to pose the fundamental question of the   171
system, means to ask about the "is," that is, about the being of beings as a whole. (This "is" is not "logical," that is, according to formal logic, but rather "logical" in Hegel's sense, in a metaphysical, and therefore theological manner.) Yet this is the question that is the subject of discussion and that receives an answer in the core section. In this way, the inner connection between "the distinction between ground and existence" and the proper point of inquiry in the question of pantheism thus becomes clear.

---

[1] {TN: 'all is God.'}

That "evil" comes to be the guiding theme in the Freedom Treatise, however, points to the fact that evil, as Schelling conceives it, constitutes the most extreme diremption and repulsiveness against beings as a whole and within beings as a whole. This is the sharpest rift that endangers a "system," that is, the *sustasis* of beings. And precisely this rift must be metaphysically developed as such and comprehended as the jointure of the system. It is not, for instance, a matter of mitigating this diremption.

Evil achieves its proper and essential actuality only in spirit, namely in the creaturely spirit that, as selfhood, is able to place itself the farthest away from God and against God, and claim the whole of beings for itself. Evil is only when it is at one with freedom, which is to say, the latter only is in relation to evil. Evil, however, is not merely the opposite of the good, separated from it, but rather it belongs to the good and to the distinction between good and evil; *the good "is" evil* (341).

If, therefore, freedom is determined as the capacity for good *and* evil (not "or"), then Schelling does not mean here freedom of choice but rather freedom as the metaphysical jointedness and binding into the discord itself – as the struggle and the endurance of the latter.

Only by thinking through these connections is the semblance dispelled that the Freedom Treatise, through its discussion of evil, gets stuck in the path of a one-sided treatment of the question of freedom. 172 Yet the question of freedom, conceived as the fundamental question of the system, is also not to be thought in the sense of a theological theodicy, but rather as a *"systemadicy"* – a justification of absolute metaphysics as the truth of beings as such and as a whole.

Why does Schelling's *Philosophical Investigations into the Essence of Human Freedom* . . . treat of evil? Because the system is supposed to be thought? But why is this the case? (See below, p. 174). The system is "beyng" at its most intimate – the standing together of beings as a whole – at the point where it should *endure* the most extreme diremption and not, say, balance it out. Thus, this most extreme discord must be unfolded and brought into its stance {*Bestand*} and standing ground {*Bestandgrund*}. This discord is evil in the sense of the independent insurrection {*selbständigen Aufstandes*} of the creaturely spirit, in its seizing of the ground's self-craving from out of the intimacy with the primal ground.

But why, then, is this treatise on system a *freedom* treatise? Because in human freedom, and *as* human, evil properly *is* {*eigentlich seiend ist*}. In the freedom of the *human*, the most extreme discord in beings properly *is*. (How is anthropomorphy to be grasped on this basis?)

Freedom is "a capacity for good *and* evil" (352), *not*, for instance, a capacity for good "*or*" evil (not *libertas indifferentiae*, not freedom of choice); for, the good, and the good precisely, "is" also evil, and evil "is" the good (341). (This becomes comprehensible only on the basis of the metaphysical fundamental distinction between existence and ground of existence; for it is only on the basis of being as it is thus determined that the "is" of these propositions becomes thinkable in the correct manner.) Freedom (freedom and necessity) is the centerpoint of the system.

But why is the system inquired about? Because what is being asked about is the beingness of beings as a whole – the truth of beings; and, indeed, in such a way that truth means certainty = securing of the representing of representedness; availability of beings on all sides; beings in the unconditionality of their being with respect to every condition   173
– certain of themselves in toto; yet beingness thought as "subjectivity." (See the treatise on Nietzsche's metaphysics) (Evil and Hegel's "negativity.")

Why is the Freedom Treatise, which addresses the "system of freedom" in its innermost centerpoint, a treatise on evil?
(See Recapitulations and Course of the Interpretation, pp. 126–127.)

Is evil merely a phenomenon in and through which freedom may be made clear, or is the system a system of freedom because freedom is essentially related to evil, evil consisting, however, in the most extreme diremption – the *apostasis* from the *sustasis*, indeed *in* the *sustasis*? Indeed, since the most extreme adversity, and precisely it, still belongs, and must be able to belong, to the innermost of the system – but this adversity as insurrection of the self-craving of spirit is freedom – freedom therefore belongs to the question concerning the center and the central ground of the system.

Evil and negativity;
Negativity and the nothing;
Evil and the distinction between ground and existence.

Transitional Reflection on Hegel

Transitional Reflection on Hegel[a]

Hegel and Schelling: their fundamental metaphysical position viewed from the perspective of the "distinction."

Hegel: *the true – truth ("certainty") – that which actually is – "actuality"*: (22 [II, 14]).[1]

1. The true is not only substance, but also just as much subject; (22 [II, 14]); (27 and following [II, 19 and following).

   Substance is essentially subject, and, indeed, absolute subjectivity. (22 [II, 14]) Every "content" "*is*" its reflection {*Reflexion*} into itself.

   Substance as immediate consciousness of the object; (22 [II, 14]).

   Hegel thinks *substantia* in a way that is not only not Greek and not Leibnizian, but Hegelian.

2. In the "concept," truth possesses the "element" of its existence; (15 [II, 7]).

   Self-becoming (23 [II, 15])

   "*pure* self-cognizing {*Selbsterkennen*} in absolute otherness"; (28 [II, 20]).

   what is simply other, but with respect to what is at first only One, and indeed self-knowing therein;

   the ether of science (28 [II, 20]);

---

[a] See Martin Heidegger, "Negativity: A Confrontation with Hegel Approached from Negativity (1938–1939, 1941)," in *Hegel*, trans. Joseph Arel and Niels Feuerhahn (Bloomington: Indiana University Press, 2015).

[1] All quotations in the Transitional Reflection without indication of location are drawn from vol. II of Hegel's *Gesamtausgabe* (ed. Glockner).

why "element" and "ether"?
3. The true is the whole; the system; (24 [II, 16])
   what fulfills itself in its development;
4. The absolute is spirit, "the actual"; spirit is "science" (28   175
   [II, 20]); thus "system of science"; spirit as the absolute, as
   system, as subject;
5. The true is bacchanalian frenzy (becoming) (44 and following [II, 36 and following]); (not outward succession, but
   rather surpassing *in itself*; sublation, threefold)
Truth – actuality; "being" as becoming; being and negativity

On Hegel's fundamental metaphysical position on the basis of the
"Preface" to The Phenomenology of Spirit.
Take as a starting point the different variations on the one theme: "*The*
true is spirit."
This includes:
   1. The true is what is certain, and what is certain is what is unconditionally certain, that is, certain simply of itself as a whole, as certain of
the self-knower, that is, of self-consciousness.
   2. "Spirit is self-consciousness"; see Introduction to B. (139–148 [II,
131–140]).
   Clarify the theme by means of the sentence:
   "The true [is] not to be grasped and expressed as *substance*, but
equally as *subject*." (22 [II, 14])
   "Substance" and "subject" as terms of metaphysics. What do they
mean? How are they used here by Hegel?
   "Substance" – for Hegel, this is neither Aristotelian nor Leibnizian,
                   but rather, in their relation, both the immediacy of
                   knowing (consciousness of) *and* the immediacy of what
                   is known (being).
   "Substance" is therefore – as it is *thus* determined – already subject,
that is, *self-consciousness*. That which is, in its beingness (being), is *self-*
consciousness. Self-consciousness, however, is: becoming-conscious
of oneself in essence; *desire*; and this only in "*recognition*," subject to
subject; in other words, "*pure self-cognizing in absolute otherness*" (28
[II, 20]).
(Otherness {*Anderssein*} not, for instance, simply the being of the other   176
{*das Sein des Anderen*}!)
   The *Phenomenology of Spirit* properly begins only with B. Self-
consciousness; and A. is only the transposition into consciousness as
abstraction – the utmost finitude of self-consciousness. (From the start
one must therefore think *in such a way* that one thinks on the basis of

"self-consciousness" and, indeed, "spirit," and not think in a Kantian manner, for instance, on the basis of perception, in which, then, the I of transcendental apperception is first discovered as condition and highest point.)

The beginning of the *Phenomenology of Spirit*, in the sense of the beginning of the presentation, is not the "*inception* of the *Phenomenology*." This is why it is precisely "self-consciousness" – the first glimmer of the true – that can be presented only in an insufficient manner in the sphere of consciousness. The development remains unconvincing so long as thinking fixates on the finite and has not taken the leap into the in-finite in advance. All critiques of Hegel, which miss the mandatory transitions here, make a misstep and, moreover, make "the essential history of spirit" into a "schoolbook" matter.

The *mathematical* is not capable of dealing with the sheer unrest of life. (44 [II, 36])

On Hegel's "Preface" (to *The Phenomenology of Spirit*)
1. the guiding principle: the actual (the true) is "spirit";
2. the metaphysical principle: substance is equally subject; (self-consciousness is the concept of spirit).
3. Interpretation of main passages 22 [II, 14], 27 and following [II, 19 and following], 37 [II, 29], 44 [II, 36]; 49 [II, 41].
4. pure self-cognizing in absolute otherness:
   (the ether as such; self-consciousness and diremption; "the sock")
   (the "phenomenology of spirit")
5. Negativity (the "dialectic");
6. *The system* (the overcoming of the mathematical); (no element of the "concept";) time (44 [II, 36])
   177   (in what way never fully presented)
7. Hegel's and Schelling's "distinction"
   "Negativity"
   (their consensus in essentials)
The danger here, as well:
   The formalism of the mechanism of "sublation";
   The "zing" of thesis, antithesis, synthesis
   Arbitrary examples!
   Whereas everything is historical! "phenomenology"
The Phenomenology of Spirit
   Its presentation in the work is the attempt to bring the absolute into knowledge as what is *first*, and, indeed, the absolute as "becoming";

The ether as such (that is, the essence of truth here is the true); absolute metaphysics; *"pure self-cognizing in absolute otherness"*
(Negation of negation ["the concept"] – as simple [infinite] negation)
(28 [II, 20])

"self-cognizing":	*that is, self-appearing in essence*, that is, *recognition of the recognizance of selfhood; self-being*: that in which and as which the I is, as well as its object and the relation between them *"cognize"*: *belong to*!
"pure":	fully and unconditionally, that is, accomplishing itself on the basis of the unconditional; and, indeed, pure subjektity – precisely in the recognition of reciprocal self-recognition;
in otherness:	the self as self-appearing "is," as the self, the other of itself; as the unconditional, it is the conditional, indeed such that it recognizes the latter in itself as its "own"; this, however,
"absolute":	that is, in-finite; not restricted to or splintered into this or that finite thing, but rather simple;

178

unconditional certainty as recognizance of the essential stages belonging to it;

Subjectity and actuality
Hegel's *Phenomenology*; *the transition from consciousness to self-consciousness*
Consciousness "is" already self-consciousness and is therefore already *desire*. Precisely this does not emerge at first, however; but it nevertheless belongs to the determination of the *subjectum*. (Leibniz, Descartes)

Actuality as subjektity
"Knowing" as existing:
the transcendental is only integrated, not decisive, and not merely "extended" into the unconditional, as in the sense of relative and absolute idealism; the beginning of the *Phenomenology* is here misleading.
Negativity as no-saying and recognizing.

On the interpretation of the Phenomenology of Spirit
1. For the first elucidation, thinking through transcendental reflection ("consciousness") is indeed necessary, but not sufficient. It is misleading when merely *it*, as finite, is then transposed into the unconditional. This neo-Kantian interpretation of Hegel (along the

lines of the difference between relative and absolute idealism) mis-recognizes the fundamental metaphysical question concerning the actuality of the actual.

2. The latter is spirit as absolute certainty; yet being certain is being in Leibniz's sense – *repraesantare* as *nisus* and *exigentia* (*nisus ad existendum* = *essentia*; *exigentia essentiae* = *existentia²*). But even this thinking of substantiality as subjectity does not suffice, not even when experienced absolutely. Rather, what is

179 3. necessary: the first, the importance of which Schelling recognizes above all and which he continually renews in ever different ways: the fundamental experience that becomes aware of the highest being *as the first* in the absolute. [The absolute difference.]

Hegel's Preface to the *Phenomenology of Spirit* (difficulties)

The conventional, royal road to take in philosophy is to read prefaces and reviews, in order to get an approximate idea of the subject."
"The ultimate royal road in studying is thinking for oneself."
"Those who speak so much against philosophical systems *over-look*, in a *determined* system, the fact that it is a philosophy; a fact as paramount as the oak being a tree.³

Hegel
1. *Thinking on the basis of the unconditional* – also, and precisely, every beginning; thus, in the *Phenomenology* the first section, "A. Consciousness," already as "B. Self-consciousness" (see Introduction, 139–148 [II, 131–140]);
   here the *Phenomenology* properly begins; A. is only a prelude to the beginning, an entry into it; see 22 [II, 14]: substantiality as subjektity (not only the objective);
2. the unconditional as un-conditional *certainty*:
   the latter is the essence of *truth*; see 182–190 [II, 174–182]
3. unconditional certainty as actuality (*actualitas*), *existentia* of the subjectum; subjectity;
   deliberate knowledge as *self-recognition*;
   Recognizance as being-in-and-for-oneself; (*certitudo* and *assensus*)
180   Recognizance and appearance – "*idea*";
   the power to bring the other to itself and let it stand in itself;

---

² {TN: 'exertion toward existing = essence; demand of essence = existence.'}
³ "Aphorismen aus der Jenenser Zeit" nos. 52–54, in *Dokumente zu Hegels Entwicklung*, ed. J. Hoffmeister (Stuttgart: 1936), p. 369.

4. Subjectity and diremption {*Zerrissenheit*} and one-ness of un-conditional unification; (not "mending," but passing through diremption;) "the sock"! Aphorism from the Jena period, no. 64[4]:
   "Better a mended sock than a torn {*zerrissener*} one; not so with self-consciousness."
   Torn self-consciousness is better than the mended one. Why?
5. The major difficulty: to grasp how the human can know and be the absolute; in other words: how the path from finite self-consciousness to the absolute; thus already asked in an inadequate manner; the decisive point lies precisely in this: that the human only "is" in the absolute; *that the latter is the first and nearest*;
   this leap is the inception; with this leap, the leap into the "diremption" of subjectity; and everything springs from this leap; if it is not carried out, then nothing can be carried out;

Hegel develops the absolute.

Schelling experiences the absolute, or, more precisely, he displaces everything into this experience, on the basis of which Hegel, to a certain extent, also thinks.

(See Hegel, "Aphorisms from the Jena period," no. 34:
"The questions for which philosophy has no answer are answered in the sense that they should not be posed in this way.")

Negativity; divisiveness and diremption
Its origin lies in unity as an in-finite unity. Unity unifies as a whole inasmuch as it recognizes each one, each time, into its essence {*ins Wesen anerkennt*}, and yet sublates it *as* essence in its one-sidedness in order to maintain for itself, in such a recognition, the unconditional in the recognizance.

See *Phenomenology of Spirit* (143 [II, 135]): "The unity is split in two   181
because it is an absolutely negative or infinite unity; and because *it* is what *persists*, difference, too, has independence only *in it*."

Absolute diremption *is* as the recognizance of the unconditional certainty that, in itself, willing its essence, wills *in*-finity as becoming, that is, the absolute unrest of becoming, a becoming in which the shapes of self-consciousness "are" and emerge in their for- and against-one-another.

The merely colorful vision of the sensible world and the empty night of the supersensible beyond:
especially as withdrawn into the spiritual day of the present (147/48 [II,

---

[4] See "Aphorismen aus der Jenenser Zeit," op. cit., p. 370.

139/40]), that is, of modernity and of the essence of its truth as absolute certainty.

Truth as certainty (recognition)

Veritas as <u>*adaequatio*</u> *determines itself as* <u>*certitudo*</u> of the represented and of representing, that is, of being-representing {*Vorstellendseins*} (as *actus*; *actualitas*); becoming certain; judgment as *assensus*.

This being-certain is nothing additional but rather the essential ground of the representing of the represented. In being-certain lies *assensus* (agreement {*Zu-stimmen*}); in agreeing: holding oneself assured and being sure; agreeing as recognizing; recognizing and subjectum.

In the realm of truth as certainty, recognition becomes the essential determination of the being of beings as *subjectum*. It only comes to its decisive unfolding where truth as certainty is taken seriously in an unconditional way, in Hegel's *Phenomenology of Spirit*. Letting otherness stand in itself and nevertheless knowing it as one's own, without insisting on a one-sided dependence. Cognizing oneself in absolute otherness.

Negativity (Hegel – Schelling)

Is negativity the state of re-presenting, interpreted (as thinking) on the basis of the latter, and, indeed, the state of re-presenting as *subjectivity* (*assensus*)? Is it first grounded in re-presenting as such, insofar as the latter is taken unconditionally? Or does negativity go back to a distinction that belongs to an inceptive contra-diction?

(Necessity and freedom

Schelling

Ground   —   Existence)!

In what way is what is posited here only apparently something different? Here, too, negativity is the between of the will, which, as will, is dichotomous in itself (why and from where?).

Will of the ground and will of the understanding

\ /

"Love"   (unity)

Why is this opposition "the centerpoint of the system"?
Where is the archetype?
In what way is dialectic possible? And system?

Negativity

As *distinguished distinguishing*, it is the self-re-presenting re-presentation. Re-presenting and (*self-*)*distinguishing*; re-presenting, consciousness, knowledge, self-knowing knowledge, and pure negativity are the *same*. However: how does dis-tinguishing (*dia*) come to have priority in the essence of re-presenting, precisely? (As presenting itself forth {*Sich-dar-stellen*}; appearing.)

Why is distinguishing grasped as "negation"? Because the "no" has in itself an in-between and transitional character; the "yes" is what simply remains. "No" is *away from as toward*, the energy of movement, of becoming. But where does this "no" come from – in such a role? To where is everything thus brought (in the realm of unconditional representing)?

Negativity and un-conditionality; the *un-* as the path {*Weg*} of the conditional; taking away {*Weg-schaffen*}, putting behind oneself and yet raising it up {*Auf-heben*}; the "labor" within the utterly secured ab-solute.

Negativity   183
The I – pure negativity (25 [II, 17]);
the sublating of "existence" {*"Daseyn"*} – first negation (32 [II, 24]);
dividing – the enormous power of the negative;
       the energy of thinking, of the pure I; (34 [II, 26])
       krinein;
the disparity between the I and substance (object) is the difference of negation in general (37 [II, 29]); "soul" (54 [II, 46]); distinguishing as comprehending – concept; "time" – "the existing {*daseyende*} concept itself"; (44 [II, 36]) (not yet – now – no longer);

"reflection" {*"Reflexion"*} (49 [II, 41]) – not dogmatic, where the I
                        is only the basis!, but rather
                        turning-back-into-oneself,
                        into self-knowing;
Negativity and subjectivity – the most extreme *against*:
for Hegel: the immediacy of mere "existence" {*"Dasein"*}, the
                most extreme form of abstract externalization ↔ that
                which in absolute knowledge is unconditionally mediated in relation to itself;
                the not and no arises in the essence of subjectivity, of
                "I-represent-before" {*"Ich-stelle-vor"*};
for Schelling: the not is difference {*Differenz*} from out of in-difference
                {*In-differenz*} – ("of love") [subject]
                ground (nature), eternal past, the oldest revelation ↔
                the existing one {*der Existierende*}.

With respect to "division" (negativity) and "distinction" – "contradiction":

the outermost limits for Hegel:　　the immediacy of consciousness and absolute self-knowledge

the outermost limits for Schelling: nature as eternal past; contraction, closure; ground – and the human, evil; what exists {*Existierendes*};

184　*Negativity and recognition*

Dividing is not separating, but rather the opposing of the other, and indeed of the other as the other to the one; therein the necessity and proper essence of otherness is recognized. Only in recognizance does *that which recognizes* come to *itself* and to the fullness of its essence.

In the easily misinterpreted "certainty" and in "being certain" seems to lie absolute egoism, and that precisely is not the essential core of the absolute.

Recognizance and love (*volo ut sis*[5]); love (Schelling) as what lets ground be effective.

Recognizance: struggle, danger, death, reciprocal self-recognition and therein the recognizance of the unconditional; the unconditional, for its part, as that which properly recognizes.

Hegel and Schelling: where they agree – therein also the difference {*Differenz*}

1. actuality: the absolute – spirit
2. the absolute as system
3. actuality – contradiction (negation) – distinction
4. actuality – becoming (will)
5. actuality as self-revealing.

But:

Spirit:

　　　　Hegel:　　science
　　　　Schelling:　love

System:

　　　　Hegel:　　system "of science"
　　　　　　　　　(concepts – freedom; "logic")
　　　　Schelling:　system "of freedom"

---

[5] {TN: 'I want you to be.'}

Division:
Hegel: negativity of the subject, "of thinking" as the self-thinking of spirit, of knowledge; (recognition)
Schelling: the distinction in willing as the self-willing 185 of love; (letting the ground be effective)

Becoming:
Hegel: spirit's coming-into-itself; world spirit
Schelling: creation, redemption, the human.

And yet: in spite of everything, at bottom the same passion for the same and therein precisely the split between the two thinkers; their discord is *the* attestation of their unity.

Summary (our relation to the metaphysics of German Idealism)
(prejudices: collapse, decline, not [essence])

"Diremption" – distinction
"Recognition": the power to bring the other to itself and let it
not as mere subjection stand in itself, thus bringing, in the other, the
rather as mastery opposition into its essence; therefore, first grounding "unity" for itself into its essence, bringing it to revealability; see Schelling: love – "letting the ground be effective"

The *Phenomenology of Spirit* (not to be taken as the "psychology of the senses");
Comparison with Schelling – in various respects; the system (Hegel always presented it; "system of science," "logic," "encyclopedia");
Metaphysics;
Schelling – "Freedom Treatise"; "pseudo-problem"; "freedom of the will."
Hegel and the system: 186
The system and the essence of metaphysics (see p. 94–96, 98 and following);
Metaphysics as truth of beings as whole;
Essence of truth each time according to the revelation of being;
Beings as a whole corresponding to:
 1. *akrotaton on – timiōtaton*[6] (Aristotle)
 2. *koinotaton (on hēi on)*[7]
    polysemous *hēi*
 3. *analogon*
    (the human).

[6] {TN: 'highest being – most honored.'}
[7] {TN: 'commonest (being as being).'

The Confrontation with the Metaphysics of German Idealism and with Metaphysics in General

The decisive confrontation {*Aus-einander-setzung*} with Schelling's "system of freedom" is carried out in the realm attained by the interpretation of the "core section" by way of the "preliminary reflection."

Here being itself is said in its essence as the beingness of beings. *Ousia* is comprehended in the sense of presencing (*idea*), and indeed unconditionally in a modern manner as subjektity: as willing. This "essence" of beingness is sufficient (according to I/7, p. 350) for all of the "predicates" that are attributed to being as if they were self-evident.

Here it is a matter of seeing that this interpretation of being as willing (the determination of primal being, that is, of being in its essential origin), is not an arbitrary "view" on the part of Schelling, but it is also not a historiographically conditioned reckoning of earlier views. On the contrary, being {*Sein*} reveals itself, but as beingness {*Seiendheit*}. The essence of every truth of beings (that is, every metaphysics) is contained in this alone. The first characteristic of this is that being is at once *koinotaton* and *akrotaton* (*timiōtaton, theion*), the most universal, highest, and emptiest for apprehension – *idea*. But this at the same time belongs to that which, in its meaning, properly is, to the *agathon* which, *epekeina tēs ousias*,[1] en*ables* and is capable of this. The *akrotaton* becomes the *primum ens, absolutum*, and this is then interpreted in a "Christian" manner, and what is Christian is "metaphysically" interpreted, in turn. As *akrotaton* (later *actus purus*), that which most is {*das Seiendste*} takes over "being" as mere "idea," in the sense of being thought, being re-presented {*Vor-gestelltheit*}, which belongs to everything, inasmuch as everything, according to this idea, is effected {*bewirkt*} and caused (created) as something effected and

---

[1] {TN: 'beyond beingness.'}

effecting (the actual) {*gewirktes Wirkendes (Wirkliches)*}. As a result, it also belongs to the truth of beings, as a further characteristic, that beings, in the sense of a "correspondence" to being in general, develop 188 in each case in various stages.

The three perspectives on the truth of beings (metaphysics) are therefore:

being (beingness) in general, *koinotaton*;

see the modification in modern metaphysics in the sense of the transcendental;

Kant's concept of reason:

    1. synthesis in general – highest genus – totality,

    2. principle – faculty – the unconditional; unity (*Cr. P. R.* A 651).

       Regarding 1. formal synthesis – the "I think in general"; to what extent it is at the same time analytic in itself;

          hen – on: in the Greek sense: presencing, persistence, gatheredness, *logos*.

       Regarding 2. the demand for completeness – *noema, noumenon*; intuition in thoughts, *intellegere*, reason as human faculty;

          "teleology" – *logos – telos – ratio*

          "rules" (*Cr. P. R.* A 647, B 675)

          As the highest concept of reason, "God" is the highest condition of possibility of all that is thinkable (*Cr. P. R.* A 334);

          Unconditional necessity as "the true abyss of reason."

The highest being that effects and incorporates everything, *akrotaton*; the manifoldness of each correspondingly effected being, *analogon*. (Concept of analogy in Kant, see *Proleg.* and *Cr. P. R.* A 177.)

The origin and necessity of analogy lies in the unified projection of beings upon beingness as what is most universal (the one), which at the same time requires of this highest one the causation for all beings – and their manifoldness – that fall under the universal. Beings must satisfy the *koinotaton*, while at the same time being caused by the *akrotaton*, 189 but in such a way that precisely what is effected and is not the highest cannot be {*seiend sein*} in the one and the same sense (*univoce*) as the first cause, and yet it must be in the sense of *koinotaton*, insofar as it is at all.

One turns, then, to the "analogy" of beings for help with the "explanation" of the manifoldness of beings and the solution of the problem of pan-theism (conceived in a purely metaphysical way); yet it explains nothing and illuminates nothing, but rather only confirms and reinforces the darkness that resides over the distinction between *koinataton* and *akrotaton*, as well as over its origin (being as *idea* – groundless *phusis*), indeed such that being, in the manner of a first inception, itself presses, as it were, into the projection of beings upon beingness.

Ever since the interpretation of *ens* as *certum* and *subjectum* (self-consciousness and independence), this "analogizing" in the interpretation of beings as a whole and of their manifoldness is then joined by the antithetics of consciousness and self-consciousness that consequently (constrained by the truth of beings [*koinotaton* – *akrotaton*]) leads to absolute self-consciousness (knowledge – will) and, as a result, demands the dialectic.

The architectonics of Scholastic philosophy (*metaphysica generalis* and *metaphysica specialis*, culminating in *theologia rationalis*) is only the doctrinal reverberation of the uncomprehended truth of beings, which was definitively established by Plato as idealism (grasped metaphysically) and was prepared, in the first inception of the naming of being as *phusis* and *alētheia*, as that which also overtakes metaphysics, such that the latter could never of its own accord, not even from out of the whole of its history, be in a position from which to know the first inception essentially. Relapsing, it can but misinterpret it. (The last misinterpretation of the first inception by Nietzsche.)

Through the questioning on the basis of the other inception (springing into the truth of beyng), everything in particular is overcome that, in the questions of metaphysics, springs from analogy and the dialectic. But thus, a confrontation between inception and inception now commences. The saying of beyng becomes an entirely different one. In this confrontation, the distinction between being and beings must first be recognized as such, interrogated, and retracted. (See *Mindfulness*[2] and *Overcoming*.[3])

(The theological character especially of modern metaphysics is not grounded first of all in its dependence on a Christian way of thinking, but rather in the essence of all metaphysics.)

Show how through "analogizing" and "dialectics" the metaphysical construction is determined more closely;

the anthropomorphy of the metaphysical construction, that is to say, explicitly:

190

---

[2] Martin Heidegger, *Mindfulness*, trans. Parvis Emad and Thomas Kalary (London: Bloomsbury, 2016).

[3] "Die Überwindung der Metaphysik" (1938/39) in GA 67.

| God – | God-human – | Human (evil) |
| Creation | Redemption | [sin] |

"Nature" essentially as ground, but mastered in God; however: possibility of elevation into the highest spirituality; in what way the metaphysical construction already includes, as all metaphysics has since the beginning, the distinction between being and beings. (See *Overcoming*[4] and *History of Beyng*[5])

What this distinction says in Schelling in its formal schema:

being = that which *only is* {*das* nur Seiende}, in which the self is not itself;

beings = where *beings* have found themselves in themselves and have laid claim on beings;

thus, in each case, beings are themselves distinguished in accordance with beingness;

now, however (beyng-historical): beingness as being – in opposition to beings in every manner; here it is not a matter of a simple reversal of the Schellingian "distinction" between being and beings, but rather a going back to the first-inceptive *question* concerning *beingness*; (where an indecision, and indeed an unknowable one, remains and preserves itself in the inception;)

what is called "ontological difference {*Differenz*}" in "Being and Time."

On the clarification of the essence of "metaphysics"
the distinction between
1. *on haplōs*[6] – *koinotaton*
        akrotaton
        analogon
2. Distinction between *ti estin* and *hoti estin*,[7] *essentia – existentia*
3. Distinction between "ground and existence" ("subjectivity")
    eternal return of the same? – will to power
    but reversal of the subject.

In what way these distinctions were already grounded on that between beings and being; whether and how this is still a "distinction" at all; the unknown, undecided distinction that sustains all metaphysics (ontological difference).

---

[4] Op cit.

[5] Martin Heidegger, *The History of Beyng*, trans. William McNeill and Jeffrey Powell (Bloomington: Indiana University Press, 2015).

[6] {TN: 'being simply.'}

[7] {TN: 'what something is,' 'that something is.'}

Overview of the Transformation of Being as "Actuality"

Overview
of the transformation
of being as "*actuality*"
The history of being as metaphysics
"subjectity"
"existence"
What properly takes place {*sich ereignet*}
Transition: Kant – German idealism;
perceptio – subjectity – certainty;
"system" (in the specifically modern sense) – essentiality, being;
Descartes – Leibniz – Kant;
Kant: the postulates of empirical thinking in general and *Critique of Judgment* § 76.

what does it mean for actuality – human and nature – to be interpreted in this way?

beingness as representedness, objectivity {*Gegenständlichkeit*};

"objective," objectivity {*Objectivität*} with regard to transformed subjektity, a characteristic of the latter;

being as representedness, *Gegenständlichkeit*; subjectivity; absolute metaphysics;

the meaning of transcendental truth;

Kant's concept of actuality:

doubled (see Leibniz)

1. freedom as metaphysical reality
   freedom – will – reason! (Leibniz – Hegel)
   representing striving.
2. *Objectivität*
   representing as intuitive thinking.

Include:

Kant: on the only possible argument   194
  Cr. of P. R.   *Objectivität* and existence as modality
                        (principles)
  Cr. of Pr. R. the "fact" of freedom
  Cr. of J.   § 76
Hegel: actuality as certainty
         certainty as unconditional
         certainty and recognition – *assensus*
         self-consciousness as desire
Emphasize more acutely *assensus* and *certum* already in Descartes.

Absolute actuality as absolute "idea"
Idea – doxa – revealability – glory;
theologically, the *maiestas dei, gloria, doxa theou*;[1]
the innermost essence of God as glorification of himself – insofar as
he exists;
existence and glory: becoming revealed to oneself, but as subjectity;
see Schelling, Freedom Treatise (399).

existentia; *Leibniz – Schelling – Nietzsche*
<u>vis</u> *primitiva activa*:[2]
    the capacity that inclines {*das mögende . . . Vermögen*}, requires,
reaches out for presencing;
vis and "will"
         will as self-willing; beyond itself
         enjoinment {*Fügung*} of the *will* and the *self*
                  Schelling: will *as* love
                  Nietzsche: will *to* power
                  Schelling: nothing for itself (or beyond itself)
                  Nietzsche: command, beyond itself.
Why, in the fulfillment of metaphysics, *anthropomorphism* becomes
necessary in a beyng-historical manner:
For Schelling and – in a different way – for Nietzsche, anthropomorphism is expressly affirmed and called for. Why?
In what way the insight into the relation of being to the human becomes   195
possible and necessary – and at the same time essentially restricted and
therefore one-sided – for metaphysics, and then announces itself as
explicit anthropomorphism.

---

[1] {TN: 'majesty of God, glory, glory of God.'}
[2] {TN: 'primitive active *force*.'}

"Existence"

Existence	brought into relief as actuality (work-ness {*Werkheit*}) in opposition to truth as correctness of the propositional statement, and that means, co-determined by this;
Existence	marked off as actuality (effectedness {*Gewirktheit*}) in opposition to possibility and effecting {*Bewirken*}, and that means, determined by these;
Existence	determined as actuality (objectivity) by way of truth as correctness of judgment and equated with it;
"Existence"	related as actuality (effectiveness {*Wirkendheit*}) to the correctness of representation as the effecting {*Bewirkung*} of this correctness.

Thus, we ultimately have a murky composite of previous determinations of *existentia*, a murkiness that, however, since it is not at all considered – out of ignorance of its provenances – awakens the illusion that the concept of existence is fully transparent and self-evident.

Schelling's distinction and the restriction of the concept of existence to the ground of the essence of being as actuality, and of actuality as will and of will as will of the understanding (spirit) and of spirit as love;
the polysemous formulation of the distinction;
essentially: the *selfhood of the actual*, but not transcendentally, and not simply "actuality" as opposed to possibility,
"Leibniz," rather.
Starting with Schelling: the exceptional status given to "existence" as that which exists, and the latter comprehended as the self; "existence" and "that which exists" used by Schelling himself in an equivocal and contradictory way.

196   The narrowing to human being – regression to Descartes; restriction to "faith" – once again backwards;
all with the help of modern philosophy; and then "philosophy of existence"

Schelling's "distinction" ("existence"):
not in relation to *ousia* (presencing), 1. and 2.,
    not in relation to *actuality, actualitas, potentia, actus*, but rather in relation to *exigentia*, willing as self-willing;
    but *the same* distinction – in the transformation of *ousia* to willing {*Wollung*} via *actualitas*; the same distinction as between *potentia* and *actualitas*, thought only unconditionally and in a Leibnizian and Kantian manner;

with Schelling's distinction the *what* and the *that* already *disappearing*; finally in Nietzsche;

starting from the will (as essence of actuality and existence), the emphasis on existence is then promoted– initially as universal, then, because it is self-being, restricted to *Christianity*;

in Schelling, within German metaphysics, the term "existence" receives a particular emphasis, and indeed within the distinction: ground and existence;

existence – actuality, as actuality now in the modern sense of subjektity, selfhood (Leibniz);

yet metaphysically unrestricted: *Deus*, stone, speck of dust.

Metaphysics as history of being
essentially: 1. being as presencing, actuality
             2. priority of beings, being as *koinon*
             3. truth as *homoiōsis*, certainty
             4. the human as *animal rationale*
             5. the distinction between beings and being (beingness); the distinction of beingness into what-being and that-being;

see Nietzsche metaphysics.

Being as actuality   197
Work-ness – *energeia*;
Actuality as causality; *actualitas*; *esse actu*; *ens creatum*;[3]
Actuality as *esse certum*[4] – objectivity – representedness;
Actuality as *substantialitas* of the *monas* – *existentia* – *exigentia*;
Actuality as will;
Actuality in the whole of metaphysics as "subjectity."

Being – actuality – will and system
Only when being comes into the essence of willing (*exigentia*) does the "system" appear as its fundamental trait. But why is "the will to power" in opposition to "the system"? Because it is the ground of the systematics of any system whatsoever. (System and organization: *ergon* – organ)

On "system" see *History of Beyng* and "Overcoming," First Continuation.[5]

Nietzsche rejects the "system" in the "petty" and external sense of

---

[3] {TN: 'actuality; being in act; created being.'}
[4] {TN: 'being certain.'}
[5] Op. cit.

an artificial, scholarly bumbling piecing together of contents. This rejection follows from "power," as will to power, being systematic in an unconditional sense, as the "system" of all possible "systems," which are thus only "conditions" of the will to power itself. The *ability to have at one's disposal* the mode and activation, the duration and retraction of these "systems" is the systematics that befits the will to power. To it also belongs the ability *not* to come forward, but rather to act as though it were not.

In what way "re-presenting" becomes essential for being (beingness) (taking effect – will – representing).

198 The difference between *noein* and *re-praesentatio*:

noein: ap-prehension {*Ver-nehmung*}, lingering in the unconcealed as what rises-presences;

    noein   idea   (Plato)
    noien   einai   alētheia   (Parmenides)

re-praesantare: the delivery of the re-presented as of what is present – in re-presenting (not *alētheia*);

on the basis of this difference also rests the differentiation of that which is determined as "thinking" and "concept" in relation to *noein* and *repraesantare*; see also the corresponding transformation of the *a priori* (on Kant's *Prolegomena*);

see the historical distance between Aristotle's *noesis noēseōs*[6] and the unconditional self-knowing of the absolute in Hegel's metaphysics;

each time "*zōē*" and "life," but "being" and "truth" transformed, admittedly *within* the same fundamental essence of metaphysics.

Actuality and will

Taking effect {*Wirken*}: as effecting {*Be-wirken*} (re-presenting!) and in that respect *self*-ef-fecting {Sich-*Er-wirken*};

Taking effect: as bringing-something-before-oneself {*etwas Vor-sich-bringen*}, delivering and in that respect re-presenting;

Taking effect: in itself backwards and forwards;

        will – re-presenting in itself; *changement*; re-presentation – willfully;

   Re-presentation, thus *re-praesentatio*;

        the essential distinctness vis-à-vis the presence {*Praesenz*} of *ousia* – presence {*Anwesenheit*} in

---

[6] {TN: 'thinking of thinking.'}

what is unconcealed, on the basis of this and as this;

re-praesentare: back to that – which at the same time brings-before-itself, beyond itself;

in that respect: in the fore and back the essencing of the "self"; why this initially as "I"?

Supplement (Leibniz)

The nothing and being (Of the inception)
Leibniz: *Car le rien est plus simple et plus facile que quelque chose.*[1]
This is why it can rightly be asked first of all, under the presupposition
of the principle of reason {*Grund*}:
Pourquoy il y a plustôt quelque chose que rien?[2]
    (*Principes de la Nature et de la Grace, fondés en raison*, no. 7)
    The nothing is simpler and easier than any beings.
(Simpler and easier in which respect? With respect to representing and
pro-ducing.)
    Of beings; thus, with respect to beings.
    The nothing in distinction to beings.
    But how do matters stand with the nothing in relation to being?
In this respect the nothing is *not* simpler and not easier than being; for
being must first essence in order for the nothing to essence. The essencing of beyng (is for the latter neither easy nor difficult); already plenty,
however, for reflection and thinking.

Leibniz: *modi existendi* (Couturat, *Opuscules et fragments inédits de
    Leibniz*, p. 473; see 437)[3]
    <u>*Perfectio*</u>   *est magnitudo realitatis.*[4] (p. 474)
              est gradus essentiae.[5] (24 Theses, no. 11/17)

---

[1] {TN: "After all, the nothing is simpler and easier than something." Leibniz,
"Principles of Nature and Grace," in *Philosophical Texts*, p. 262 (trans. mod.).}

[2] {TN: "why is there something rather than nothing?" (ibid.).}

[3] Hildesheim 1961 (unchanged reprographic reprint of the 1903 edition). {TN:
'modes of existing.'}

[4] {TN: '*Perfection* is a magnitude of reality.'}

[5] {TN: 'is a degree of essence'}

<u>*Subjectum*</u> *est, cui aliud ens inhaeret, quod dicitur adjunctum.*[6]
(p. 475)
aequalia – aequalibus[7]
Leibniz: "24 Theses"
see Gerhardt VII, pp. 289–291; see Couturat:

1. *Ratio* est in Natura, cur aliquid potius existat quam nihil. Id con-   200
sequens est magni illius principii, quod nihil fiat sine ratione, quemad-
modum etiam cur hoc potius existat quam aliud rationem esse oportet.[8]

To *Natura* (essence of beings as beings (as <u>*existens*</u>, because *existens*
as *perceptio – apperceptio* [*potius*])) belongs *ratio* as "ground"; *reor –
logos, hupokeimenon*;
causatio – causatum
effectus – effecting {*Bewirkung*}
actus – actualitas
Natura – rerum natura sit uniformis[9] (to de Volder, Gerh. II, 270)
see *Principes de la nature* . . . no. 6.

2. Ea ratio debet esse in aliquo Ente Reali seu causa. Nihil aliud enim
causa est, quam realis ratio, neque veritates possibilitatum et *necessita-
tum* (seu negatarum in opposito possibilitatum) aliquid efficerent nisi
possibilitates fundarentur in re actu existente.[10]

Natura requires *ens reale*.[11] *Realitas* = *existentia* (*actu*); but *existentia*
is not simply actuality {*Wirklichkeit*}, but rather *effecting* {*Erwirkung*}
as essential taking effect and thus the actual.

Realitas: not simply "*whatness*" {"*Sachheit*"} as *quidditas*.

Real distinction vs. mental (ideal) = *possibile*.

---

[6] {TN: 'A *subject* is that in which some being inheres, which is called an adjunct.'}

[7] {TN: 'equals – in equals.'}

[8] {TN: "There is a *reason* in Nature why something exists rather than nothing. This is a consequence of that great principle that nothing happens without a reason, just as there must be a reason why this exists rather than another." Here and for the other theses below, we have drawn, with occasional modifications, on Lloyd Strickland's translation, available at http://www.leibniz-translations.com/theses.htm.}

[9] {TN: 'the nature of things is uniform.'}

[10] {TN: "This reason must be in some Real Being, or cause. For a *cause* is nothing other than a real reason, and truths about possibilities and *necessities* (that is, where the possibility of the opposite is denied) would not produce anything unless the possibilities were founded in an actually existing thing."}

[11] {TN: 'a real being.'}

See Letter to de Volder, 30 June 1704, Letter to de Volder 11 October 1705.[12]

3. Hoc autem Ens oportet necessarium esse, alioqui causa rursus extra ipsum quaerenda esset cur ipsum existat potius quam non existat, contra Hypothesin. Est scilicet Ens illud ultima ratio Rerum, et uno vocabulo solet appellari DEUS.[13]

4. Est ergo causa cur Existentia praevaleat non-Existentiae, seu *Ens necessarium* est *Existentificans*.[14]

Praevalentia of *existentia* over the *non existentia*; thus it is clear why *potius aliquid quam nihil*,[15] even though the latter is *plus simple et plus facile*.[16]

201 *Principes de la nature . . .* no. 7.

5. Sed quae causa facit ut aliquid existat, seu ut possibilitas exigat existentiam, facit etiam ut omne possibile habeat conatum ad Existentiam, cum ratio restrictionis ad certa possibilia in universali reperiri non possit.[17]

Existentia = *essentiae exactum*; *exigendum*.[18]

6. Itaque dici potest *Omne possibile Existiturire*, prout scilicet fundatur in Ente necessario actu existente, sine quo nulla est via qua possibile perveniret ad actum.[19]

verbum desiderationem; *possible* = *existentiam exigens*; *existentia*: *exactum possibilitatis exigentiae*.[20]

---

[12] Gerh. II, 267–272 and 278 and following.

[13] {TN: "Now this Being must be necessary, otherwise a cause would in turn have to be sought outside it for why it exists rather than not, which is contrary to the Hypothesis. Plainly, this Being is the ultimate reason for Things, and it is usually referred to by the single word GOD."}

[14] {TN: "There is, therefore, a cause on account of which Existence prevails over non-Existence, in other words, the *necessary Being* is *Existifying*."}

[15] {TN: there is 'something rather than nothing.'}

[16] {TN: 'simpler and easier.'}

[17] {TN: "But the cause which brings it about that something exists, or the fact that possibility demands existence, also brings it about that every possible has a tendency toward Existence, since in general a reason for restricting this to certain possibles cannot be found."}

[18] {TN: 'existence = essence having been exacted; what is to be exacted.'}

[19] {TN: "So it can be said that *every possible is Existence-seeking*, as it is founded on an actually existing necessary Being, without which there is no way a possible may attain actuality."}

[20] {TN: 'word desire; possible = demanding existence; existence: having exacted the possibility of demanding.'}

7. Verum hinc non sequitur omnia possibilia existere: sequeretur sane si omnia possibilia essent compossibilia.[21]

8. Sed quia alia aliis incompatibila sunt, sequitur quaedam possibilia non pervenire ad existendum, suntque alia aliis incompatibilia, non tantum respectu ejusdem temporis, sed et in universum, quia in praesentibus futura involvuntur.[22]

9. Interim ex conflictu omnium possibilium existentiam exigentium hoc saltem sequitur, ut Existat ea rerum series, per quam plurimum existit, seu series omnium possibilium maxima.[23]

10. Haec etiam series sola est determinata, ut ex lineis recta, ex angulis rectus, ex figuris maxime capax, nempe circulus vel sphaera. Et uti videmus liquida sponte naturae colligi in guttas sphaericas, ita in natura universi series maxime capax existit.[24]

11. Existit ergo perfectissimum, cum nihil aliud sit quam quantitas realitatis.[25]

Omnitudo; (the how-much-ness of *realitas* as such, that is, the allness)
See Couturat: Leibniz *Opuscules: Perfectio est magnitudo realitatis.*[26]
(p. 474)

12. Porro perfectio non in sola materia collocanda est, seu in replente tempus et spatium, cujus quocunque modo eadem fuisset quantitas, sed in forma seu varietate.[27]

in what way? the same *essential level*, that is, magnitude of present   202
whatness; see no. 16.

13. Unde jam consequitur materiam non ubique sibi similem esse,

---

[21] {TN: "However, it does not follow from this that all possibiles exist, but it would if all possibles were compossible."}

[22] {TN: "But because some things are incompatible with others, it follows that certain possibles do not attain existence. Some possibles are incompatible with others not only with respect to the same time, but also universally, because future possibles are enfolded in present ones."}

[23] {TN: "Meanwhile, from the conflict of all possibles demanding existence, this at least follows, that there Exists that series of things through which the greatest amount exists, that is, the maximal series of all possibles."}

[24] {TN: "Further, this series alone is determinate, just as of lines is the straight line, of angles the right angle, and of shapes the most capacious, namely the circle or sphere. And just as we see liquids naturally collect in spherical drops, so in the nature of the universe the most capacious series exists."}

[25] {TN: "Therefore what exists is the most perfect, since [perfection] is nothing other than quantity of reality."}

[26] {TN: 'Perfection is a magnitude of reality.'}

[27] {TN: "Further, perfection is not to be located in matter alone, that is, in something filling time and space, whose quantity would have been the same in any event, but in form or variety."}

sed per formas reddi dissimilarem, alioque non tantum obtineretur varietatis quantum posset. Ut taceam quod alibi demonstravi, nulla alioque diversa phaenomena esse extitura.[28]

14. Sequitur etiam eam praevaluisse seriem, per quam plurimum oriretur distinctae cogitabilitatis.[29]

15. Porro distincta cogitabilitas dat ordinem rei et pulchritudinem cogitanti. Est enim *ordo* nihil aliud quam relatio plurium distinctiva. Et confusio est, cum plura quidem adsunt, sed non est ratio quodvis a quovis distinguendi.[30]

16. Hinc tolluntur atomi, et in universum corpora in quibus nulla est ratio quamvis partem distinguendi a quavis.[31]

(see no. 12)

17. Sequiturque in universum, Mundum esse *kosmon*, plenum ornatus; seu ita factum ut maxime satisfaciat intelligenti.[32]

18. *Voluptas* enim intelligentis nihil aliud est quam perceptio pulchritudinis, ordinis, perfectionis. Et omnis dolor continet aliquid inordinati sed respective ad percipientem, cum absolute omnia sint ordinata.[33]

19. Itaque cum nobis aliqua displicet in serie rerum, id oritur ex defectu intellectionis. Neque enim possibile est, ut omnis Mens omnia distincte intelligat; et partes tantum alias prae aliis observantibus, non potest apparere Harmonia in toto.[34]

(*res?*)

---

[28] {TN: "From which it follows that matter is not everywhere alike, but rendered dissimilar by forms, otherwise there would not obtain as much variety as possible. Not to mention what I have demonstrated elsewhere, that otherwise no diverse phenomena would have existed."}

[29] {TN: "It also follows that that series has prevailed through which there arises the greatest amount of what is distinctly thinkable."}

[30] {TN: "Further, distinct thinkability gives order to a thing and beauty to the thinker. For *order* is nothing other than a distinctive relation of many things, and confusion is when many things are present but there is no way of distinguishing one from another."}

[31] {TN: "This rules out atoms, and in general any bodies in which there is no reason for distinguishing one part from another."}

[32] {TN: "And it follows in general that the World is a *cosmos*, full and adorned, that is, made in such a way that it is fully satisfying to an intelligence."}

[33] {TN: "For intelligences, *pleasure* is nothing other than the perception of beauty, order, and perfection. And every pain contains something disordered, albeit relative to the percipient, since absolutely speaking all things are ordered."}

[34] {TN: "Consequently, when something in the series of things displeases us, that arises from a defect of our understanding. For it is not possible that every Mind should understand all things distinctly, and the Harmony in the whole cannot appear to those who observe only some parts rather than others."}

20. Ex his consequens est in Universo etiam justitiam observari, cum *Justitia* nihil aliud sit quam ordo seu perfectio circa Mentes.[35]

see *Principes de la nature* . . . no. 9: "Et comme la *justice*, prise fort généralement, n'est autre chose que la bonté conforme à la sagesse . . ."[36]

(see Nietzsche – on "justice")

21. Et Mentium maxima habetur ratio, quia per ipsas quam maxima varietas in quam minimo spatio obtinetur.[37]

"*Mentis*, inquis, *agendi modi obscuriores* sunt. Ego putabam claris-simos esse, et claros distinctosque pene solos." (To de Volder 21 January 1704 [end])[38] 203

22. Et dici potest Mentes esse primarias Mundi unitates, proxi-maque simulacra Entis primi, quia rationes distincte percipiunt neces-sarias veritates, id est rationes quae movere Ens primum et universum formare debuerunt.[39]

23. Prima etiam causa summae est *Bonitatis*, nam dum quantum plurimum perfectionis producit in rebus, simul etiam quantum pluri-mum voluptatis mentibus largitur, cum *voluptas* consistat in percep-tione perceptionis.[40]

24. Usque adeo ut mala ipsa serviant ad majus bonum, et quod dolores reperiuntur in Mentibus, necesse sit proficere ad majores voluptates.[41]

---

[35] {TN: "It is a consequence of this that justice is observed in the Universe also, since *Justice* is nothing other than order or perfection in respect to Minds."}

[36] {TN: "And since *justice*, taken very generally, is nothing other than goodness in conformity with wisdom." Leibniz, *Philosophical Essays*, p. 210.}

[37] {TN: "And the greatest consideration is given to Minds, because through them one obtains the greatest possible variety in the smallest possible space."}

[38] Gerh. II, 265. {TN: "'The modes of action in the mind,' you say, 'are too obscure.' I thought they were most clear; indeed, that they alone are clear and dis-tinct." Gottfried Wilhelm Leibniz, *Philosophical Papers and Letters*, ed. and trans. Leroy E. Loemker, 2nd edn. (Dordrecht: Kluwer, 1989), p. 535.}

[39] {TN: "And it can also be said that Minds are the primary unities of the World and the closest likenesses of the first Being, since they distinctly perceive necessary truths, that is, the reasons responsible for moving the first Being and forming the universe."}

[40] {TN: "Also, the first cause is of the highest *Goodness*, for while it produces as much perfection as possible in things, it simultaneously bestows as much pleasure as possible upon minds, since *pleasure* consists in the perception of perception." Couturat notes the last word should probably read: *perfectionis*, 'of perfection.'}

[41] {TN: "So much so that evils themselves serve a greater good, and since Minds experience pains this must be necessary to advance to greater pleasures."}

Editor's Afterword

The present text – volume forty-nine of Martin Heidegger's *Gesamtausgabe* {*Collected Works*} – occupies a certain special position within the second division, "Lecture Courses 1919–1944": not only due to the fact that it was delivered over the course of both the first trimester and the summer semester of 1941; but also because, from a formal point of view, both parts of the text differ significantly from each other: the first part (first trimester of 1941) is held in the style of a lecture course while the second part, by contrast, is characterized by the reflective and sketch-like style of seminar notes.

Yet Heidegger's text is conceived of as a unity, which is already apparent on the surface of the text from the frequent cross-references as well as the continuous pagination of the manuscript written by Heidegger on A4 paper in landscape format.

Heidegger's entry in his seminar book[1] also gives us information about the relation between the two parts as well as their in-between status. It runs as follows for "Trimester 1941": "Lecture course and tutorial on Schelling, *Philosophical Investigations into the Essence of Human Freedom* . . . – An introduction to the metaphysics of German Idealism"; and for the "Summer Semester '41" (the division into trimesters having been once again abandoned): "Study group: Schelling, On Human Freedom . . . see Trimester 1941."

The break in the unified conception of the text is marked among other things by the "Recapitulations," which were customary for Heidegger's lecture courses; they are limited to the "First Trimester" and extend from the recapitulation of 14 January to the recapitulation of 11 March. The first trimester 1941 must have concluded, then, with

---

[1] {TN: A notebook Heidegger kept with titles and attendees of his seminars. Available in the Deutsches Literaturarchiv Marbach.}

the session of 18 March; and, in terms of content, evidently with the fourth chapter of the first part, which, together with the third chapter – likely also because the trimester was drawing to a close – turned out to be relatively succinct. The subsequent text (§§ 16, 17), then, also clearly has a summarizing and transitional character: both sections lead, starting from the "Preliminary Reflection" of the first part – which is of significant interest, above all because of Heidegger's self-interpretation of "Being and Time" – to the proper discussion of the text, to the interpretation of the "core section," that is, to the elucidation of the distinction between ground and existence. The protocols for the summer semester seminar – as a rule, protocols were written for Heidegger's seminars – are not extant or their whereabouts are unknown. This gives us reason to suspect that the seminar also retained something of the style of the lecture course.

In accordance with the unified conception of the text with respect to its theme and content – the "elucidations of 'Being and Time'" in the "Preliminary Reflection" are not an end in themselves, but rather have as their starting and end point Schelling's distinction between ground and existence – I broke the text into sections throughout; many of the section titles were specified by Heidegger himself or, when that was not the case, they emerged without difficulty from Heidegger's text and in Heidegger's terminology.

The "Recapitulations," which Heidegger himself conceived of as the third part of the manuscript and numbered continuously from pages 1 to 12, were not incorporated into the lectures of the first trimester. Given that they bear the title "*Recapitulations* and *Course* . . ." on the cover sheet, breaking them up would have destroyed Heidegger's intention – to demonstrate the course of the lectures in its unified path-like character.

The sections "Preliminary Glimpses and Directives," "On the Confrontation with the Metaphysics of German Idealism and with Metaphysics in General," and "Overview of the Transformation of Being as *Actuality*" are paginated separately in the manuscript with lower-case Latin letters or Arabic numerals. The extent to which they were integrated into the progression of lecture course and seminar could no longer be discerned.

By contrast, the "Transitional Reflection on Hegel" – which contains numerous supplements – is continuously paginated 52–53d. They were undoubtedly set apart by Heidegger himself and considered to be a unified reflection. On the title and outline page of a typescript, the following handwritten note by Heidegger is found next to the bullet point

206

207

"Transitional Reflection on Hegel": "As an excursus to this, *Hegel – Negativity* 38/39." (This text is in preparation and will appear in Part III of the *Gesamtausgabe*.)[2]

In editing this volume, I had at my disposal Heidegger's manuscript, as well as the typescript version by Fritz Heidegger reworked by the former in blue ink and lead pencil. The manuscript is preserved in full, along with a number of supplements, all of which are incorporated, except for the Leibniz supplement. Of the typescript version, there are available a complete bound (carbon) copy and two incomplete and unbound identical copies with various marginal notes, corrections, etc. furnished by Heidegger.

The typescript version prepared by Fritz Heidegger was collated with the manuscript; transcription errors were corrected, omissions transcribed, and keywords, elliptical phrases, sentences, and supplements were partially relocated. Heidegger's marginal notes in the typescript versions were incorporated – in accordance with the editorial guidelines – into the present text. The citations were checked and, when necessary, made to match the original; Heidegger's additions, annotations, etc. were placed in square brackets. Complete bibliographic references are given each time with the first citation. Footnotes with Arabic numerals are the editor's;[3] footnotes (or just their text) with lower-case Latin letters are Heidegger's.

It was necessary to retain the note-like character of the "seminar style" in the second part; more developed formulations would have – where they would have been possible, even in the case of a missing transcription – forced the subject matter, indeed they might have pushed in an interpretive direction contrary to Heidegger's intention. Only the punctuation had to be handled in a more discriminating manner for the sake of a better comprehension of the text; above all, the dash, which Heidegger uses as a universal sign, was here given more concrete form. In cases of doubt – it is well known, indeed, that punctuation marks, too, contribute to the semantics of the text – the dash was always preserved.

The manuscript cover sheet with the indications "1940/prepared for 1941" and "see lecture course from S.S. {summer semester} 1936"

208

---

[2] {TN: now in *Hegel* (GA 68), ed. Ingrid Schüssler. Published in English translation as "Negativity: A Confrontation with Hegel Approached from Negativity (1938–1939, 1941)," in *Hegel*, trans. Joseph Arel and Niels Feuerhahn (Bloomington: Indiana University Press, 2015).}

[3] {TN: When, that is, they are not placed into curly brackets, which signify additions by the translators.}

bears the title "A *New Interpretation* of *Schelling*, Investigations into the Essence of Human Freedom and ... (Confrontation with 'Metaphysics')"; page 1 of the manuscript, in contrast, bears the heading: "Metaphysics of German Idealism. Schelling, Philosophical Investigations into the Essence of Human Freedom and the Matters Connected Therewith. 1809." The title of the typescript undoubtedly approved by Heidegger, "The Metaphysics of German Idealism: A New Interpretation of Schelling's Freedom Treatise," as well as Heidegger's handwritten note from 1945 found in Jean Beaufret's papers, "Lecture courses and seminar tutorials since the appearance of 'Being and Time'" – which lists "The Metaphysics of German Idealism (Schelling)" for the Summer Semester of 1941 – ultimately determined, then, the order of title and subtitle. This is also justified by the text itself, since Heidegger's interpretation is launched by the maxim that the metaphysics of German Idealism reaches its peak in Schelling's Freedom Treatise (see § 1).

Point I of the typescript's outline (now § 11, b) bears the typed inscription "I. Preliminary Reflection on the Distinction between Ground and Existence. (Elucidations of 'Being and Time')"; on this inscription is a handwritten note by Heidegger: "under revision 1943." This revision was done – alongside two supplements inserted by Heidegger himself – on the old manuscript pages, above all by way of marginal annotations, deletions, and interlinear additions.

209

For their kind assistance in the editing of this volume – with questions of detail and regarding the conception of the whole – my heartfelt thanks to Dr. Hermann Heidegger, Prof. Dr. Friedrich-Wilhelm von Herrmann, and Dr. Hartmut Tietjen. I remain indebted to Mark Michalski for his proofreading, and to Dr. Eva Zeltner, to political-science graduate Hans-Peter Hempel, and to Dr. Hans-Helmuth Gander for their help in many ways.

Günter Seubold
Würzburg, late Summer 1990

Glossaries

German–English Glossary

abbauen – to dismantle
Abendland – West
abendländisch – Western
Abgrund – abyss
abhandeln – to treat of, deal with
Abhandlung – treatise
Absolute, das – the absolute
absolvieren – to absolve
ahnen – to divine
Aktualismus – currentism
Allheit – allness
Aneignung – appropriation
anerkennen – to recognize
Anerkenntnis – recognizance
Anerkennung – recognition
Anfang – inception, beginning
anfänglich – inceptive
Angst – anxiety
Anschauung – intuition
Ansprechung – addressing
Anspruch – claim
Anthropologie – anthropology
Anthropomorphie –
    anthropomorphy
Anthropomorphismus –
    anthropomorphism
anwesen – to presence

Anwesung – presencing
Auf-stellung – setting up
Aufbau – structure
aufheben – to sublate
Aufhellung – illumination
Aufruhr – insurrection
Aufstand – uprising
Auseinandersetzung –
    confrontation
Ausgesetztheit – exposedness
Basis – basis
Bedenken – misgiving
Befehl – command
Bedingung – condition
Befindlichkeit – disposition
Begierde – desire
Beginn – beginning
Begriff – concept
Bei-sich-selbst-sein – being-at-
    home-with-oneself
Bekümmernis – concern
Beständigkeit – constancy
bestehen – to persist, consist
bestimmen – to determine,
    destine
Bestimmung – determination
Bewegtheit – movedness

Bewegung – movement
bewirken – to effect
Bewußtsein – consciousness
Bild – image
bilden – to form
Boden – firm soil, solid ground
Bodenständigkeit – rootedness
bösartig – malevolent
Böse – evil
Bosheit – malice
Centrum – *centrum*
Da-sein – Da-sein
Dar-stellen – presenting forth
Darlegung – exposition
darstellen – to present
Dasein – Dasein
Dauer – duration
Denken – thinking, thought
Destruktion – destructuring
Dialektik – dialectic, dialectics
Differenz – difference (German always marked to distinguish from Unterschied)
Dimension – dimension
Ding – thing
echt – genuine
Egoismus – egoism
Egoität – egoity
eigen – proper, own
Eigenheit – ownness
eigens – specifically
Eigenschaft – property
eigentlich – proper, authentic
eigentümlich – peculiar
Ein-bildung – formation through the imagination
einbilden – to imagine
Einheit – unity
Einzelne, der – the individual
ekstatisch – ecstatic
Element – element
Endlichkeit – finitude

entrücken – to transport
entscheidend – decisive, authoritative
Entscheidung – decision
entsprechen – to correspond
Entwurf – projection
Entzweiung – diremption, divisiveness
er-streben – to strive to attain, to strive to bring to
erblicken – to glimpse
ereignen, sich – properly to take place
Ereignis – appropriative event
Erfahrung – experience
Erkenntnis – cognition, knowledge
Erklärung – explanation
Erläuterung – elucidation
Erörterung – discussion
Erschlossenheit – disclosedness
erstreben – to strive
Erwirkung – effecting
Erzeugung – generation
ewig – eternal
Ewigkeit – eternity
Ex-sistenz – ex-sistence
Existenz – existence
existenzial – existential
Existenzialien – existentials
existenziell – existentiell
Existenzphilosophie – philosophy of existence
Frage – question
fragwürdig – questionable, worthy of question
Freiheit – freedom
fügen – to join, conjoin
Fügung – enjoinment
Gang – course, trajectory
Gefüge – jointure
Gegenkraft – counterforce

Gegensatz – opposition
Gegenstand – object, matter
Gegenständlichkeit – objectivity
Gegenwart – the present
Geist – spirit
geistlich – spiritual
Geschichte – history
geschichtlich – historical
Geschichtlichkeit – historicality
geschicklich – destinal
Geschöpf – creature
gewaltsam – violent
Gewesene, das – that which has been
Gewesenheit – having-been
Gewißheit – certainty
geworfen – thrown
Glaube – faith
Gläubiger – believer
Gott – God, god
Gottheit – divinity
Größe – magnitude
Grund – ground, (as prefix) basic or foundational
grund-haft – ground-like
grundlos – groundless
Gründung – grounding
Gute, das – the good
Güte, die – goodness
Heil, das – salvation
Herkunft – provenance
herrisch – masterful
herstellen – to produce
Historie – historiography
historisch – historiographic
Historismus – historicism
Ichheit – I-hood
Idea – Idea (Greek transliterated as *idea*, with italics)
Idealismus – idealism
Idee – idea (Greek transliterated as *idea*, with italics)

In-der-Welt-sein – being-in-the-world
Indifferenz – indifference
Individuum – individual
innerweltlich – inner-worldly
Innerzeitigkeit – within-timeness
Innestehen – standing-in
innig – intimate
Insistenz – insistence
Inständigkeit – persistent steadfastness
Instanz – jurisdiction, instance
Klärung – clarification
Kommende, das – what is coming
Konstruktion – construction
Kosmos – cosmos
Kraft – force
Kreatur – creature
Lichtung – clearing
Liebe – love
Macht – power
Magie – magic
Manifestation – manifestation
Maß – measure
Mensch – human
Menschentum – humanity
Menschheit – humankind
menschliches Sein – human being
Menschsein – the being of the human
Menschwerdung – incarnation
Metaphysik – metaphysics
Mitte – center
Mittelpunkt – centerpoint
Möglichkeit – possibility
nachdenken – to ponder
Natur – nature
Neuzeit – modern age
neuzeitlich – modern
nichtig – null
nichts – nothing

Nichts (capitalized and without article) – Nothing
Nichts, das – the nothing
Not – need
Notwendigkeit – necessity
objektiv – objective
offenbaren – to reveal
Offenbarkeit – revealability
Offenbarung – revelation
Offene, das – the open
Offenheit – openness
offenkundig – openly manifest
offensichtlich – manifest
ontisch – ontic
Ontologie – ontology
Ordnung – ordering, order
Originalität – originality
Pantheismus – pantheism
Personalität – personality
Personhaftigkeit – personhood
Phänomenologie – phenomenology
Präsenz – presence, presentness
Raum – space
Reale, das – the real
Realität – reality
rechnen – to reckon, to calculate
recht – correct, right
reell – real
regellos – without rule
Riß – rift
Sachheit – whatness
scheiden – to divide
Scheidung – division
Schicksal – fate
Schöpfung – creation
Schuld – guilt
Seele – soul
sehnen – to long
Sehnsucht – yearning
Seiendes – beings, that which is, a/the being

Seiendheit – beingness
Sein, das – being
Seinheit – ipseity
Seinsvergessenheit – forgetting of being
Seinsverständnis – understanding of being
Selbstbejahung – self-affirmation
Selbstbewußtsein – self-consciousness
Selbstheit – selfhood
Selbstsein – self-being
Seyn – beyng
Sinn – meaning, sense
sondern – to differentiate
Sorge – care
Spekulation – speculation
Sprache – language
Stimmung – attunement
streben – to strive
Subjectität – subjectity
Subjekt – subject
Subjektität – subjektity
Subjektivismus – subjectivism
Subjektivität – subjectivity
Substanz – substance
Sucht – craving
Synthesis – synthesis
Systasis – systasis
System – system
Tat – act
Tätigkeit – activity
tauglich – suitable
Technik – technology
Tod – death
trennen – to separate
übereignen – properly to assign
überliefert – traditional
Übermächtigung – overpowering
übernehmen – to take on, take over
Umschlag – changeover

Un-fug – dis-jointure
unbedingt – unconditional
Unbedingte, das – the
  unconditional
Unendlichkeit – infinity
Ungrund – unground
Universum – universe
unsterblich – immortal
Unterscheidung – distinction
Unterschied – difference
Unterschiedenheit –
  differentiatedness
Untersuchung – investigation
Unverborgenheit –
  unconcealment
Unwesen – non-essence
Urbild – archetype
Ursache – cause
Ursprung – origin
ursprünglich – originary
ver-stehen – to under-stand
Verfallen – falling prey
Vergangenheit – the past
Verhalten – comportment
verhüllen – to veil
Verklärung – transfiguration
vermitteln – to mediate
Vernunft – reason
Verschiedenheit – distinctness
versetzen – to displace
Versöhnung – reconciliation
Verstand – the understanding
verstehen – to understand
verwahren – to preserve
Verwandlung – transformation
verwirklichen – to actualize
vor-stellen – to re-present
vorhanden – present, present at
  hand
vorstellen – to represent

Wahrheit – truth
Walten – to prevail
Wassein – what-being
Welt – world
Weltanschauung – worldview
Werden, das – becoming
wesen – to essence
Wesen, das – essence, essential
wesenhaft – essential
Wesenheit – essentiality
wesentlich – essential
Wesung – essencing
Widerwärtigkeit – repulsiveness
Wille – will
wirken – to be effective, to act
wirklich – actual
Wirklichkeit – actuality
Wirklichsein – being-actual
Wirksamkeit – effectiveness
Wissen – knowledge
wissen – to know
Wissenschaft – science
wissentlich – consciously,
  knowingly
wollen – to will, to wish
Zeit – time
Zeitalter – age
Zeitigung – temporalizing
zeitlich – temporal
Zeitlichkeit – temporality
Zentrum – centrum
Zerrissenheit – diremption
Zeug – equipment
Zu-kunft – the to-come
Zukunft – future
Zusammenhang – connection,
  nexus
zusammen-stellen – to present
  together
Zwietracht – discord

English–German Glossary

absolute, the – das Absolute
absolve – absolvieren
abyss – Abgrund
act – Tat
act, to – wirken
activity – Tätigkeit
actual – wirklich
actuality – Wirklichkeit
actualize, to – verwirklichen
addressing – Ansprechung
age – Zeitalter
allness – Allheit
anthropology – Anthropologie
anthropomorphism –
  Anthropomorphismus
anthropomorphy –
  Anthropomorphie
anxiety – Angst
appropriation – Aneignung
appropriative event – Ereignis
archetype – Urbild
assign, to – übereignen
attunement – Stimmung
authentic – eigentlich
authoritative – entscheidend
basis – Basis
becoming – das Werden
beginning – Beginn, Anfang
being – das Sein
being of the human, the –
  Menschsein
being-actual – Wirklichsein
being-at-home-with-oneself –
  Bei-sich-selbst-sein
being-in-the-world – In-der-Welt-
  sein
being, a/the – ein/das Seiende
beingness – Seiendheit
beings – Seiendes
believer – Gläubiger

beyng – das Seyn
calculate, to – rechnen
care – Sorge
cause – Ursache
center – Mitte
centerpoint – Mittelpunkt
centrum – Centrum
centrum – Zentrum
certainty – Gewißheit
changeover – Umschlag
claim – Anspruch
clarification – Klärung
clearing –Lichtung
cognition – Erkenntnis
command – Befehl
comportment – Verhalten
concept – Begriff
concern – Bekümmernis
condition – Bedingung
confrontation –
  Auseinandersetzung
conjoin, to – fügen
connection – Zusammenhang
consciously – wissentlich
consciousness – Bewußtsein
consist – bestehen
constancy – Beständigkeit
construction – Konstruktion
correspond, to – entsprechen
cosmos – Kosmos
counterforce – Gegenkraft
course – Gang
craving – Sucht
creation – Schöpfung
creature – Geschöpf, Kreatur
currentism – Aktualismus
Da-sein – Da-sein
Dasein – Dasein
deal with, to – abhandeln
death – Tod

decision – Entscheidung
decisive – entscheidend
desire – Begierde
destinal – geschicklich
destine, to – bestimmen
destructuring – Destruktion
determination – Bestimmung
determine, to – bestimmen
dialectic/dialectics – Dialektik
difference – Unterschied or (with
 the German interpolated)
 Differenz
differentiate, to – sondern
differentiatedness –
 Unterschiedenheit
dimension – Dimension
diremption – Entzweiung,
 Zerrissenheit
dis-jointure – Un-fug
disclosedness – Erschlossenheit
discord – Zwietracht
discussion – Erörterung
dismantle – abbauen
displace, to – versetzen
disposition – Befindlichkeit
distinction – Unterscheidung
distinctness – Verschiedenheit
divide, to – scheiden
divine, to – anhnen
divinity – Gottheit
division – Scheidung
divisiveness – Entzweiung
duration – Dauer
ecstatic – ekstatisch
effect, to – bewirken
effecting – Erwirkung
effective (to be) – wirken
effectiveness – Wirksamkeit
egoism – Egoismus
egoity – Egoität
element – Element
elucidation – Erläuterung

enjoinment – Fügung
equipment – Zeug
essencing – Wesung
essence – das Wesen
essence, to – wesen
essential – wesentlich, wesenhaft
essentiality – Wesenheit
eternal – ewig
eternity – Ewigkeit
evil – Böse
ex-sistence – Ex-sistenz
existence – Existenz or (with the
 German interpolated) Dasein
existential – existenzial
existentials – Existenzialien
existentiell – existenziell
experience – Erfahrung
exposedness - Ausgesetztheit
exposition – Darlegung
faith – Glauben
falling prey – Verfallen
fate – Schicksal
finitude – Endlichkeit
force – Kraft
forgetting of being –
 Seinsvergessenheit
form, to – bilden
formation through the
 imagination – Ein-bildung
freedom – Freiheit
future – Zukunft
generation – Erzeugung
genuine – echt
glimpse, to – erblicken
god/God – Gott
good, the – das Gute
goodness – die Güte
ground – Grund
ground (solid) – Boden
grounding – Gründung
ground-like – grund-haft
groundless – grundlos

guilt – Schuld
having-been – Gewesenheit
historical – geschichtlich
historicality – Geschichtlichkeit
historicism – Historismus
historiographic – historisch
historiography – Historie
history – Geschichte
human – Mensch
human being – menschliches Sein
humanity – Menschentum
humankind – Menschheit
I-hood – Ichheit
Idea – Idea
idea – Idee
idealism – Idealismus
illumination – Aufhellung
image – Bild
imagination – Einbildung
immortal – unsterblich
incarnation – Menschwerdung
inception – Anfang
inceptive – anfänglich
individual – Individuum, der
   Einzelne
infinity – Unendlichkeit
inner-worldly – inner-weltlich
insistence – Insistenz
instance – Instanz
insurrection – Aufruhr
intimate – innig
intuition – Anschauung
investigation – Untersuchung
ipseity – Seinheit
join, to – fügen
jointure – Gefüge
jurisdiction – Instanz
knowingly – wissentlich
knowledge – Wissen, Erkenntnis
language – Sprache
long, to – sehnen
love – Liebe

magic – Magie
magnitude – Größe
malevolent – bösartig
malice – Bosheit
manifest – offensichtlich
manifestation – Manifestation
masterful – herrisch
matter – Gegenstand
meaning – Bedeutung, Sinn
measure – Maß
mediate – vermitteln
metaphysics – Metaphysik
misgiving – Bedenken
modern – neuzeitlich
modern age – Neuzeit
movedness – Bewegtheit
movement – Bewegung
nachdenken – to ponder
nature – Natur
necessity – Notwendigkeit
need – Not
nexus – Zusammenhang
non-essence – Unwesen
nothing – nichts
Nothing – Nichts
null – nichtig
object – Gegenstand
objective – objektiv
objectivity – Gegenständlichkeit
ontic – ontisch
ontology – Ontologie
open, the – das Offene
openly manifest – offenkundig
openness – Offenheit
opposition – Gegensatz
order – Ordnung
ordering – Ordnung
origin – Ursprung
originality – Originalität
originary – ursprünglich
overpowering – Übermächtigung
own – eigen

ownness – Eigenheit
pantheism – Pantheismus
past, the – Vergangenheit
peculiar – eigentümlich
persist – bestehen
persistent steadfastness –
   Inständigkeit
personality – Personalität
personhood – Personhaftigkeit
phenomenology –
   Phänomenologie
philosophy of existence –
   Existenzphilosophie
possibility – Möglichkeit
power – Macht
presence – Präsenz
presence, to – anwesen
presencing – Anwesung
present – vorhanden
present at hand – vorhanden
present together, to – zusammen-
   stellen
present, the – Gegenwart
present, to – darstellen
presenting forth – Dar-stellen
presentness – Präzenz
preserve, to – verwahren
prevail, to – walten
produce, to – herstellen
projection – Entwurf
proper – eigen, eigentlich
property – Eigenschaft
provenance – Herkunft
question – Frage
questionable – fragwürdig
re-present, to – vor-stellen
real – reel
real, the – das Reale
reality – Realität
reason – Vernunft
recognition – Anerkennung
recognizance – Anerkenntnis

recognize – anerkennen, erkennen
reckon, to – rechnen
reconciliation – Versöhnung
represent, to – vorstellen
repulsiveness – Widerwärtigkeit
reveal, to – offenbaren
revealability – Offenbarkeit
revelation – Offenbarung
rift – Riß
rootedness – Bodenständigkeit
salvation – das Heil, Erlösung
science – Wissenschaft
self-affirmation – Selbstbejahung
self-being – Selbstsein
self-consciousness –
   Selbstbewußtsein
selfhood – Selbstheit
sense – Sinn
separate, to – trennen
setting up – Auf-stellung
soil (firm) – Boden
soul – Seele
space – Raum
specifically – eigens
speculation – Spekulation
spirit – Geist
spiritual – geistlich
standing-in – Innestehen
strive to attain or bring to, to –
   er-streben
strive, to – erstreben, streben
structure – Aufbau
subject – Subjekt
subjectity – Subjectität
subjectivism – Subjektivismus
subjectivity – Subjektivität
subjektity – Subjektität
sublate, to – aufheben
substance – Substanz
suitable – tauglich
synthesis – Synthesis
systasis – Systasis

system – System
take on/over, to – übernehmen
take place, properly to – sich
ereignen
technology – Technik
temporal – zeitlich
temporality – Zeitlichkeit
temporalizing – Zeitigung
that which has been – das
Gewesene
that which is – das Seiende
the nothing – das Nichts
thing – Ding
thinking – Denken
thought – Denken
thrown – geworfen
time – Zeit
to-come, the – Zu-kunft
traditional – überliefert
trajectory – Gang
transfiguration – Verklärung
transformation – Verwandlung
transport, to – entrücken
treat of, to – abhandeln
truth – Wahrheit
unconcealment –
Unverborgenheit
unconditional – unbedingt

unconditional, the – das
Unbedingte
under-stand, to – ver-stehen
understand, to – verstehen
understanding of being –
Seinsverständnis
understanding, the – Verstand
unground – Ungrund
unity – Einheit
universe – Universum
uprising – Aufstand
veil, to – verhüllen
violent – gewaltsam
West – Abendland
Western – abendländisch
what is – das Seiende
what is coming – das Kommende
what-being – Wassein
whatness – Sachheit
will – Wille
will, to – wollen
wish, to – wollen
within-timeness – Innerzeitigkeit
without rule – regellos
world – Welt
worldview – Weltanschauung
worthy of question – fragwürdig
yearning – Sehnsucht

Greek/Latin–English Lexicon

Prepared by Ian Alexander Moore and Rodrigo Therezo

Greek–English Lexicon

a-lētheia – un-forgetting,
un-concealment
aei – always
agathon – good
aitia – cause
akrotaton – highest

alētheia – truth
analogos – analogical
apostasis – standing away from
apousia – absence
archē – source
arithmos – number

boulēsis – will
chronos – time
doxa – opinion, glory
dunaton – potential
dustasis – bad standing
eidos – form, outward look
einai – being, to be
ek-stasis – standing out
en-ergeia – at-work-ness
energeia – actuality
entelecheia – actuality (more literally 'maintaining oneself in a state of completion')
enuparchon – inherent, constituent
epistēmē – knowledge
ergon – work
erōs – love
genesis – generation
hen – one
hulē – material
hupokeimenon – underlying thing
hupostasis – standing under
kataphasis – affirmative proposition
kinēsis – movement
kinoumena – things moved
kinounta – things moving
koinotaton – commonest
megethos – magnitude
metochē – participation
metabolē – change
morphē – shape
noein – think, apprehend
on – being, that which is
orexis – desire
ousia – substance, beingness, estate
pan – all
panta – all things
parousia – presence
philia – love
phusis – nature
poiēsis – making
proaireton – what is deliberately chosen
ptōsis – grammatical case
sumbainen – to come together
sumbebēkota – attributes, accidents
sustasis – standing together
technē – art
telos – goal, end
theon – divine
theos – god
topos – place
zētēsis – search

Latin–English Lexicon

accidens – accident
actu – in act
actualitas – actuality
actus – act
adaequatio – making equal
agere – to act
animalitas – animality
animus – mind, intelligence
apperceptio – apperception (perception of oneself)
appetitus – faculty of desire
causa – cause
certitudo – certainty
cogitare – to think
conatus – effort
conservare – preserve
creare – to create
creatio – creation

creatum – what is created
deductio – deduction
desiderium – desire
elevare – raise up
ens – being, the/a being
essentia – essence
ex-sistentia – standing out
exigentia – demand
existentia – existence
formaliter – formally
gradus – degree
intellecus – intellect
intelligere – understanding
intuitus – intuition, view
materialiter – materially
mens – mind
natura – nature
nihil – nothing
nisus – exertion
nunc stans – standing now

perceptio – perception
personalitas – personality
principium – principle
prius – prior
propensio – inclination
quidditas – whatness, essence
ratio – reason, account
rationalitas – rationality
reor – I reckon, I deem
repraesentare – to represent
sempiternitas – perpetuity
subjectum – subject, that which
   has been cast under
substans – standing under
substantia – substance
tollere – cancel
universum – universe
veritas – truth
vis – force